C. Brad Faught is Associate Professor and Chair of the Department of History at Tyndale University College in Toronto. A graduate of the Universities of Oxford and Toronto, he is a Fellow of the Royal Historical Society and a Senior Fellow of Massey College at the University of Toronto. He is author of *The Oxford Movement: A Thematic History of the Tractarians and Their Times* (2003); *Gordon: Victorian Hero* (2008); *The New A–Z of Empire: A Concise Handbook of British Imperial History* (2011); and the forthcoming *Clive: Founder of British India*.

T0258302

To Anthony Hamilton Millard Kirk-Greene

Scholar, Mentor, Friend

INTO AFRICA
The Imperial Life of Margery Perham

C. BRAD FAUGHT

BLOOMSBURY ACADEMIC
LONDON • NEW YORK • OXFORD • NEW DELHI • SYDNEY

BLOOMSBURY ACADEMIC
Bloomsbury Publishing Plc
50 Bedford Square, London, WC1B 3DP, UK
1385 Broadway, New York, NY 10018, USA

BLOOMSBURY, BLOOMSBURY ACADEMIC and the Diana
logo are trademarks of Bloomsbury Publishing Plc

First published in Great Britain by I.B. Tauris 2012
Paperback edition published by Bloomsbury Academic 2020

ISBN: HB: 978-1-8488-5490-1
PB: 978-1-3501-6348-5
ePDF: 978-0-8577-2132-7
ePub: 978-0-7556-3072-1

Typeset by 4word Ltd, Bristol

To find out more about our authors and books visit
www.bloomsbury.com and sign up for our newsletters

CONTENTS

LIST OF PLATES

1. A casual Perham family pose taken about 1902 when Margery was seven.
2. Perham on camelback at the pyramids at Giza, Egypt with unidentified group, 1930.
3. Perham on horseback in Darfur, Sudan, 1937.
4. Perham *c.* 1900.
5. Harry Rayne as a lieutenant in the King's African Rifles, Nairobi, 1915.
6. Lord Lugard, the great man of African empire, as Perham knew him in 1935.
7. Perham on horseback at Hargeisa, British Somaliland in 1921.
8. Perham with Bror Blixen and two unidentified hunters, in Tanganyika, 1930.
9. Perham with General Yakubu Gowon, Head of State of Nigeria, in Lagos, 1968.
10. A characteristically animated Perham talking with native women in Darfur, Sudan, 1937.
11. Edgar Perham *c.* 1915 in the uniform of the West Yorkshire Regiment.
12. Perham on camelback in Hargeisa, British Somaliland, 1921.
13. Hugh Cholmondeley, 3rd Baron Delamere, by Bassano, 1930.
14. Perham with the other members of the St. Hugh's College, Oxford, Women's Hockey 1st XI, 1916.
15. Perham as a new history don, recently returned from Sheffield, St. Hugh's College, Oxford, 1925.

PREFACE AND ACKNOWLEDGEMENTS

Born in 1895 in the twilight of the Victorian age but at the point when the British Empire was reaching its apotheosis, Margery Perham's life was lived within the shaping contours of imperialism, particularly that practiced by her compatriots in Africa. Her own direct exposure to Africa – her 'love affair' with the continent – began in 1921 and within a decade had become the organizing principle of her life for its remaining fifty years. During that half-century she became the leading British expert on colonial governance in Africa, writing copiously, lecturing, advising, travelling, defending, and cajoling in ways that were both defining of her character and personality, and demonstrative of her belief in the high moral purpose of what the British were doing there. Her base was Oxford University, and for much of that time more specifically Nuffield College, and from these precincts of what were then bastions of male privilege she entered the equally masculine world of the Colonial Office and the Colonial Service. There were a number of firsts in Perham's life but surely one of the most impressive is the essentially *sui generis* nature of her professional work among the men of empire.

That work took her on numerous journeys to Africa, the experience from which she channelled into acute observations and policy recommendations. Her career was full of government documents and conference proceedings, but behind all of these professional requirements was a tenacious personal attachment to Africa – romantic in many respects – that makes it necessary to view Margery Perham, in part at least, as one of those intrepid visitors to the outposts of empire, especially other women such as Mary Kingsley, Mary Slessor, and Gertrude Bell. Like them, she visited exotic out of the way places, exhibited physical courage and endurance, and regularly found herself in the company of people utterly unlike herself. The mature Perham of the Colonial Office brief would eventually become her defining identity, but before that there was the young Margery of the Tanganyikan buffalo hunt taken with the roguish Bror von Blixen, Karen Blixen's impossible sometime husband. This biography seeks to capture them both, as it does also Perham's indispensable later work as a publicist in explaining African nationalism to the British people better than anyone else and therefore helping to ready them for the end of empire in Africa in the 1960s.

The work that follows is divided into nine essentially chronological chapters. Perham's life was extraordinarily full and productive, and most of it is well-documented. The result of this is a Gladstone-sized archive of some 770 boxes, the Perham Papers, kept at the Bodleian Library of Commonwealth and African Studies at Rhodes House in Oxford. I have relied heavily upon this collection of letters, diaries, records, policy drafts, photographs, and ephemera to distill her life story. Equally, I have leaned upon Perham's own voluminous collection of published works, encompassing as it does history, biography, fiction, lectures, policy prescription and newspaper and magazine letters and articles. Of vital importance too has been the work of others who have spent much time over the years writing about Perham or cataloguing her papers and generally keeping her memory alive. In this respect the work of Patricia Pugh and Mary Bull especially has been indispensable. I would like to thank them, and also all those others who were happily willing to be interviewed. Though this number is naturally dwindling with the passage of time their vivid memories of Perham have given much to my understanding of her life and character.

The debt to others in researching and writing a book is always large. To that end, I would like to thank the staff of Rhodes House Library, especially Lucy McCann, archivist, for their consistent help in making the Perham Papers readily available to consult, and for always being prepared to bring up 'just one more box'. Also, I am grateful to St. Hugh's College, Oxford, and to Amanda Ingram, archivist, for welcoming me to consult the Perham material in their possession. My thanks to Anthony Rayne, Margery Perham's great-nephew, for granting me permission to reproduce many of the photographs in this book. Tyndale University College in Toronto, where I teach, has been greatly supportive through the provision of research grants for this project for which I am thankful. The wise counsel and support of Dr. John Darwin of Oxford, and Emeritus Professors David Fieldhouse of Cambridge and Trevor Lloyd of Toronto – all of whom are leading historians of the British Empire, and some of whom knew and worked with Perham – is much appreciated. Dr. Lester Crook, Senior Editor at I.B.Tauris, has overseen this project in his usual highly amiable and professional style, and I would like to thank him and the other Tauris staff –

especially his colleague in history, Senior Editor Joanna Godfrey and Production Editor, Cecile Rault – for bringing it to fruition. My wife, Rhonda, and our children, Claire and Luke, have exhibited sustained forbearance in allowing for my regular transatlantic trips to the archives over the past few years, and to them I am grateful also. Finally, I would like to thank Anthony H.M. Kirk-Greene, Emeritus Fellow of St. Antony's College, Oxford. A distinguished historian of the British Empire in Africa and heir to Perham's work on its administration, he suggested writing her biography to me and over its gestation has been unstinting in providing help and encouragement. I first met Tony when I was an undergraduate in Canada at the very outset of my interest in Africa and the British Empire, and subsequently throughout my time as a graduate student in Oxford and ever since during my years as a professional historian he has been both a mentor and friend. This book, in great appreciation, is dedicated to him. Its shortcomings, needless to say, belong to me alone.

1

CHILDHOOD AND YOUTH:
A PROPER GIRL

Swallowed up now by the burgeoning conurbation that is modern Manchester, the small English Midlands town of Bury has lost much of its independence as being firmly of Lancashire. But in the last years of Queen Victoria's long reign, such was not yet the case. In those days its dissenting heritage, dating from the religious upheavals of the sixteenth and seventeenth centuries, remained strong, as did its almost equally robust Church of England character. Bury was a quiet, if not sleepy place, hugging the banks of the River Irwell and located about midway between the bigger neighbouring towns of Bolton and Rochdale. But with its rail-line laid out in 1846 and its storied regiment of fighting men, the Lancashire Fusiliers, Bury could claim to be almost their equal, if not in size then at least in reputation. Nonetheless, then as now, it was an out of the way place for most people and, given Britain's ongoing North–South divide portrayed famously in the Victorian fiction of Benjamin Disraeli and then later Elizabeth Gaskell, perhaps not the most auspicious of towns in which to be born. But that is where, on 6 September 1895, Margery Freda Perham entered the world. 219 Walmersley Road, the Perhams' house, was one similar to that of their middle class neighbours, functional and with no pretensions to grandeur; indeed, it was much like the one they would move to subsequently in Harrogate, a slightly larger and newer house located at 36 Old Kent Road. But together they would be the starting point for Margery Perham's remarkable Oxford to Africa journey, one that would take her far beyond the familiar streetscapes of a late-Victorian market town.

Frederick Perham, Margery's father, born in 1854, was tall and swarthily handsome and, as a successful wine and spirit merchant, a suitably respectable member of the middle classes in an age that demanded it. Her mother, Marion Hodder Needell, one year her husband's junior, was nurturing and

demure, but thanks to a grandmother who had been a novelist, had a literary disposition, which she passed on to some of her seven children, most
notably to Margery. As the youngest child and second daughter amongst
five surviving sons, Margery was especially beloved and was pulled very easily into the rough and tumble games of her elder brothers.

Frederick and Marion Perham had married in 1881 in the parish church
of Netherby, Dorset, her home county. The move north to Bury, nearer
Frederick's home, would soon follow, as did the children in quick succession, beginning with Arthur in 1884 and joined soon by Cecil, Wilfrid,
Oliver, and Edgar, and one other girl, Ethel. Not long after Margery's birth
Frederick decided to move the family a little further north still, to bustling
Harrogate in North Yorkshire. Well known as a spa – and, increasingly in
the emergent age of the package holiday, a tourist-town – Harrogate had
more to offer him as a merchant, as well as to his growing family. There,
on the edge of the Yorkshire Dales, the children thrived amidst an outdoor
and sporting life. Sturdy and fearless, young Margery took easily to sport,
attempting to keep up with her brothers in riding, rambling, shooting, and
golf, and from an early age was a thoroughgoing tomboy, as such young girls
used to be called.

In those turn-of-the-century years, as the Victorian era drew to a close,
Margery Perham's life was a round of innocent pleasures, of first school-
ing, of Sunday attendance at the Anglican parish church of St. Wilfrid's,
recently built and where her father served as warden, of scrapes, and of
childhood diseases. In one of the earliest examples of her writing extant, as
a seven-year-old in the spring of 1903 she reported to her elder sister Ethel,
then aged fifteen, that 'Spring cleaning has nearly finished. My measles has
[sic] run away, it has been very naughty to me'.[1] In this brief postcard sent
from Harrogate to Ethel who was away at school in Bangor, North Wales,
we see a matter of fact tone mixed together with whimsy, traits that would
come to define the writing style of the adult Perham. In the meantime, in
the pre-vaccination world of the first decade of the twentieth century, she
suffered through her share of childhood scourges, surviving them all and in
1904, like other children of her social class, was sent away to school, south
to Windsor to attend St. Stephen's College, an institution for girls run by the
St. John Baptist Clewer Sisterhood. Founded in 1849, this Anglican order
was closely connected with raising 'fallen women', and notably in this regard
to the legacy of Prime Minister W.E. Gladstone's 'rescue' work amongst the
prostitutes of Piccadilly and elsewhere in central London, which he carried
out during much of the latter part of his storied political career. The college,
as Perham would have known it half-a-century later, had nothing to do with

work among the 'penitents', as the streetwalkers were called. But it was a school that still strongly emphasized service to the poor and dispossessed and its ethos took root in the young Margery.

The great attractions of the school, however, and those that mark the six years she spent at Windsor, were a continuing love of sport, and of excellence in the classroom. 'Little Midget', as Edgar nicknamed her then – itself a measure of reciprocal jocularity – 'do you play La Crosse [sic] now? It must be a very silly game according to you'.[2] Silly or no, she played all the games and continued to do so after leaving St. Stephen's in 1910 for the bigger and rather more august surroundings of St. Anne's School, Abbots Bromley in Staffordshire. Founded by Canon Nathaniel Woodard in 1874 in the full flush of Victorian anglo-catholicism, and the coincidentally strong push for education for girls and women, St. Anne's School would prove to be an inspired choice for the fifteen-year-old Perham. She spent four glittering years there, during the last of which she was head girl. The adolescent Perham, it seems, was a human whirlwind. She played hockey, lacrosse, tennis, and cricket, was various grades of prefect, edited the school newspaper, and, as if to keep the school itself on the straight and narrow, was 'chapel bellringer'.[3] She was completely taken up with life at St. Anne's and especially with the inspiration provided by one of her teachers, Mildred Roechling, who taught history and would go on to become headmistress of a leading school in Nova Scotia. Upon (unsurprisingly) winning an open scholarship in history to St. Hugh's College, Oxford in 1913, Perham asked to have it deferred for a year on account of little money available from home by which to supplement her £30 per annum award. The school of course was very happy to have her around for another year, and at Speech Day in 1914, the headmistress, Miss Anne Rice, extolled Perham's virtues, calling her 'one of the most excellent heads the school has known, vigorous not only in scholarship, but also in power for good'.[4] To reinforce the point, Margery then carried off that year's school prizes for languages and general literature. Her mark on St. Anne's was significant and today both the Perham Society, a discussion group for senior students that in her era was called the Political and Social Problems Club, and Perham Hall, the school's main entry-way, speak of her impact there.[5]

Throughout her years at St. Anne's, Perham's filial relationship with her brother Edgar had deepened significantly, far outstripping that she had with any of her other four brothers. He was just two years older than she, and letters between them passed back and forth regularly. These letters are full of the exuberance of youth, as well as with the over-seriousness that is part of adolescence too. Along with the lighthearted and steady use of nicknames: 'Midget-fidget'; 'Midge'; 'Heavenly Virgin'; Edgar's tone could also turn dark and occasionally lapse into regret, a hint of bitterness, or even sarcasm. Margery's obvious prowess at games was a source of brotherly pride for Edgar, but not unreservedly so. 'A supreme moment of joy', was the way he described his reaction to her success at cricket in her last year at St. Anne's. But then, in the same letter, his tone changes quickly as he goes on to say such joy 'gives me more pleasure than many things that happen in this family – for we are having a tense time of it at present'. Unfortunately, there is no way now to clarify his reference. Perhaps the looming war – these words were written in July 1914 – was casting a pall over the Perhams like it did over so many other English families during that summer when the lamps began to go out all across Europe. More likely, however, was a continuing tension in the relationship between Edgar and his father, not of course unusual in the paternal dynamic, but possibly exacerbated by the fact that Margery's success on the sporting field – traditionally a site for manly achievement – contrasted sharply with his own lack of the same. This, it seems, was something for which he believed his father was partially responsible: 'It is regrettable that Father has always been willing to give the opportunity', he wrote while praising Margery for her ability along the 'games line, [but] he has been careless as the result'. Meanwhile, Edgar was hopeful that Margery's own sometime angular relationship with their mother had settled into the 'sweetest and most amicable terms possible'.[6]

Margery and Edgar's sibling relationship had itself always been one of fun and action and (melo)drama. Music and dancing, recitation and acting, all were part of their Edwardian childhood and youth. Much of what they did, it appears, they did together. One summer, for example, probably about 1913 while back home in Harrogate, they both participated in a community 'Grand Concert' in which Edgar on piano played a sonata by Beethoven and Margery recited 'The Lioness', a rather purple poem, but interestingly with a notional African theme.[7] The event seems to have been a ringing success.

Edgar's diary and notebooks from these early years are a revealing compendium of jottings and diagrams, of pictures and caricatures, and of poetry and history. They contain numerous references to Margery, as well as simple pencil sketches of them both. In one of the now yellowing notebooks there is a poem entitled, 'To Margery'. It contains five stanzas, the final one finishing off with the not very flattering, perhaps even hurtful, words: 'All the world knows – you are plain!'[8] Put it up to the sometime biting tongue of childhood, perhaps, although even by then it must have been becoming clear to Edgar that his overachieving sister was anything but plain.

By the time Margery left St. Anne's she had reached her full height of 5'10". Photographs of the period reveal her to have thick lustrous brown hair, which she usually wore in a fashionable bob. Her complexion was clear and she had highly penetrating hazel (sometimes described as brown or grey-green) eyes. She exuded intelligence and physicality. She would not have been described as beautiful in a conventional sense, but her height, her confidence, her ability both to think and to do made her very attractive nonetheless, if not intimidating. While no record exists of youthful romance one can surmise that for most awkward teenage boys Perham might have been entirely too mature and too accomplished to risk asking out.

Given her natural self-confidence Oxford's approach filled Perham with anticipation rather than trepidation. Women had been going up to the University since the 1870s, although it still was not permissible for them to be awarded degrees. Her college would be St. Hugh's, a relatively recent women's foundation established in 1886 and located in leafy North Oxford, where ultimately she would read for a degree in Modern History, the same course taken by the emerging Arabist and friend of T.E. Lawrence, Gertrude Bell, some thirty years earlier and with whom Perham would later bear comparison. Bell was the first Oxford woman undergraduate to be placed in the first class by the examiners in Modern History, astounding them with both her knowledge and her forthrightness.[9] Perham would do much the same thing. But that would come later. In the meantime, during those last months before Oxford, a time, it was remarked upon widely, of especial warmth and beauty in England, and before Europe descended into four years of darkness, Perham enjoyed her last full summer of adolescence. Turning nineteen in September she readied herself for the emotional excitement and intellectual stimulation of undergraduate life, and yes, for the opportunities it would offer her for sport and exercise, the latter being 'a very necessary thing in Oxford,' according to the sometime sedentary Edgar.[10] Her parents, especially her father, were liberal in the sense that they expected their daughters to gain a university education and once the finances were in place to do so, Perham's way was thus clear to go. And so in October 1914, at the beginning of Oxford's academic year, she arrived at the place from which she would never really, or for very long, leave for the rest of her life.

2

OXFORD UNDERGRADUATE: AMIDST THE DREAMING SPIRES

A few years prior to that glorious prize-winning Speech Day at St. Anne's in the spring of 1914 and the setting off for Oxford later in the autumn Margery Perham had written a poem with the romantically teenaged title, 'The Song of the Wind'. In it she writes of going 'round the world, round the world, round the world I go forever'.[1] As a piece of foreshadowing of a life of doing much that very thing it works rather well, but in the short term her world was to be comprised simply of Oxford, which was then, in October of 1914, on the cusp of experiencing the shattering impact of the First World War, one that would be both anonymously large and, tragically for Perham as for countless others, intimately small.

Like her co-matriculants Perham arrived in Oxford at the start of Michaelmas Term. Her brother Edgar, having gone up in 1911, was near to taking his degree but, like so many of his peers, went off to war instead. He had spent the previous three years as a Scholar at The Queen's College but once war was declared in August was eager to march off to the European continent in order to defy Wilhelm II, the hated German Kaiser and, unfortunately for most British patriots, the grandson of Queen Victoria.

The Oxford to which the young and fresh-faced Margery Perham had arrived was still the heavily masculine society it had always been through its 800 years of history. The advent of a handful of women's colleges beginning with Lady Margaret Hall in 1878 had not done much to alter Oxford's essentially male ethos, and its few hundred women students existed in a kind of demi-world of educational semi-legitimacy and, as far as their thousands of male counterparts were concerned, social amusement. On the other hand, women were at Oxford to stay and the high tower of academic achievement soon enough would be scaled, even if the university refused to honour it formally until 1920 when it began to award degrees to its graduating women members.[2]

Perham's own college, St. Hugh's, in which she took up residence in early-October, was located in verdant North Oxford. Known as 'donland' for its preponderance of married fellows who had begun to colonize the area once celibacy ceased to be a requirement of the colleges for their academic staff in 1882, St. Hugh's sits between the Woodstock and Banbury Roads, the main thoroughfares leading into the city from the north. Then as now it is the most remotely located of all the colleges (although, Wolfson College, built much later for graduate students, is similarly located to the east) and maintains a greensward exceeded in size only by the historic and palatial Christ Church, Oxford's grandest college. Nearby too are the University Parks, a magnificent tract of parkland running over to the Cherwell River, the home of languid punting in the late spring and summer, and to that other less public pastime of occasional nude bathing at the bend in the river known naughtily from the Victorian era as 'Parsons' Pleasure'.

If Oxford in those days was still, in Evelyn Waugh's famously nostalgic description from *Brideshead Revisited*, 'a city of aquatint', its lingering glow was about to depart abruptly with the onset of war. Indeed, that golden Oxford, where, to quote Waugh again, 'in her spacious and quiet streets men walked and spoke as they had done in Newman's day', disappeared forever in the autumn of 1914 just as Margery Perham trooped off with the other freshers to the Sheldonian Theatre for that annual rite of passage known as the matriculation ceremony. Her early education may have been, in her later overstated estimation, 'chaotic', but once having become a member of both college and university it would settle down very quickly into the steady rhythm of reading and tutorials, the traditional hallmarks of academic life for Oxford undergraduates.[3]

Outside of academic work Perham's youthful religiosity, inspired principally by her father's stout anglo-catholicism, found ready expression in the home of its modern progenitor, the Oxford Movement.[4] She attended college chapel services regularly and on Sunday could be found worshipping at various of the High Anglican churches in the city, especially St. Barnabas, located a short cycle ride away from St. Hugh's behind the massive building that is Oxford University Press. At St. Barnabas's, the Tractarian religious ethos promoted by the early Newman and later maintained so assiduously by his onetime fellow travellers John Keble and Edward Bouverie Pusey still animated its clergy and people. Perham's dutiful faith would soon be tested by the enormous waste and tragic loss of the war, but early discordant notes can be found independent of that, such as her comment after a service in February 1915: 'Heard Mr. Ronald Knox at St. Barnabas. If this is modern preaching I've had enough'.[5] Knox, just a few years older than Perham and a brilliant classicist, was fellow and chaplain of Trinity College but would, in 1917, leave the Church of England, a la Newman, to become a Roman Catholic. Evidently, he was not an ideal preacher for Perham's own brand of loyal Anglicanism as there can be little doubt that her faith was deeply rooted and owed nearly everything to the shaping influences of home and school. Perham's faith too pushed her initially in the direction of the academic study of theology, as evidenced by her taking the Divinity Moderations in second year, a kind of rehearsal for Schools, the final year set of examinations upon which the class of an Oxford undergraduate's degree wholly depends.[6]

For Perham, the stark transition of leaving the all-female society of St. Anne's School for the largely all-male society of Oxford was cushioned by the presence of Edgar. Early on he was a wealth of information about Oxford's often arcane ways and their warm and chatty relationship made evident by their correspondence mark them as especially close. As the year 1914–15 proceeded Edgar decided, however, to do what was fast becoming a cliché – 'his bit' for the war effort.[7] The Battle of the Marne in September of 1914 ensured that the war's predicted brevity – its being 'over by Christmas' – would sink into the waist-high mud of the fast-developing Western Front. And with it the early giddy public support for the war sank likewise. Perham's own view of the war was governed always by the fact of Edgar's decision to enlist. She maintained a 'Contents Strictly Private' diary of the war from beginning to end and already, in November of 1914, her initial enthusiasm for the great crusade against the Kaiser was starting to wane. 'I had my fill of soldiers today', she wrote. 'Watched the men in the Parks for 2 hours … . The grim earnestness of the men was very marked …'.[8]

Amidst the descending gloom of war as it stretched into 1915, however, ordinary undergraduate life continued apace. Perham's strong interest in history, cultivated especially at St. Anne's, was given full scope to develop at Oxford. She produced her required weekly essays for her college tutor, G.S. Woods, on, for example, why 'The Tudors deserved to fail in Ireland', or, 'The Study of History', a rather sweeping effort. Her conclusion in the latter offering is supremely whiggish in its optimism: 'Is the prospect entirely gloomy. No. New events, new elements may come in that at present cannot be visualized'.[9] Perhaps she was thinking of the war.

Such a malleable, essentially optimistic, outlook would mark Perham's thinking always, whether as a relatively callow undergraduate, or later as a hardened and sophisticated analyst of British colonial policy in Africa. What comes through too from her early student days is a practicability in her nature that, in some ways, goes against type in defining the contemplative Oxford don – whose ranks she would later join. In the meantime, the war pressed on relentlessly during that year. Continuing to ruminate on it in the autumn of 1914, she writes: 'It does not take a Christian to make a good soldier, but it does take a soldier to make a good Christian. We must wrestle, & fight, & pray. The calm & the visions come at the end of the Bible – the rest is action. So with us'.[10]

For Perham, it is evident that her Christianity was a powerful animator, which is why as the war closed in on her life, as it did on the lives of so many of her contemporaries, her dependence on both its power to explain and on its capacity to succour deepened. In 1916, that dependence on her faith would be tested in a way that had never happened before, or would again.

Edgar Perham was just twenty-two years old when he marched off to war as part of the hastily dispatched British Expeditionary Force or, as the Kaiser had sneered, that 'contemptible little army'. Contemptible it may have been initially; still, it was the kernel of the future million-man British Army, the largest volunteer force in the history of the world until that point in time, and Edgar was an enthusiastic member of it from the outset. In physique he was sturdily built and just this side of handsome with a shock of brown hair and a forthright manner of speaking. Contemporary photographs show him wearing his uniform and great coat proudly, the young army peacock on his way to battle. Edgar loved his youngest sister deeply, a love that was reciprocated fully and rather exclusively. The two-year gap in their ages had never meant much to either of them and indeed, when speaking publicly later about her five brothers Perham saw no need to elaborate on any of them other than Edgar.[11]

As fairly close-in-age children they had spent much time together in play, whether outdoors or in the nursery. Their surviving ubiquitous notebooks bulge with the collected poetry and prose of those early years. In 1906, for example, the eleven-year old Margery wrote 'Ode to a Brother' in which she rhapsodizes that 'the earth holds no face for me but thine'. In response, Edgar wrote a poem extolling the virtues of their companionship entitled simply, 'Midget and I'.[12] In our psychoanalytical age perhaps there is a reflexive desire to read something sexual into such an intimate exchange. But to do so would be to put on their warm and close relationship a completely wrong complexion. Theirs was an intense sibling relationship, a union of brother and sister as soul-mates, but nothing more. And whatever their ages, they could always speak to one another in a 'grown-up mood', as Edgar wrote to her from Oxford in the summer of 1914. Their complete trust in one another and their joint desire to be *understood* is palpable in the letters. A year into the war Edgar wrote of their friendship as being 'a permanent truth, immortal & imperishable'.[13] His letters became increasingly elegiac in tone as the war continued, matching its course, which, for the British especially, would reach a tragic mid-point in the summer of 1916 at the Somme.

Nearly a century later the slaughter of the battle of the Somme retains its capacity to shock and repel, so stark are the numbers. At the end of 1 July 1916, the first day of the battle, 60,000 mainly British troops lay dead or wounded in the steaming mud of northern France, a single day's harvest of death unmatched in the annals of Britain at war.[14] Given its well-documented history the allied campaign of that summer of blood requires no reprise here. The constant desire for a breakthrough along the static Western Front had guided allied strategy for the first years of the war but by 1916 the difficulty of doing so had caused a change in strategy to one of attrition. Preparedness mixed with fresh troops and an unwavering commitment to besting the enemy through dogged survival was now the great strategic animator. British high command, led by General Sir Douglas Haig, argued desperately that such a campaign was both possible and necessary. From July until December of 1916, therefore, the effort continued even though the casualty rate was horrendous and the ground gained small.

As a 2nd lieutenant in the West Yorkshire Regiment, Edgar Perham found himself in the midst of the Somme cauldron from the outset. In expected fashion he had moved closer and closer to the action, finally experiencing the trenches – 'a sea of mud' – for the first time in October of 1915, and then, for awhile at least, becoming 'fearfully busy'. Having arrived at the front lines meant to Edgar that he had 'done what I joined to do'.[15] To fill the long hours of restless excitement before the whistle would blow and the action recommence he had brought with him various books, including Dickens's *Pickwick Papers*: 'By Jove they are good once you get moving in them'.[16] His spirits were high as he wrote home about 'grand' night attacks and the 'great fun' of tracking German airplane movements through his field glasses.[17]

Such reports continued steadily from the Front – 'if people knew how one longs for letters out here they would be writing all day long', he wrote to his mother in October – but as 1915 passed into 1916 their jauntiness diminishes and is replaced by an air of resignation verging on despair. Amidst the literary 'delights of *Pride and Prejudice*, which I have just finished' and the less satisfying *Great Expectations*, the demoralizing impact of what First World War historian Paul Fussell would later call the 'Troglodyte World' was now weighing heavily upon Edgar.[18] His letters to Margery in the spring of 1916 are almost unrelentingly dark, although as always Edgar does his best to maintain an optimistic tone. 'We are now back in the trenches, up to the knees in melted snow and mud – the trenches all falling down with the thaw as with shellfire', he reported in March. But 'it's a gay life' nonetheless, he finishes with a flourish.[19]

For Perham and her parents of course there was no way of knowing the precise location in France where these events were taking place. British Army censorship withheld battlefield movements, but the tone of the letters made it clear that Edgar was in the thick of the fighting. Between reporting that life is 'cheap' out here, and that I am 'dog tired' and 'distraught with trench warfare' it was clear that he was approaching maximum exposure to life at the Front.[20] A week into the brutal Somme campaign, nursing a minor leg wound, and with death all-around him, he wrote with a sense of resignation that 'my life is now a matter of moments'.[21] And, tragically, it was to be so. The West Yorkshires were fighting at Delville Wood, a zone of intense action and heavy casualties near the town of Longueval, and led by the initial major wartime engagement of the South African 1st Infantry Brigade.[22] On 20 July 1916, six days after the battle had commenced Edgar wrote his last letter to Margery. Reporting that he was 'terribly down in the dumps' owing to the loss of 'some of the best fellows on Earth', including his commanding officer 'whom the whole battalion worshipped', he asked plaintively: 'will the war ever be over?'[23]

Four days later on the 24th of July the war indeed came to an end for Edgar Perham as he kept his regulation steel helmet on firmly and struggled through the killing ground of Delville Wood. In his last letter to his sister he had told her lightly that 'I seem to be Achilles, utterly immune from wounds'.[24] But the maw of death that was the Somme claimed Edgar too, shot and killed that day in his twenty-fourth year, his helmet proving no defence against German lead. The dreaded telegram from Buckingham Palace announcing his death was received by the Perhams on 16 August. Edgar was gone. Poignantly, his last letters would not be received until after the knowledge of his death, which only added to the family's pain. For Perham, the sense of loss at Edgar's death was overwhelming, and her grief, it seems, could not be assuaged. As she would do so often at points of crisis in her life, she took up pen and paper in an attempt to cauterize the deep psychic wound left by Edgar's violent death. On three tiny cards and in cramped handwriting she poured out her anguish over her beloved brother's loss. 'You left me to the solitude of a grief which is not for words', she opined. And yet the words kept coming. Later, it would seem that the

Christian faith itself had failed her in this her greatest hour of need. At the time, however, she leaned upon it heavily in order to try and absorb the deathblow and understand its meaning and impact. 'Life has got to be lived', she continued, in a paean written to the departed Edgar, 'the truth has got to be faced bravely, victoriously, for God's sake, for yours, for mine, for the World's. The World may see the victory; it must not see the tears. God sees them. Does he let you see them? Does he let you see & fear for me, as I pray for you?'[25]

Edgar's death in the midst of the British Expeditionary Force's summer of slaughter in 1916 left Margery Perham in a kind of lingering stupour. After an excruciating few months of grief she returned to Oxford in October for her final year, but there was little that was anticipatory in doing so. Oxford itself, where the war was cutting a wide swathe of death through a devastated undergraduate population, seemed to lack most of its usual charms. For Perham, it became clear that the enduring pain of Edgar's loss was best dealt with through work and so she dug hard into her third year of reading and essay writing leading to a date at the Examination Schools in June of 1917.

Her performance in the week-long marathon of Finals was brilliant, defying the depressed mood that had dogged her all that year. The intensity of examination writing at Oxford has produced failure in many an otherwise brilliant student – most famously, perhaps, John Henry Newman. Perham, however, would not be among them. Of the thirty-one women examined in Modern History in Trinity Term 1917 she was one of just four to be placed in the first class.[26] Traditionally, such an outstanding performance made an academic career available, if desired, although in the case of women no such trajectory was much considered, or offered. Indeed, following such a course was highly unlikely. Oxford itself had only a handful of women dons and they were restricted to the women's colleges. Perham herself displayed no such academic ambitions at the time, but her highly impressed examiners along with her tutor, Woods, thought otherwise and encouraged her to enter upon a life of university teaching if, for no other reason, than it was her wartime duty to do so![27]

The options available to her in this regard were few and restricted to so-called Redbrick or provincial universities, however. No Oxbridge appointment for Miss Perham. This reality came to mean a post as assistant lecturer in history at the University of Sheffield. Having gained full university status only in 1905 Sheffield was very new and, compared to the assorted glories of Oxford, utterly without appeal. But with her parents having embarked upon a peripatetic retirement lifestyle of living in the Channel Islands and holidaying in the South of France, and therefore with really no home to which to return and no obvious other job to take up, Perham reluctantly accepted Sheffield's offer.

In later years Perham's view of the time spent at Sheffield was unremittingly negative: the 'worst' time of her life. Undoubtedly, as her decision in 1920 to take a year's leave would make clear, her state of mind worsened the longer she was there. But such was not always the case if the level of her engagement in the life of both the university and the city are taken into account. Sheffield may have been 'grimy' as she called it, but as a Yorkshirewoman heading to the Midlands for a first job it would be unreasonable to see it wholly as a form of banishment.[28] And so having just marked her twenty-second birthday at the beginning of September Margery Perham arrived in Sheffield, younger than many of the students she was about to teach, the most junior member of the history staff, and, quite plainly, its only woman.

3

IN EXILE AND INTO AFRICA: FROM SHEFFIELD TO SOMALILAND

The city of Sheffield, in the autumn of 1917, had a population of about 185,000 people spread over its signature hilly topography. A bustling industrial burgh long known for its steel production – ranging from the swords and bayonets that had equipped Britain's eighteenth and early-nineteenth-century army to contemporary high-quality cutlery – it was not, on the other hand, anyone's idea of a university town. Like the other so-called Redbricks of the time, the University of Sheffield was seen – certainly from the scholarly uplands of Oxford and Cambridge – as hopelessly provincial with its unlucky staff existing in a form of academic exile. In retrospect, such was certainly the view of the place held by Margery Perham, but this unremittingly gloomy perspective would take some time to form. At first, she relished her new life as a young Sheffield history don and was 'determined to be independent'.[1]

There is something highly admirable about the youthful Perham, on her own in an unfamiliar city midway through the Great War. Apart from the tragically increasing number of war widows there were not many (unmarried) twenty-two year old women making their own way in the world, especially as a budding academic professional. Accordingly, the much-prized independence she now exercised was not easily financed on the meagre university salary she received of just £100 per annum. Everything was expensive, especially food, she complained regularly to her mother that first autumn. Exacerbating her money troubles were those of transport because she found she could not easily ride her bicycle to the university on account of Sheffield's ubiquitous and steep hills.[2] As a result Perham became a regular on a 'clanging tram', as she described it, which took her to and from rental accommodation located on the outskirts of town, before later acquiring a motorcycle.[3]

No. 1 Summerfield in Broomhill, the rambling mid-Victorian house where she rented a room, was the best she could afford. Unsurprisingly given the era, the house was 'full of men' only therefore, and in her blithely suggestive phrase, which probably made her upstanding parents blanche, 'impregnated with masculinity'.[4] Having grown up in a household brimming with brothers, putting up with a bathroom 'full of razor straps and shaving appointments' could not have been as awful Perham made it sound. Indeed, for someone with little apparent romantic and almost certainly no sexual experience, a boarding house full of young men must have provided a certain hormonal frisson to an otherwise drab domestic scene. Still, her later reminiscences of Sheffield, of sitting 'down to a piece of steak and a pudding both of which I had cut into four portions to last for four days', or of walking out on the nearby moors there to sit on the soot-encrusted heather and contemplate the 'dark bare horizon' are almost uniformly grim.[5]

This (retrospective) bleakness was deepened by Perham's frosty reception at the hands of her fellow members of Sheffield's history department. Numbering about six and all men, they looked with suspicion upon this female high-flyer fresh from Oxford. In some ways, and just as well, she could afford to ignore them. Working up her inaugural lectures would prove – as it always has done for embryo academics – to be an all-consuming exercise and very hard going. 'It is all I can do to keep pace', she wrote to her mother that first term. 'I have to give 3 on one day, which leaves me rather exhausted... . I cannot say I like lecturing'.[6]

The Sheffield Senior Common Room, with its clubby atmosphere of jackets with elbow patches and acrid pipe smoke was an unwelcoming environment for Perham, and in an echo of a Ladies' Annexe at a Pall Mall club, she was quickly ushered out of it and into a tiny and unheated room nearby. 'This', she was told firmly by one of her putative colleagues, 'is the Ladies' Common Room'.[7] Sexism of this blunt type at that time is almost too common to bear much comment. But it weighed heavily on Perham, especially when professorial privilege seemed to extend to attacks on things she assumed, properly speaking, were personal, such as her Christian faith. But unaccountably within her first month at Sheffield she had a disagreement over this very matter with Dr. John Baker, holder of the chair in history. As she recounted in one of her frequent letters to her mother, in the course of a discussion with Baker about religious matters, he had exploded with the comment: 'If you are High Church I shall sack you'.[8] He accused Perham of 'acting a part' in this regard, and that if she truly was a Tractarian – in reference to Newman and Pusey and the other Church of England reformers of the 1830s and 40s and their anglo-catholic successors – then the only honourable thing to do was to become a Roman Catholic. This sort of attack naturally was as deeply wounding as it was inappropriate, and a shocked and 'extremely angry' Perham simply went silent in front of Baker in response, refusing to answer the threat and waiting for him to apologize, which, finally, and to her satisfaction, he did.

Enduring this degree of blatant animus had the effect of driving Perham even more deeply into her academic work. Eventually she began to enjoy teaching, and her students were voluble enough to let her know she was good at it. All along, however, and despite Perham's unhappiness, her appointment at Sheffield had been big news at her old school, as was the first class degree at Oxford that had preceded it. The St. Anne's 'School News' of December 1917 sang Perham's praises, congratulating her 'heartily' on such serial successes.[9] Meanwhile, as if to put a balm on the wound opened by Professor Baker's intemperate comments, his daughter, a Sheffield undergraduate, attended one of Perham's lectures and told her afterwards that she found them to be both charming and interesting. While not quite sure what to make of 'charming' as a term of endearment for a history lecture, Perham was grateful for the endorsement nonetheless.[10]

As her first year at Sheffield progressed, and as Perham's comfort and confidence in the lecture hall increased, her letters home became lighter in tone. She was teaching the modern European history syllabus, which gave her ample opportunity to delve into the causes of the ongoing war, and about which – as we shall see – she would soon be lecturing to British troops. Meanwhile, between lunch and tea at the residence of the Vice-Chancellor, Sir W. Henry Hadow: he has a 'ripping house', and steady comments about her other activities both indoors and out: the weather is 'rippingly fine', Perham was certainly pushing back the gloom that had descended upon her shortly after her arrival.[11]

In the spring of 1918, and as the end of her first academic year at Sheffield approached, Perham accepted the invitation of the YMCA to lecture to British soldiers stationed across the Channel in Northern France, as well as nearer home in the great martial gathering place that was the Salisbury Plain, as part of its educational scheme. By then, the war was showing clear signs that it must soon be over. The Americans had finally dispensed with their overstretched claim of neutrality the previous year and enthusiastic doughboys by the hundreds of thousands now were steaming across the Atlantic bound for the Western Front. The Germans were not quite ready to admit defeat, however, and prepared steadily that winter for their last great offensive, Operation Michael, that would come beginning in March. But the beleaguered allies, buoyed up critically by the fresh American troops, resisted this last ferocious drive across the churned up wasteland of Arras and Amiens and in so doing made it look more and more that the day when the guns might fall silent along the Western Front could not be far off.

In this penultimate phase of the war Perham, ever conscious of doing her duty, gave a number of lectures to what proved to be – in the main – rapt and impressed audiences of war-weary Tommies, as well as to colonial troops. Whether on the Salisbury Plain or across the Channel in Le Havre, she endeavoured to explain to the men how and why it was that almost all of Europe had gone to war back in 1914. Naturally, the memory of the fallen Edgar was strong during these assignments, but she seems to have almost revelled in the experience. Especially enjoyable was the response of troops from the Empire. 'I found the Colonials keener than the English', she wrote after an address in April. 'They used to come crowding round after the lecture and ask when you were coming again'.[12]

The novelty of a young and attractive woman speaking with authority on Prussia, Germany, and Bismarck – the latter a perennially favourite topic of hers – likewise caught the fancy of the press. In particular, the (London) *Morning News* covered her lecture to a mass of New Zealand troops in Le Havre under the headline: 'For Lady Readers: Lecturing to Soldiers, A Girl's Experience in France'. After noting that there were upwards of a thousand troops in the audience, the unidentified writer goes on to quote Perham as calling the experience the 'finest sensation I have ever had in my life'.[13] Certainly she had now mastered the art of the lecture, putting to rest forever her disappointing first efforts at Sheffield. Indeed, Perham's forthrightness combined with her obvious femininity elicited a chivalrous response from some of the men gathered to hear her speak. In a rather poignant letter Perham received shortly after she had addressed a large body of English troops in Le Havre in mid-April 1918, the writer, one Corporal Thomas Knight, asks after her safety following the lecture. In plain and mildly ungrammatical language he confirmed to her that 'I am sure I am very glad to hear that you got home alright becaus [sic] I know what being in the streets is Miss, in Havre at night, Miss, with us soldiers'.[14] Miss Perham, no doubt, was charmed.

Less charmed, however, was she once some of these same troops began to demobilize in the autumn of 1918 and return home to enroll in university, including a few of them in her courses at Sheffield. The signing of the Armistice in November meant the release of thousands of servicemen, many of which began to attend university around the country. Consequently, the undergraduate population at Sheffield swelled to some one thousand from about half that figure. Many of these young men had had their educations interrupted by the war and, considering the high number of their former comrades who now were dead, they can only have considered themselves uncommonly lucky to be back reading for their degrees. Additionally, and herein the problem seemed to be situated for Perham, there were many students older than the typical undergraduate and, arguably because of the government's provisions made to accommodate 'demobbed' soldiers, of a lower standard academically than their pre- and wartime peers. For Perham, coping both with mostly male students who were older than she was herself, and some of whom demanded considerable remedial help, was highly difficult and began to take its toll during the 1918–19 academic year. As she remarked to her mother, I 'intend to have over the coals two young men who come to my lectures & who have not been behaving too well. I don't look forward to it I can tell you as they look as old as I am… .'[15] Over the next year the strain would only worsen. Her archive is rather silent about this vexed period, but it is clear that she took on too much work in the form of personal outside tuition and remediation. Exacerbating her woes was an ongoing shortage of money. 'It [Sheffield] is no place for the poor', she complained to home.[16] There was also the further complication of an intense, but failed, romance with a Sheffield colleague, Vincent Tourner, with which to contend. Not much is known of him, but their brief relationship was ended by Perham. His letters form a small, sad cache in her archive and date from the autumn of 1919. The last of Tourner's seven missives to Perham is immediately post break-up and is overwrought with the language of unrequited love: 'You may imagine what I am feeling & going through just at the present time: the world is dead … . Tomorrow will be the first day for four weeks that I will not see you: & I will feel a terrible loneliness; will you think of me a little?'[17]

The genesis and course of this romance are impossible to recover now, so many years later, but the letters reveal that Perham was reluctant to commit herself to Tourner, just as she was reluctant or unable to commit to any other suitor, either then or later. She had, in the past, engaged in some vigorous discussions of love, marriage, and sexuality with Edgar, and even more pointedly, with her brother Wilfrid, known to the family as 'Willie'. A 1915 letter from him, for example, commends her for holding a traditional stance on pre-marital sexuality, while at the same time containing a revealing comment about himself: 'Your argument appears to be sound about keeping yourself for one man … . So far as that goes I have succeeded in keeping myself pure for one girl, though it has not been through any piety on my part as I have tried to be bad, but something in my temperament has kept me from availing myself of other men's experiences'.[18]

Altogether, by 1920, Perham was in severe psychological straits. Later she would complain of having been 'crushed by overwork' and of being assailed by 'personal troubles and isolation'.[19] A later age too would likely have diagnosed her as suffering from clinical depression. As it was, she was given urgent medical advice to take a long rest, which, to Perham's surprise and lifelong joy, ended up being spent in the highly unlikely location of British Somaliland. If Sheffield increasingly had the air of exile about it, then a trip to the Horn of Africa, to far-off Somaliland, meant adventure and freedom. She could not wait to go.

In today's world the Republic of Somalia encompasses the old British Protectorate of Somaliland, which, since 1991, has proclaimed itself as the 'Republic of Somaliland' in an unrecognized bid for freedom from the larger surrounding republic it deems to be illegitimate. But however defined, contemporary Somalia is a byword for savage anarchy, seafaring piracy, and crippling poverty. It is a country that routinely ranks near the top of those international scales that measure the assorted miseries of failed states. The per capita GDP of Somalia is around US $800, putting it in the bottom two percent of the world's nations. Somalian politics pit clan against clan in a protracted bloody civil war, at the centre of which is a weak, corrupt, and impoverished coalition government that is able to exert very little control over the country's 246,000 square miles.[20] By all measures – as I write not even the Internet can penetrate the country – Somalia is a place very few, if any, would consider going for a rest cure. But ninety years ago much was different there and that is precisely where Margery Perham chose to go, leaving England on the last day of 1920.

In Sheffield, Perham's weakened state of mind and her need for a long period of rest had been recognized by the increasingly sympathetic department chair, Dr. Baker, as well as by the University administration. Beginning in the autumn of 1920, therefore, she was granted a year's leave of absence. As Perham tells it, Africa had always occupied a large place in her imagination and it quickly emerged as *the* place in which this necessary period of rest should be spent.[21] Clinching its attractiveness, however, and in most practical ways making the trip possible, was her sister Ethel's residency in Somaliland.

Ethel, eight years Perham's senior, had gone out to British East Africa in 1910 intending to serve as a missionary with the (Anglican) Church Missionary Society, which, since its inception in 1799 with the heroic abolitionist William Wilberforce as its vice-president, had come to have a significant presence in equatorial Africa, especially in the field of education. Romance intervened in these well-laid plans, however, in the form of a dashing New Zealander who was just then travelling the Imperial trail of adventure mixed with commerce. Henry 'Harry' Rayne had arrived in South Africa at the turn of the century. He proceeded to fight alongside his countrymen in the Boer War, afterwards moving north to hunt elephant and buffalo in East Africa just as it began to open up to British settlement at the behest of the tireless colonial visionary, Hugh Cholmondeley, 3rd Baron Delamere, and then moved north further still to the region of Somalia, to what was then called Jubaland, a rump of territory dividing British Somaliland from that contiguous piece of land claimed by Italy. Here Rayne settled down in a semi-permanent way to grow cotton. Returning from a selling and reprovisioning trip to London in 1910 he met, wooed, and successfully proposed to a rather star-struck Ethel Perham. By the time their ship lay in the roads off Mombasa they had determined to marry straight away; straight away did, in fact, turn out to be the next year, but when they did marry it was done rather grandly at the coastal town's recently built Church of England cathedral.[22]

Thereafter, a decade of rough and ready frontier living ensued, with child-bearing, warfare, Harry's entry into the Colonial Administrative Service, and the bringing to heel of Somaliland's so-called 'Mad Mullah' just prior to Margery Perham's arrival in 1921. The Mad Mullah episode ranks as one of the mythic set-pieces of British Imperial history in North Africa, a concerted attempt to stamp out what was seen as Oriental extremism standing in the way of Western order and good government. The Mad Mullah's proper name was Abdullah Hassan. Born in Somalia in 1856, he grew up devout in the Islamic faith, working for two years as a teacher of the Qur'an, then becoming radicalized by his pilgrimage to Mecca to perform the Hajj in 1894. The next year he encountered the British directly at Berbera, as well as the presence elsewhere in Somalia of Italian Roman Catholic missionaries. Both sets of European Christians he took to be potentially destructive of the faith of his Muslim co-religionists. Eventually exacerbating his heightened state of mind was a dispute over the theft (he claimed it was a gift) of an official garrison gun, which the British accused him of having committed. Hassan chose this moment in 1899 to strike back against them, together with their Ethiopian collaborators under King Menelek II, as well as against the Italians. The result was a protracted twenty-year struggle, comparable in some ways to the Mahdi's earlier struggle against the Anglo-Egyptians in the Sudan, which came to an end only after the First World War when the British concentrated their efforts in a joint air and land campaign. Beginning in January 1920 Hassan's stout network of forts was smashed and his control over the Somali hinterland broken. The British then offered him terms of surrender, which were rejected peremptorily. By December Hassan was dead anyhow, having succumbed to influenza.[23]

The dusty epic of the Mad Mullah speaks to Britain's long interest in the region, although not necessarily to its rationale. Such interest had been sparked mainly by the peregrinations of Richard Burton and John Hanning Speke in 1854–55. Later, of course, this intrepid pair would find great fame – and suffer an almost equally famous personal falling-out – over the search for the headwaters of the Nile.[24] But in mid-century, they were mostly unknown soldier-adventurers out to penetrate territory which no European had ever seen, even though Somalia was located only a short distance across the Gulf of Aden from its eponymous port, the most important British coaling station, or 'coal hole', in the Middle East. By the turn of the century, Berbera, the main Somali port, had become the transshipment point for a steady supply of meat from the hunting grounds of the Horn of Africa. Nicknamed the 'butcher shop', Berbera served the booming India trade that, since the opening of the Suez Canal in 1869, had become a veritable nautical highway for British ships bound especially for Bombay and thence to the Far East.

For Major Harry Rayne, M.B.E., M.C., after almost twenty years now an 'Old Africa hand' and a decorated soldier from Britain's First World War engagements against the Germans in East Africa, the prospect of ending the Mad Mullah's irritating insouciance toward the British was tantalizing. Rayne participated in the final campaign against him and his 'dervishes' with great enthusiasm, as recounted in his memoir, *Sun, Sand and Somals* (1921). On the ground the Somaliland Camel Corps pursued the dervish, while from above the Royal Air Force tracked and bombed them: 'The magic of the Mad Mullah, that had for so long held his followers together, was useless against the magic of the bird-men above', he gushed.[25] Published only a year after the campaign's success, Rayne's book is part *Boys' Own* adventure tale told in the style of Rider Haggard, and part amateur anthropology. In the aftermath of the war, Rayne had been appointed District Commissioner of one of the now recontrolled territories of Somaliland centred on the southern town of Hargeisa. He took on the task with relish and with a good deal of pride. After all, as he saw things, 'British prestige in Somaliland had been entirely restored and the country, after twenty years of unrest, is at last at peace'.[26] And so it was that into this remote corner of the *Pax Britannica* came twenty-five year old Margery Perham early in 1921.

Despite Perham's growing enthusiasm for Somaliland, spiked by letters from and then a trip home by Ethel in 1920, going there was hardly a sure thing. Her parents did not think it was either quite proper, or –

more pointedly – likely to be of much use in providing the kind of rest it was thought their daughter needed in order to recover her health. But once Somaliland became her choice – and for Perham there really seemed to be no other – she was determined to go at all costs. By this point in their lives Frederick and Marion Perham had confirmed their rather rootless retirement lifestyle in the Channel Islands and the South of France, with very little time spent near their children in England. As such, as Perham had experienced now for a number of years there was no real 'home' to which to go, save the one she might forge for herself. And so, after a half-hearted attempt to please her mother by engaging briefly in a rest cure at a hotel in the Lake District – which she seemed to regard as a cure worse than the disease – Perham began earnest planning for her departure for Somaliland. And when at last it came – on the S.S. *Kaiser & Hind* from Tilbury on 31 December 1920 – she experienced nothing but a febrile 'Joy, Joy. I ran up on to the topmost deck, hatless in the wind & rain, & laughed aloud as the gap of dirty green between us and the dock swirled and widened… .' Perham's youthful freedom and exuberance very nearly jump off the pages of her unpublished and tattered 'Somaliland Diary' as she describes the inaugural moment of this great adventure, a beginning shared with Ethel and her two young sons, Robert and Wilfrid, who would make the journey with her.[27]

Travelling by ocean liner in 1921, one could expect a voyage of about three weeks from England to Somaliland, down the European coast and in past the storied strategic choke point of Gibraltar, across the azure Mediterranean Sea, south along the Suez Canal and through the Red Sea, into port at Aden and then at last, across the Gulf, to the Somaliland shoreline and the port of Berbera. The route constituted the main part of the so-called Passage to India and in that respect for many was the lifeline of the modern British Empire. These were the great years of ocean voyages, of mammoth Peninsular & Oriental liners on their way to India or elsewhere, when the long, measured journey allowed travellers to absorb climatic and time changes slowly, when on-board friendships and romance might blossom, and when a true appreciation of distance was made. For Margery Perham, this trip to Somaliland was the first great journey of her life and she radiated anticipation of what it might hold in store.

At first flush, after the excitement of departure, the voyage did not hold much, however, other than an immediate acquaintance with sea-sickness. But ever stout in the face of physical discomfort: 'I do not admit to being sick', she wrote a day into the passage, she could not overlook the fact that 'I have a headache, & oh it is heaving. Everyone is the colour of an evening paper'.[28] Soon enough, however, Perham found her sea-legs, the sun came out, and the fun began. So too, once having reached Gibraltar, did her encounter with Africa, which, she wrote rather grandiloquently, 'frowned heavily at the sister continent … in sweat & death must she be sought and subdued'.[29] Such language is clearly indicative of the way in which her generation approached the apparent perils of the Dark Continent, and it does little good almost a hundred years later and in what is apparently a more culturally sensitive time to downplay the degree to which Africa was seen by contemporaries as a fearsome, savage place. There is little doubt that Perham was feeling both trepidation and exhilaration at the prospect of entering Africa, a frame of mind reinforced by her first sight of it.

In the meantime, the voyage out was becoming exceedingly convivial, 'glorious', as Perham described it in her journal, full of food and drink, conversation and dancing. One of the young soldiers on board, Corporal Townsend, reminded Perham, happily so, of the lost Edgar. And the ship's ascetic skipper, Captain MacClanaghen, became the subject of some friendly verse: 'Captain Mac is tall and thin, we hope he has no more to grow, on the decks he stalks along, like an automatic crow'. A fancy dress ball capped off the voyage, with Perham dressed rather daringly as 'a sort of courtesan', then adding, 'quite successful'. The waning days of the journey also brought a cricket match, a concert, and, alas, much sadness for its impending end. Port Said was made, then the Suez Canal by night and the Red Sea and finally into the Gulf of Aden with the 'menacing wildly cut [Surud] mountains on each side'.[30] Aden itself was reached on the evening of Sunday, 16 January 1921. Walking down the gangway the sights and smells of the 'Eastern night' made an immediate impression upon Perham: 'It was like a scene in a play', she wrote, adding that the old port was 'lit by torches' the light from which illumined 'a group of natives with gleaming arms and white and scarlet clothes'. From there it was off to what she found to be the inaccurately named Grand Royal Hotel, and then to a place of much greater comfort, the Club, the true spiritual home of the contemporary British overseas.

Aden, today, is the former capital and best-known city in the People's Democratic Republic of Yemen with a population approaching one million. Its history stretches back to antiquity, however, with some even regarding it as the burial place of Cain and Abel. In Perham's day, Aden was ruled as part of British India, having come under Crown control in 1838, and it was the most important port on the route to India between Port Said and Bombay.[31] A chaotic town of perhaps 50,000 people, Perham soaked up its other-worldliness, running outdoors the morning after her arrival 'to watch every camel that went by'. Alongside the camels could be seen 'black-capped Parsees, bronze-bodied Arabs, straight-legged Somalis – black as coal – standing erect in spotless clothes, checked & white'.[32] Here was the glorious East in all its variety and exoticism! Perham, as would be the case throughout her early exposure to Africa and, as Wm. Roger Louis has pointed out was always to be a feature of her apprehension of the continent's peoples, took great notice of physiogonomy.[33] Racial attributes and distinctions were of sustaining interest to her. In this she was largely typical of her era in which all manner of science and pseudo-science spoke to the existence and supposed profound meaning of racial difference. Still, Perham was especially interested in those things that marked out the African physically from other 'natives', as well as from Europeans, and her writings contain many references to such distinctions.

Perham's stay in Aden was brief, just two days. Then it was off across the Gulf to Africa and the port of Berbera. Years later she recalled being fearful of this final part of the journey, of what lay in wait for her in 'unknown, unknowable' Somaliland. However, none of this 'spasm of recoil', of 'revulsion', of 'racial fear', as she summed it up half a century onward, is evident in her record of the time. Rather, she seems to have been excited and happy to 'shake off the sand of the Grand Royal from our feet' and make the short trip to her penultimate destination.

Unsurprisingly, the cattle boat, the *Woodcock*, which took Margery and Ethel and the boys over to Berbera was dingy and overcrowded and noisy, replete with all manner of passengers and livestock. Perham read a novel by the light of a swinging hurricane lamp and managed a good sleep nonetheless. By evening of the next day the 'white walls and flat roofed bungalows of Berbera' had come into view. Approaching the port and peering 'eagerly in search of signs of welcome & celebration', Perham was disappointed to see that 'there were none' but soon enough a 'dilapidated car' approached the landing and, once disembarked, they climbed in and were taken to the ship captain's bungalow located nearby the docks. There they were met by his daughter and shown to a portion of the verandah, which would act as temporary sleeping quarters. And so, on 24 January, three and a half weeks after setting out from England, Perham wrote in anticipation of what was to come, 'we began our life in the East'.[34]

Berbera was an ancient and, to Perham at least, a surprisingly fragrant port, home to the timeless export of frankincense and myrhh, and used for centuries by Arabs and others as one of the main points of entry into Africa. Its population was comprised of 'Barbarians', at least as far as the Romans had been concerned. Much closer in time to Perham's visit, however, in April 1855, Burton and Speke's encampment at Berbera had been attacked by local tribesmen, confirming for the two explorers, one supposes, the Roman view. In any event, a ferocious struggle ensued that saw Burton take a spear through the face, which left him with the jagged scar that gave him the slightly sinister look he bore thereafter, while Speke was taken prisoner and brutalized.[35] By 1921, however, Berbera, while still a potentially violent place, had also become the ramshackle capital of British Somaliland and home to a few thousand people, many of whom, it seemed to Perham, were to be found in the prison located next door to the captain's bungalow. 'It was a new experience for me', she noted a few days after arriving, 'to see the lines of prisoners with water tanks bowing their shoulders & chains clanking between their knees walking up & down in front of a guard armed with lash & rifle'. Despite the apparent harshness of the prison routine, she concluded wryly that on the strength of its provision of shelter and three square meals a day incarceration was popular and there was 'some competition for sentences'. Perham's first impressions of Berbera were thus contradictory, she concluded, save for the fact that without the British presence conditions would be truly unimaginable.[36]

Meanwhile, in anticipation of heading inland about 200 miles to Hargeisa, their ultimate destination where Harry Rayne was stationed, Perham spent considerable time in a saddle on the back of a 'nettlesome' pony sent to Berbera for just this purpose. The town's terrain was sandy and rough, good for learning the rudiments of African horsemanship, and together with a move to a more accommodating bungalow, Perham was fast beginning to really enjoy herself. At the new house 'I chose the upper room, & to my joy am able to sleep upon the roof. It is flat & smooth & white; & the nights upon its surface are a pure delight and a luxury of new sensation ... . The nights – oh the Eastern nights. What can the Westerner know ...' .[37]

Perham's rapturous – even semi-erotic – welcoming of her new life in Berbera was tempered, however, by the ongoing unease caused by the Mad Mullah's last stand and by the government's imposition of a new tax. This unease was particularly true at Hargeisa, and amongst the small British community in the capital the ongoing tense situation in the southwest part of the Protectorate was talked about incessantly. Such was especially the case at Government House where Margery and Ethel were invited to dine early in February. As far as such standard colonial-era buildings went, Berbera's edition of it was rather humble, but the centrality of its place in the town and Protectorate belied its simplicity. For Perham, whose subsequent African journeys would usually be centred upon the government house in a given colony, this first trip to the seat of local British power initially proved to be 'nerve wracking'. Dinner was served on the same table that had lately been used to dispense local justice, and once everyone had sat down Perham found herself on one side of the Governor, while Ethel sat on the other. Dressed for the occasion 'in our best', they were the only women present in the dining room. But the food was good and plentiful, and the Somali servants, the 'boys', as everyone called them, were well turned out. The Governor, Sir Geoffrey Francis Archer, knighted the previous year for his success against the Mad Mullah, was a fast-rising member of the Colonial Administrative Service who would go on to serve in a gubernatorial capacity in Uganda in 1922 and then in the Sudan two years later.[38] Tall and handsome, as if pre-ordained to rule, not surprisingly he proved to be a good conversationalist too and Perham was put at her ease by him immediately. The fragrant smell of jasmine wafted through the air and when it came time for the two women to depart, they did so with a laugh over one of the servants describing them as Rayne Sahib's 'two wives'.[39]

As enjoyable as these early days in Berbera had become they were anxious nevertheless to join Harry in Hargeisa. However, given the highly-charged atmosphere there, doing so quickly – or perhaps at all – was growing doubtful. The Governor told them flatly that no women were to go there, going so far as to say that their best course of action in fact was to sail back to Aden and then for home! Perham politely dismissed this advice and asked for more time. Governor Archer agreed reluctantly, and so the horseback-riding and other pastimes continued. The heat continued too, although not in the blazing way that would become the norm within another month or so. Then, the 'pitiless heat' that she had exaggerated about for February would indeed become 120 degrees in the shade. In the meantime, boredom and irritation began to set in until finally Harry arrived in Berbera to escort them personally to Hargeisa.

For the Perham sisters the fact that their original welcome was less than embracing, and that Harry himself had not been there to greet them, had been both troubling and annoying. Initially, Perham had thought that simple indifference had caused Harry to remain in Hargeisa. But she soon found out differently and was prepared to wait until the situation had settled down enough for him to undertake the 200-mile journey overland. The dangers for Rayne were real. There remained strong popular feeling in the countryside for the Mad Mullah's cause, even if the paramount British had broken him and scattered most of his supporters. Still, maintaining control and the peace over a vast backcountry with only a handful of red-coated British regulars together with the Somali police and those of their countrymen who were in the Camel Corps – whose loyalty to the British was suspect – was an open question. Exacerbating the situation was the new tax, a forceful demonstration of the British occupation and therefore a focus of popular resentment.

As far away as Somaliland was from London, and its relatively small size versus other larger dependent colonies of empire, the campaign against the Mad Mullah had been followed closely in the metropolitan press. The Colonial Office, and its newly appointed Secretary, Winston Churchill, was watching the situation closely as it represented a small part of the puzzle of broader Anglo-Egyptian governance, something that would be negotiated at Cairo a short while later that year.[40] In the meantime, for Perham, Somaliland existed in a 'pause, awaiting comment & command from home'. Of course, on the ground such a pause was artificial. In Somaliland decisions had to be made, and such decisions would have an immediate and telling effect on Harry Rayne, as well as on herself. In this way, the air, she believed, was full of 'small portents'. Respect from Somalis was lacking, she observed, and she shuddered at the fact that even war-hardened Harry 'starts violently at a sudden noise in the town'. If this was what it was like in Berbera, what would it be like on trek to distant Hargeisa, she wondered? Harry, it seemed, was just about ready to go nonetheless, and despite the dangers so too was Perham – if only the Governor would give his blessing. 'Well, I wanted adventure', she confided to her diary, '& it is in the air with a vengeance'.[41]

The Governor indeed reluctantly agreed to their going to Hargeisa and on 3 February he held a big dinner to mark their impending farewell: 'Everyone was there', Perham observed with satisfaction. The dinner was lavish, twelve courses featuring buck, oysters, plum pudding, and champagne. Three days later on 6 February their entourage was about to duly depart; the accompanying camel train was loaded and waiting. But they failed to leave. All the while Rayne had been receiving up to the minute telegrams about the 'excited state' of people in Hargeisa and therefore he chose to delay their departure.[42] After much discussion and some sleepless nights he finally decided to go back to Hargeisa alone, which he did on 9 February, leaving the Perham sisters in agitated frustration in Berbera for a while longer. They made the best of it again, however, sailing along the coastline and riding their surefooted horses along the beach and inland, and, in Margery's case, experiencing the excitement and emotion of an intense attraction to one of the young officers, whose name she does not reveal. 'Feeling very depressed this morning', she wrote on 19 February, 'emotional & lonely … . I wonder why I get so absurdly fond of people … . Though I cannot be in love with him, I do not want to lose him'. It can only be surmised that marrying a soldier was hardly an acceptable course of action for Perham. As she had found in Sheffield, few of the men she met seemed right for her. Like one of them there, Harold Ewbank – who described himself as 'The Castaway' and naturally resented it when she told him that he was 'wholly unsuited' to be her husband – her current infatuation would not work either. Sometimes, as we shall see, it would be circumstance or marital status that proved impossibly problematic for Perham to overcome in her search for a partner. In the end, of course, she would simply run out of suitors, although this fact never really seemed to bother her unduly. Part of the emotion Perham was feeling too regarding the young officer in Berbera she attributed to seeing 'aspects of Edgar' in all such officers. But much of her angst, it is fair to say, was owing to the interminable waiting upon events in the African coastal heat that was starting to bear down on her like a 'furnace'.[43]

A week later the situation in Hargeisa had not improved and the Governor was about to leave for Cairo to see Churchill, who just then was convening the conference that would settle, at least for a season, the geographical and political issues of the Anglo Middle East that had remained unresolved from the First World War and the Paris Peace Conference. Joining him in the deliberations there would be such emergent Arabist luminaries as Gertrude Bell and T.E. Lawrence.[44] Meanwhile, at Hargeisa, Rayne had had some further trouble over the application of the new tax regime, 'which', noted Perham ruefully, 'it needed machine guns to settle'. He would be returning to Berbera shortly, however, and she expected that their moment of departure now, at last, was approaching. She was right, but alas, the stay in Berbera would stretch a further six weeks filled with what was now the usual round of sailing, riding, and dinner parties. The period was spiked, too, with a bout of sickness for Perham, in the form of mild blood poisoning. But April finally brought with it their long-anticipated departure for Hargeisa, and on the morning of the 12th 'half of Berbera turned out to see us wedge ourselves, our staff, and the last of our goods into three cars. Then we started out in cavalcade along the track through the maritime plain'.[45] Perham's African adventure, properly speaking, had begun.

The seven-day journey to Hargeisa would be tackled first by car, then by mule, and finally by pony. To begin, the road was in rough shape and the grade fairly steep, eventually rising some 5,000 feet from the coastal plain to the 'jagged dignity' of the inland mountain ranges, called Sheikh and Daallo. Animal life was visible almost immediately too, with jackals being the most in evidence. The driving was intricate. Hairpin turns at increasingly higher elevations abounded, and it did not seem to help to repeat to one another that the journey had been made safely many times before. 'Nothing could reassure fears', Perham wrote later, 'that proclaimed the slightest mistake would plunge us into a death, ready, visible, & spectacularly horrible'.[45] Two days into the journey 'the cars stopped because they could go no further'. After a short rest the small party mounted four mules and began a twisting, snake-like ascent through an 'unearthly' field of 'stones of every shape and size and from these sprang cactii'. To add to the otherworldly topography and atmosphere, the close and brooding clouds chose this moment to open up and down poured 'sheets of rain' turning this stage of the trek into a hellish experience. So distressed was Perham by all of it that she later wrote categorically: 'I hated the place'. But, like so many climbers and trekkers, the awfulness of the ascent is worth it once the summit is reached. And Perham was no different: 'When we reached the top all these things were forgotten. There were ponies waiting'. So, too, was rudimentary accommodation. They had broken the back of the trek. Hurrying on now they passed through the town of Burao and then stopped at the whitewashed and picket-fenced bungalow of the District Commissioner, unearthly British in its own way, and then struck out across the vast 'waterless desert' plain that lay in advance of Hargeisa, reaching it on 19 April, a week after setting out from Berbera.[46]

Today with a population of well over a million, Hargeisa then was a hard-scrabble town of a few thousand people. Located in the Galgodon highlands, it is tucked into a valley but at an elevation of about 4,400 feet. The climate, therefore, unlike that at the coast, is temperate and equable, the temperature never falling much below 13 degrees Celsius, or rising above 32. At the time of Perham's visit forest cover came right down to the edge of the town, and the surrounding countryside, both woods and savannah, teemed with game such as leopard, lion, kudu, warthog, and antelope. Hargeisa had been inhabited for thousands of years but in its modern iteration dating from the proclamation of the Protectorate of British Somaliland in 1888, it had become an increasingly important outpost of British rule, a process that would culminate in 1941 when it would be named the Protectorate's capital.

To the wider world, however, Hargeisa was little known then, just as it is today. But to Perham, no African town ever came close to occupying the pride of place she gave to it. Hargeisa was 'my *first* Africa', she later said, and despite a career that would see her crisscross the continent and visit most of the great African capitals, none ever impressed itself upon her as much as did that first one.[47] She would be there for five months, a period of time crammed with experience and intensity of living, the kind that had a lifetime's impact on her, even if in later years she seemed mildly embarrassed by her own youthfully romantic apprehension of it. Perham's Hargeisa days would provide her with what she would grandly call, 'An African Philosophy', in which she rhapsodized that 'with a strong body I indulged my greatest desire, that for physical achievement. I rode through the dawn, along the hills at sunset. I rode furiously … . I destroyed wild things and ate them'.[48] In this ecstatic, almost primal entry into Africa Perham's words are highly reminiscent of those of Karen Blixen, whose joyous first years in British East Africa especially, of hunting and trekking, she described as being the happiest of her life.[49]

The months in Hargeisa did not, however, start impressively. Instead, her first diary entry, made nine days into her stay, records a rather dreary existence, of waiting for the rains to come so that the parched earth and gaunt animals – 'standing listlessly under the trees with stark ribs and angular haunches' – would come back to life in that remarkable way of nature that seems to belong most starkly to Africa. Soon enough, however, and even though the land continued to 'pant for rain', Perham was thundering around on her pony, playing tennis, and hunting with abandon: 'No rule against shooting sitting birds!' in abundantly endowed Hargeisa.[50] She was also gaining her first direct exposure to colonial governance by attending the court proceedings over which Harry Rayne, as District Commissioner, presided. These initial impressions of the D.C. at work were deep ones and would form the basis of what she regarded as the human face of the British Empire, especially in Africa: just, upright, and incorruptible. That it happened to come in the form of Harry Rayne, about whom Perham initially idolized and probably loved, made it that much more personal. Together with going on trek, the whole experience of colonial frontier life was beginning to overwhelm Perham with a great sense of the romance of her own existence at that moment, in contrast with what she assumed lay in store for her back home in Sheffield.

Perham's diary entries for June and July 1921 especially are peppered with references to riding, playing polo, and shooting – 'on the way home I shot a splendid silver fox, stone dead through his heart, & brought it home' – to reading and writing, to dinner across the local Maroodijeex river at the mess of the Camel Corps and its attendant 'chinwagging.' Of the latter exercise, it seems that Harry was becoming concerned – or possibly jealous – over what he took to be Perham's rather free and easy manner and at one point during yet another 'great dinner with lots of champagne' with the officers of the mess he 'leaned over & told me not to cast my pearls before Camel Corps swine'. Perhaps it had the desired effect because her next entry in the diary is a cryptic: 'Played bridge'.[51]

In the end these pastimes were superseded by the more serious business of helping to train newly-arrived Indian troops who had been drafted into the Camel Corps. And then, in August, of going on trek with Harry up to the Abyssinian (Ethiopian) border. This self-described greatest 'thrill' of her time in Somaliland left Perham breathless in the retelling of it later. The journey did not begin well, however. The first night was dispiriting and exhausting, 'a H_LL of a night', she complained owing to caterwauling men and groaning camels.[52] But from then on it became one of the most memorable experiences she would ever have. Dining in elaborate, blue-lined tents imported from India where they had been used in King Edward VII's Delhi Durbar of 1903, and sleeping out under the vault of stars that was the African night. The sensation of moving through territory in which no European foot had ever trod and of having a close encounter with a lion who, much to Perham's relief, chose to amble off into the bush rather than attack a young woman who, nevertheless, was quite prepared to use her rifle, were the stuff of a lifetime's memories.[53]

In sum, Perham's seven months in British Somaliland were indeed 'the time of my life', as she later called it. The impact that it had on her can scarcely be exaggerated, but now that it was drawing to a close in September and a return to Sheffield loomed she became quite anxious as to her future. But back home she went nonetheless, first to Berbera through 'that grim thorny wilderness, across the oven-hot plain' and then by boat – 'thick with animal stink' – to Aden. Finally, it was on to England and in October the beginning of the new academic term.[54]

By the time Perham had visited her quite relieved parents, organized new housing, and set her courses for the term the students had begun to arrive. She had been away from Sheffield for almost a year. 'But now I was back in … the winter slush' and, apparently, hating it.[55] But it was not nearly as bad as she later recounted. In fact, the years from 1921 to 1924 saw her lead a rather exciting academic, literary, and social life in Sheffield. Inspired by her African experiences she created an Imperial history syllabus, she also acted in plays, and even more impressively, wrote a novel that reprised – in part at least – the time she had spent in Somaliland.

That first year back in Sheffield saw Perham begin to engage the subject of British imperialism intellectually in a sustained manner. In October, she launched a year-long course called, simply, 'The British Empire'. The course offered complete coverage – in a style rarely seen anymore in university history departments – from the semi-piratical days of the early East India Company down to the First World War. The length and breadth of the Empire was traversed, sometimes pithily so: 'New Zealand. Interesting story. That of a colony that began badly and ended well'.[56] She gave considerable attention of course to the role of sea-power in British overseas expansion, and to the long struggle for paramountcy in India, to which she gave pride of place to the rule of a succession of governors-general and viceroys. She forged ahead into the just developing field of comparative imperialism – always to be a topic of interest for her – by including discrete examinations of the French, German, and Russian Empires.[57] She plunged into the study of Africa, focusing, naturally, on Somaliland. For this topic she brought slides to the lecture theatre and, one can imagine, a good deal of inspiration and romance. As she explained to her students: 'Every day [in Somaliland] was marked with some incident of interest ... a long ride upon a white pony'. She dismissed the Mad Mullah as 'a lesser Mahdi', which, in point of fact, he was, and in her recounting went back to the very earliest history of Somaliland.[58]

For Perham, the year 1921–22 was not all about teaching, however. To the degree that the best teaching is in part good acting, she certainly found the right outlet for a great deal of surplus energy in the form of both writing and then taking the lead role in a dramatic play. In March of 1922 she, along with the other members of the University Dramatic Society, put on 'Aethelburga', a four act imaginative retelling of the life of the seventh-century Northumbrian queen, who, as the playbill put it bluntly, had been instrumental in converting 'the rude Northern people to Christianity'. She was vice-president of the UDS, playwright, lead actor, and persuasive promoter. And the play garnered mostly admiring reviews, especially that for her own portrayal of Queen Aethelburga: 'Miss Perham's interpretation of the part', said *The Doncaster Gazette*, 'was an absorbingly interesting piece of work.' The University Vice-Chancellor, Sir Henry Hadow, was likewise taken with the production, writing to Perham: 'you have certainly added another leaf to the laurels of the University'. Not all was sweetness and light, though, as a discordant note was offered by one reviewer who complained of a 'lack of freedom of action, which hindered the players and gave their movements a rather stilted effect'. In all, however, the play was a singular success and Perham remained active in the UDS, as well as in other city dramatic societies such as the Sheffield Playgoers, for the duration of her time there.[59]

Despite these extracurricular triumphs, however, Perham was far from uniformly happy in Sheffield. Granted, her academic life had improved, both within the classroom and with her colleagues. Gone were the earliest days of having 'Ladies Common Room' painted on the 'cupboard' that constituted her departmental space. But the causes of her breakdown – even if, as she later maintained, it was not a mental breakdown but rather one of physical exhaustion owing to overwork and alienation – had not disappeared.[60] Part of her ongoing vexation too was spiritual, as the Christianity of her childhood and youth was waning and, as we shall later see, would not be revived until the 1940s. Indeed, during this time she wrote to the Bishop of London, Arthur Ingram, an earlier acquaintance, who tried to buoy up her faith with the simple and timeless words: 'the truth shall set you free … I have found that Christ is the way, the truth and the life …' . But the blows of the war – especially Edgar's senseless death – and her new-found 'faith' – philosophy as she called it – in Africa had taken precedence over her conventional Christianity.[61]

In 1923, Perham threw herself into Africa in a new way, by beginning work on a novel that would give her the means to express what she had distilled from her time in Somaliland: 'it impressed me so deeply that I was driven to write about it. Feeling that it would be presumptuous to attempt a serious work I put my impressions into the form of a novel, *Major Dane's Garden* … . I regretted later that I had not turned my Somaliland experience to better use'.[62] In this vein she would describe her novel as a substitute for the then rather new (since 1917) Oxford D.Phil., the advanced research degree that confers upon a student the right to proceed along the prescribed path of academic life.[63] Of course, as a novel, it would never have made it through the *viva voce*, the final oral examination for an Oxford doctoral candidate. But as an analysis of British administration in Somaliland, it worked very well and, when coupled with its sharply defined characters, exotic location, and genuine romance, was an accomplished piece of work. Upon publication in 1925, as we shall see, *Major Dane's Garden* met with ready sales and a flurry of admiring reviews.

In the meantime, however, and unbeknownst to her, Perham was about to be set free from her apparent exile in Sheffield. In the spring of 1924 she was suddenly offered a fellowship and tutorship at her old college of St. Hugh's in Oxford. 'This was my chance!' was the way in which Perham later recalled her exultation, and she took the offer as a sign that her commitment to the study of Africa and of its British colonial administration was to be her life's work.[64] And so at the beginning of Michaelmas Term 1924 she once again found herself in the place where ten years earlier she had first come as a fresher, only this time she was in Oxford to stay.

4

OXFORD AGAIN AND AROUND THE WORLD

To some, such as the future Prime Minister, Harold Macmillan, Oxford after the First World War, was a city of ghosts. 'I just could not face it', he recalled later in life.[1] Margery Perham was haunted too in this regard, most especially of course by memories of Edgar, but her return there in 1924 was nonetheless just short of triumphant. Her health, both psychological and physical, had been restored fully. Her years at Sheffield had tempered her and made her justly confident in her own abilities as both a history lecturer and a writer. And, most important of all, she had a subject and a purpose. Nothing is more damaging to the spirit and prospects of an academic than a lack of singular purpose. And in the autumn of 1924, the nearly twenty-nine year old Perham arrived at her new post positively brimming with it.

A return to Oxford, and to St. Hugh's, had hardly been anticipated, however, and was occasioned by what came to be known as the 'St. Hugh's row'. An intense administrative and personal struggle at Perham's old college had been brewing for some time and in November of 1923 it went public with a thunderclap. Cecilia Ady, a widely respected Renaissance scholar and much-loved history tutor at St. Hugh's, was peremptorily dismissed on just a few days notice. She had been at the college for most of the previous twenty-three years, initially, like Perham would be, as a first class honours student in modern history before becoming tutor in the subject. For much of that time she had been the favourite of the college's Principal, Eleanor Jourdain. But latterly, as Ady's star had risen both as an academic and as a figure around college, Jourdain began to see her as a rival. There was not, it seems, room enough at St. Hugh's for two such commanding personalities, so the Principal used executive fiat to remove Ady from the Senior Common Room. Predictably, the dismissal provoked uproar both within and outside of St. Hugh's. A number of other college tutors resigned in protest over

Ady's treatment and undergraduates both at St. Hugh's and elsewhere in
Oxford denounced her dismissal as capriciously unjust. Nonetheless, the
College Council held firm in its support of Jourdain. An inquiry chaired by
the former Indian Viceroy and current University Chancellor, Lord Curzon,
would follow, which found Ady utterly blameless, citing 'a want of understanding' in the relationship between administrative and tutorial staffs.[2]
Certain constitutional reforms were recommended, and later implemented,
but the damage was done including the sad fillip to the case, the untimely
death by heart failure of Jourdain in April 1924, which, naturally, elicited its
own recriminations from some of her own many supporters.

Up in Sheffield, Perham had followed the case closely. Her ties to St.
Hugh's were warm and firm – a decade earlier she had been taught by Ady –
and her experience in the Sheffield history department had made her acutely
sensitive to the vulnerabilities of (female) academic staff to the caprices of
both administrators and colleagues. But, as it turned out for Perham, the
upset at St. Hugh's proved to be the most propitious of circumstances to
recast her own career. And she leapt at the unexpected offer to replace Ady
and to come home, as it were, to the scene of her many undergraduate triumphs, ranging from those on the hockey pitch to those of a more lasting
nature such as her sterling performance in the Examination Schools.

Perham's arrival at St. Hugh's in anticipation of Michaelmas Term 1924
coincided with that of the new College Principal, Barbara Gwyer. She was
just the third head in the relatively brief history of the college, a line which
began with Elizabeth Wordsworth, the poet's grand-niece and foundress of
St. Hugh's. Gwyer would serve for twenty-two years as Principal, until 1946,
and throughout her tenure was a firm supporter and friend of Perham. They
maintained a lively and comprehensive correspondence whether it was during Perham's five years there as fellow and tutor, or later when her formal
connection to St. Hugh's was at arm's length. 'Darling' was Dwyer's usual
epistolary greeting to Perham and good humour and intimacy pervades
their many letters to one another.[3]

Once settled into her new Oxford appointment and college digs Perham
proceeded to further develop her budding academic specialty in Imperial
history. The place of women in the University – both as undergraduates and
as teaching faculty – was only then just becoming clarified. Indeed, it was
only four years earlier in 1920 that Perham's own degree had been awarded
officially when Oxford had formalized the position of its female students.
As for the University's female staff as represented by college tutors, Perham
was one of just thirty such women. The distaff population was in Oxford
to stay, but eight centuries of almost uniform masculinity carried an almost

overwhelming weight nonetheless. While it was true that the existence of the four women's colleges (in addition to St. Hugh's there were St. Hilda's, Lady Margaret Hall, and Somerville) leavened Oxford's prevailing male-ness, there was plenty of both institutional and personal animus toward the presence of Eve in Oxford's Adamic Garden of Eden. As one St. Hugh's undergraduate recalled of her time at Oxford – as late as the 1950s: 'it was like being on the 'sidelines' of a giant male public school'.[4]

For Perham, a life of older brothers, keen athletics, robust travel, and the evident masculinity of the Sheffield history department, had effectively inoculated her against the importunities of Oxford male life. She makes virtually no mention of any offence, much less trouble, in this regard dur-ing the initial period of her Oxford teaching career. Whatever constraints sex and gender may have later placed on her career – despite a well-earned eminence in her field she was never offered a professorial chair, for example – none were apparent in 1924.

That first autumn back at Oxford Perham began to lecture on the impe-rial topics that had dominated her academic pursuits since returning from British Somaliland three years earlier. Indeed, she answered an invitation to give a talk in October at her old school of St. Anne's by offering to the admiring girls there a full-blown lecture of forty closely-written pages on that colossus of modern British imperialism, Cecil Rhodes. Though having been dead now for twenty-two years, Rhodes had not yet (notwithstanding J.A. Hobson's stinging critique of him) come in for the kind of thoroughgo-ing deconstruction that would be applied to him by later generations. Still, Perham is probing in her analysis of the singular builder of empire, conclud-ing that Rhodes was not a great man in the traditional sense but nonetheless had been 'an elemental force that rouses fear and induces awe'.[5]

The Oxford system has always allowed for considerable latitude in teach-ing and lecturing and Perham took full advantage of it to maximize her reach in the fields of imperial history and contemporary international affairs. Teaching courses such as 'British Policy towards Native Races', and the 'Mandates System', Perham plunged into the leading issues of the day, quickly establishing herself as a young but learned authority on the latest iteration of the imperial world established by the provisions of the 1919 Paris Peace Conference.[6] The other major feature of her initial years at St. Hugh's was the publication of her first book, *Major Dane's Garden*. As noted in the previous chapter, soon after returning from Somaliland Perham took her experiences from there and turned them into a novel. Though most of the writing of it occurred in 1922 in Sheffield, its publication did not occur until after her move to Oxford. The book came out in 1925, a year after her arrival at St. Hugh's, and was met with immediate critical acclaim and, gratifyingly, good sales too. Perham had negotiated with her publisher, Hutchinson & Company of London for an advance of £50, a substantial sum in those days, and a royalty rate based on sales that rose from ten to twenty per cent.[7] The contract was signed in February of 1925, and the book – dedicated 'To My Sister' and selling for 7 shillings and 6 pence – hit the shelves early that summer. Perham leaves no record of having had any difficulty in finding a publisher, and if she had done they would have been disappointed since the book was reviewed immediately and in highly positive terms. 'A clever story', wrote the reviewer in the *Times Literary Supplement* on 18 June, 'and rich in a convincing local colour'. A few days later the *Daily Mail* chimed in with the commendation that *Major Dane's Garden* was 'a novel which is both an education and a delight to read'. Then it was the turn of the *Morning Post*: 'Mr. M.F. Perham's novel' – and in giving her the honourific 'Mr.' making the mistaken assumption that such a book with its vivid backcountry descriptions simply had to have been the work of a man – 'is an unusually good example of what may be called Outpost fiction'.[8] Indeed, the book was uniformly praised. Much of its appeal centred on the captivating protagonist, Rhona Cavell, the young wife of a British military commander in 1920s' Somaliland. After going out to join her husband she is impressed deeply by the land and its people while at the same time falling in love with an idealistic and upright district commissioner, Major Dane, a character that Perham modelled on Harry Rayne.

Read today many passages of the novel sound arch and old-fashioned, even cringe-worthy. And certainly its moral tone, of wifely duty especially, is of its time. But Perham's descriptions of the Somali landscape, her creation of an exotic, colonial-era atmosphere, and its sure-handed demonstration of local knowledge are as convincing now as they were upon its publication. In the years after it came out, Perham moved steadily away from including it (and another novel, *Josie Vine*, that would follow two years later) as part of her oeuvre, mainly because a novel simply did not fit properly into the research and writing agenda of an academic. Thus, almost fifty years later and well into retirement, it came as a rather nice surprise to Perham in 1970 when *Major Dane* was republished in New York at a time when African independence had made a colonial-era novel of considerable contemporary interest. As she noted then: 'The story has been forgotten for about half a century but, astonishingly, it has been resurrected as the first of a new series of colonial novels'.[9] By then her affection for it had been restored and, indeed, as she explained to *The Times* that year: 'I think the political part of the book, particularly the fighting, will stand the test of time. But I fear the love affair is now rather dated. All my characters behave quite correctly'.[10]

Characters behaving correctly would surely have pleased her father, who enjoyed his younger daughter's initial literary success. But a steadily weakening heart meant that by the autumn of 1925 Frederick Perham was in severe decline and on 5 December he died at a clinic in Menton, France, not far from the Isle of Jersey where her parents had been most recently living. Marion Perham wrote her daughter to say that 'Father ... had suffered terribly for 24 hours, could not get his breath, it was heartbreaking'.[11] His death meant that he did not live to see the publication of *Major Dane* in the United States. There the reviews were even more glowing, but just as ready to make the mistaken assumption about gender. As *The Saturday Review of Literature, New York City*, put it: 'Soundly written, vivid and convincing, obviously by a man who knows intimately the land of which he writes...'.[12] The fact that many reviewers assumed a man wrote the book never seemed to bother Perham, however, either then or later. She simply laughed it off.

By the time *Major Dane* was published Perham had begun to move with assurance into her chosen field of imperial government. She paused long enough to publish her second and last novel, *Josie Vine*, however, which Hutchinson brought out in December of 1927. Like her first novel, it was well reviewed: 'arresting' said *The Daily Telegraph*.[13] But, unlike *Major Dane*, it was little-read and almost completely forgotten in subsequent years even though the character Josie Vine as protagonist demonstrates much that is biographical about Perham herself, including having a brother who dies in the First World War.

In academic terms, the late 1920s were years of great significance in the establishment of a tradition of Imperial and Commonwealth studies at Oxford, and Perham was quick to become one of its key beneficiaries. In what David McIntyre has recently called the development of 'The Britannic Vision' Oxford played an indispensable part in this development, and it was just such a vision, as described by McIntyre to be one of 'autonomy, freedom, and equality, combined with allegiance to the Crown', that came to animate Perham's own understanding of her formative work and how it might fit into the larger Imperial academic project of her Oxford colleagues.[14] But first she had to really become one of them herself, and the clearest recognition of that came in 1929 when she embarked on what turned out to be a world tour to investigate 'Native administration', especially that conducted by the British. If the trip to Somaliland had introduced her to Africa and the British Empire, Perham's protracted tour of a decade later would confirm her in the subject and, indeed, in her life's work.

Perham's entry into this world of imperialism and native administration had been made possible, initially, by a direct encounter with the League of Nations. On two occasions during her early years at Oxford, first in 1927 and then again in 1929, she had travelled to Geneva to observe the League's Permanent Mandates Commission in session. These visits could not have been more professionally fortuitous because it was through them that she was first exposed directly to the British representative on the PMC, Lord Frederick Lugard. By the time of his appointment to the commission in 1922 Lugard had become a legendary figure in British government and colonial circles, owing principally to his highly influential pro-consular positions in Nigeria and, to a lesser extent, Hong Kong. Perham's gradually developing teaching and research interests in the questions being debated by the PMC made Lugard the obvious choice of professional mentor, even if on the face of it the aging man of empire and the young female Oxford don might not necessarily make for a natural partnership. But very soon after first making his acquaintance a correspondence ensued followed by almost twenty years of collaboration, which would culminate after his death in 1945 when Perham embarked upon writing Lugard's biography, a two-volume magnum opus published – as we shall see – respectively in 1956 and 1960. In the meantime, the late 1920s was a period during which Perham would soak up everything she could about the workings of the British Empire in the post-First World War environment, and she did so in large part through the Lugardian lens. Indeed, by 1929, the year she departed on her world tour, she was describing Lugard as 'no longer just a famous name but a friend'.[15]

As large a part as Lugard would play in Perham's later life, her Oxford years prior to leaving on tour in 1929 were influenced greatly by those resident scholars who had spent the last generation creating there a sturdy foundation of Imperial history. Oxford as an incubator of British statesmen had long been an assumption, even a cliché, and perhaps no one exemplified the idea better than Benjamin Jowett, the Master of Balliol College from 1870 until 1893, whose task, he once half-jokingly told Florence Nightingale, was to govern the world through his pupils.[16] And with some of them, notably Lord Curzon as Viceroy of India, H.H. Asquith as Prime Minister, and Sir Edward Grey as Foreign Secretary, he may in fact have fulfilled his fanciful wish. Jowett, however, was at base a churchman and classicist, and while highly interested in the Empire, especially in India, he was not in any way an Imperial scholar. But not so long after Jowett's death in 1893 came that of Cecil Rhodes in 1902, an event that would change just about everything related to Oxford's understanding of itself as an Imperial university.

The advent of the Rhodes Scholarship in 1904, provided for in Rhodes's will and – later controversially – designed to bathe the world in the glow of British Imperialism and good government through a cadre of keen and bright young men sent forth to do so, both telescoped and sped-up this process.[17] From then until the Second World War Oxford was the epicentre of the study of the British Empire, something upon which not even J.H. Hobson's withering critique of diamonds and gold and the Boer War, *Imperialism: A Study*, published in 1902, would have much impact. These were the years when the Beit Professorship of Colonial History was established – endowed by the Randlord, Alfred Beit, apparently convinced to do so during the first course of a banquet by the champion of empire and future Dominions Secretary, L.S. Amery.[18] Hugh Egerton would hold the chair until 1920 when he was succeeded by (Sir) Reginald Coupland who would become a central figure in the history of the study of the British Empire and its successor, the Commonwealth, until his retirement in 1948.[19] He would also, in the same way, be a key person in helping to set Margery Perham on the path of becoming a similarly highly influential, Oxford-based, scholar of empire.

In 1926, the Rhodes Trust decided to establish a program by which young(ish) – no more than forty-five years of age – Oxford dons would be given a kind of travel sabbatical during which they could supplement their book knowledge with direct exposure to those parts of the world in which Britain had a particular interest or, indeed, formal responsibility. Anthony Kirk-Greene has told the story well of Perham's application to the Rhodes Trust Travelling Fund in his introduction to the edited version of the first part of her world tour, *Pacific Prelude*.[20] A full reprise of it here is therefore unnecessary. But certain features of how the travelling fellowship came about, and under what terms she first accepted, and then executed, it speak revealingly to the ways in which Perham went about establishing her career. Just what did the three or so years that eventually she spent travelling – especially through Africa – mean in the creation of herself as one of the leading Africanists of the day?

In December of 1928, during her fifth year back at St. Hugh's, Perham decided to apply to the Rhodes Trust for a travelling fellowship to take effect the following summer. In the usual cycle of academic sabbaticals she was nearing the time when she might be afforded one, and consequently had already created a twelve-month itinerary for herself, three-quarters of which was to be spent in Africa with the balance of the time in India, Australasia and the United States. These proposed peregrinations were to be in the service of examining race, and, as she put it, 'British Native Policy and increasing knowledge of the English-speaking world'. A tour of this sort would allow her to view with her own eyes those places and issues which had concerned her so greatly over her teaching career thus far. In coming before the Rhodes Trust adjudication committee Perham, of course, had no way of knowing that one of the things they would guard against would be – as it was later put – a 'joy ride' – and for some members of the committee Perham's proposed terminal three months had the relaxed air about it of taking the slow boat to America. They acknowledged that her nine-months-in-Africa plan was strong, so their suggestion was to begin with America and Australasia (India, deserving of its own tour altogether in the view of the committee, was quickly excised from the proposed itinerary) and conclude with Africa, where, it was assumed rightly, the real work of the journey would take place. Professor Coupland as one of Perham's referees was strongly supportive and in March 1929 she was awarded the fellowship. Nevertheless, the committee was convinced that changes in Perham's proposed itinerary must still be made. And so they were. After rewriting her proposal to this end and obtaining the views of a number of prominent voices on Imperial affairs – including that of Lord Lugard, the first protracted meeting of the two of them taking place in late-April in the almost-exclusively male precinct of the Athenaeum Club in Pall Mall, of which Lugard was a member – the Trustees made her award official in May. The year's fellowship would commence in July 1929 and be supported by a monthly grant of £100. Perham was now on her way.[21]

On 25 June she duly sailed from Southampton on board the 40,000 ton S.S. *Homeric*, an 'ugly great liner', in her view, belonging to the White Star Line famous for being the owner of the ill-fated S.S. *Titanic*.[22] Perham's stomach may now have been used to great sea crossings but her heart and mind were highly unsettled as she waved to her sister Ethel, just then back from Africa, who had come to see her off. Excitement, yes, was natural, but by the next morning she awoke with what seemed to be 'a great weight sitting upon my chest'.[23] St. Hugh's had granted her a leave until Michaelmas Term of 1930 so her professional life for well over a year was secure. But beyond that, fear and panic had set in as she contemplated the possibility of not being capable of 'carrying out my large and indefinite commission'.[24] For young people especially of either sex it is not unusual to be gripped by trepidation at the outset of a long journey, to, as Perham lamented, 'have little experience in travel, [and] no brazen exterior behind which to cover the fears and embarrassments which are already tormenting me in prospect'. But as a young woman the fear was even greater as again she would be operating mainly in a male-dominated arena. 'How much easier all this is,' she exclaimed, 'for men!'[25]

Nevertheless, off she went. New York was reached a week later after an uneventful Atlantic crossing. She arrived on a stiflingly humid July morning, with the Statue of Liberty rising above the harbour and giving 'every chance to impress', she remarked in admiration. Once having made port Perham was engulfed in 'the noisiest city in the world', however, but was steadied by the welcoming hand of Dr. Abraham Flexner, an eminent medical researcher and soon to be director of the Institute for Advanced Study at Princeton, who had been sent by the Rhodes Trust to meet her.[26] He was the first of many academics Perham would encounter along the way. She would spend only a few weeks in the US, however, going from New York City to Albany, and then on to Washington, D.C., Virginia, Chicago, and finally across the continent to San Francisco before embarking for the South Pacific near the end of July. Her American interlude was spent mostly in pursuit of what she termed flatly, 'this race business'.[27] And as much as the tone of her diary is mildly negative about her American experience: 'I do not think even the dullness of the great northern European plain is as dull as north-central America', there is a constant admiration for the scale and scope of US society, the sheer size of the American national enterprise that never fails to impress or even over-awe visitors.[28]

The content of Perham's Oxford teaching of the previous five years was now used to guide her itinerary and discussions over the succeeding three weeks. She was keen to probe the imperial history of North America, especially where it had touched upon contact with and governance of native Indians. The main focus of her research in this regard was the career of Sir William Johnson (c. 1715–1774). He had become Colonel of the Six Nations of the Iroquois Confederacy during the Seven Years' War and in the period leading up to the American War of Independence had hoped to establish a humane system of administration, the like of which, Perham maintained, was to be found later in the British Colonial Service in Africa. Alas, relentless white settlement and the exigencies of revolution meant segregation and, in some areas of the country, virtual extermination of the native population and Johnson's enlightened ideas did not come to pass. In the midst of America's Fourth of July celebrations Perham did her best to see some of the sites connected with his life and service, including his sturdy, brick home in Upstate New York, and to engage in conversation the state historian who was also the editor of the Johnson papers. This last, scholarly attempt failed, however, and her first foray into meeting the parameters of her 'large and indefinite commission' seemed a failure. Perham was wont to wax philosophical on a regular basis during her life, and she did so here, in the midst of America's still almost primordial vastness. 'What a country to use – what a continent to play with! Have the people been worthy of the opportunity?'[29] Her diary leaves this rhetorical question unanswered – a question she might have very easily asked of the British in Africa too – but one suspects that the unwritten answer to the question as asked in America is 'no'.

In any event, she returned quickly to New York City from this disappointing excursion north and immediately caught a train to Washington. She could not wait, it seems, to be rid of the great metropolis with its noise, congestion, and skyscrapers, arrayed, as she saw them to be, in 'monstrous formation'. She had no way of knowing of course that her flight response would be one shared by many others later that year on 29 October when the stock market crashed signaling the onset of the Great Depression. As it was, she boarded a train for the short journey to the US capital, arriving at the type of impressive rail station seen routinely in North America, which she described aptly as a cathedral of the modern age. In leaving behind New York, Perham also left behind her brief examination of the Native Indian question in order to 'face up to the negroes', as she put it directly, that even more pressing question of race in America.[30]

Washington was essentially a Southern city and accordingly its first century or so of history had been one of slavery followed by emancipation and then the creation of a large black underclass. Negroes – the term was fifty years away from being superseded by black or African-American – abounded, and it was here that Perham really began a sustained encounter with what a later generation would call race relations. Her visit to British Somaliland had gone some distance, as we have seen, in acclimating her to this world, but the disdain all around her in America for the negro came as a considerable shock nonetheless. She was aware that her own progressive, relatively colour-blind views 'would be violently condemned by most South Africans, and in this country by nearly all Southerners, and most Northerners'. The prevailing view of the negro, she averred, was patronizing and racist to the core: 'They are not to be trusted; some of them are plausible enough. They know how to talk, but as a race they are permanently inferior and must be kept in their place'. While admitting the 'innocence of my impartiality', Perham was keenly aware that the American negro's lowly place in society had come about not from being preternaturally incapable of social achievement, but rather from being torn violently from Africa and made to live in a bestial fashion for generations. Only now was this view even beginning to change, she observed, and as such the race question 'must be the main theme of all my thoughts while I am in America'.[31]

And, indeed, it was her main theme. For the next two weeks as she continued her visit to Washington, then to nearby Virginia, on to Chicago and finally west to San Francisco, her thoughts and conversations never strayed much from what has been called America's 'original sin'. To the degree that the topic did change, it was done so by others to include the culpability of the British in slavery and the Atlantic slave trade, and therefore America's inheritance of an old evil from Europe. Perham made some memorable visits to places such as Howard University in Washington, which by 1929 had become a great centre of learning and culture for African-Americans, and to the Phelps-Stokes Foundation established to promote the education of negroes in both the US and Africa. For the time Perham was remarkably egalitarian in her social and political views. Typically, however, she would remark regularly on physiognomic differences of a sort that would make later generations blush, or worse. Thus, for example, while waiting to meet the President of Howard University, Mordecai Johnson, she cast a critical eye over one of his (male) secretaries: 'The man, like so many of these so-called negroes, does not look negro at all. Lighter brown than the woman [the other secretary], he has a purely Hamitic cast of face, and would be handsome by our standards if his nose were not too thick'.[32] If nothing else this passage demonstrates Perham's then-deep unfamiliarity with miscegenation in African-American history and the range of contemporary racial types that it had produced.[33]

Occasionally, Perham's anger would flash at what she found to be the relentless revolutionary triumphalism of her hosts, as it did at Saratoga, Virginia, the site of an occasion for a British surrender during the War of Independence, and marked by a tablet. 'We stood in silence', she confided to her diary, 'looking at it and then, being determined to exercise self-control, I contented myself with the remark that I thought it was all a great pity, not so much for us, but for them'. Apparently, Perham's understanding of self-control was not shared by the Americans with her that day as 'they nearly lynched me, and it was with some difficulty that we got under way again'.[34]

Throughout her stay in the US Perham became both reliant upon and accustomed to British consular help and hospitality, a pattern begun in Somaliland and one that would become that much more apparent in her subsequent visits to the South Pacific and to Africa. Accordingly, her last evening in America was spent in the company of the British Consul-General in San Francisco, before setting out for a week's voyage to Honolulu in the Hawai'ian Islands, not yet the Fiftieth State in the American Union but under complete US control, en route for American Samoa, and her introduction to New Zealand, Australia and elsewhere in the region.

Perham departed San Francisco on the morning of 27 July. She was late for the sailing, but scrambled on board the S.S. *Sierra* where she would share a cabin with, in her view, a rather uncongenial Australian. Her predilection to take the measure of people from their physical appearance was at work immediately, as she encountered a pair of Englishmen, looking every inch properly turned out in her view, perhaps in the mode of Evelyn Waugh's fictional Sebastian Flyte and Charles Ryder from *Brideshead Revisited*. One of them, she observed, 'was strikingly handsome, tall and slim, with a long well-shaped head, brown hair brushed with a slight ripple and a feathering of red-gold; well-set grey-blue eyes, a fine nose and a rather scornful mouth'.[35] Examples of this sort of description pile up the deeper one reads in the Perham oeuvre, making her rather harsh assessment of the Howard University secretary above a little less jarring. Still, it is revealingly noteworthy that good looks counted for much in Perham's personal inventory.

After Hawai'i, Perham's first stop was Pago Pago in American Samoa. Doing so was a rather last minute decision, however, spurred by the idea of examining the relative novelty of a rare American colony having just come from the mother country itself. American Samoa, like so many other islands in the South Pacific, had been pushed back and forth between various European powers before the US, itself powerful in the region by the end of the nineteenth century, made it her own in 1899 when the whole of the Samoan archipelago was divided between the US and Germany under the provisions of the Tripartite Convention. The proto-nationalist Mau movement, in response, broke out after the First World War in Western (formerly German, but now administered by New Zealand under the League of Nations mandate system) Samoa, which had its analogue in American Samoa. But by the time Perham arrived in early August of 1929, the fiery Mau movement in American Samoa had much abated too, suppressed by the US Navy and later confirmed by a Congressional Committee in 1930. Indeed, American Samoa would continue under Washington's suzerainty, where it remains to this day.

Perham's two months in the South Pacific, culminating in Australia, were an instructive interlude before she launched herself into Africa. There is little doubt that she considered this period an interregnum leading up to the main event of her return to Africa, although this time, of course, she would enter the continent from the south rather than from the north, as she had done almost nine years earlier in Somaliland. Her diary for the Pacific portion of her tour is replete with the acute, humorous, and sometimes biting observation that is a pronounced feature of her writing. As both a don and a twice-published novelist her literary skill was considerable, and her powers of observation were superior. Accordingly, pen-portraits abound, as in 'colossal Australians' and 'rosy bronze' Samoans, 'surely the best of all colours for the human form' – as always taken up with physicality.[36] Her American experience, one of being impressed, even overwhelmed by the size and wealth of the country, was added to by the enviable way in which she regarded US imperialism having had remade Hawai'i and was now doing the same to Samoa. She was chagrined to overhear some Americans in Honolulu bemoaning the fact that in their view British imperialism, by contrast, was all about acquisition: 'You know what the British are. They take everything and give nothing. It's all those damned officials lounging about like God Almighty that blight the place'. Perham confided that 'yes, it does make you think … . I have now seen my first American "colony". The ruling power has turned upon Hawaii, a week's voyage away from the wealth of California, the full blast of her energy. She has developed the islands to their limits.'[37]

If the Colonel Blimp caricature prevailed unfairly, it was represented only occasionally in the score of British colonial officials Perham was to meet over the course of her Pacific travels. She was the first to admit that she was not the easiest of persons with whom to get on. Not given to small-talk, supremely confident in her own judgement and abilities, in other words, as she put it herself: 'an inquisitive and critical young woman', Perham might not necessarily have expected to gain the cooperation of colonial officials whose good graces were required in order to carry out her tour successfully. And yet, despite her sometime sandpapery manner, she did succeed. Later, in Africa, one exasperated official minuted that 'Margery Perham ought to be boiled in oil'.[38] But that, clearly, was an extreme response. Mostly, it seems, the officials with whom she interacted were rather charmed by the sight of this young Oxford don busily travelling along the Imperial trail, doing her best to understand colonial governance even if invariably she cast a critical eye on their execution of it. And such was especially the case, she found, in Western Samoa, the responsibility for which, as noted above, had fallen to New Zealand under the Permanent Mandates Commission of the League of Nations.

Unquestionably, Perham's view of the apparent incompetence of the New Zealanders in this respect had been influenced heavily by Lugard's own highly critical view of Western Samoa. Her April 1929 first meeting with him in London had reinforced what she had already been reading in the proceedings of the PMC that she had gone through assiduously in order to teach her Oxford course on native administration. Lugard would prove to be unwaveringly critical in his assessment of New Zealand's handling of the Mau crisis, which lasted mainly from 1927 until 1929 before sputtering out completely in the early 1930s. A nationalist up-thrust of a sort that the British would begin to see regularly in Africa after the Second World War, the Mau was successful in destabilizing Western Samoan society and, more than anything else, embarrassing New Zealand in its attempt to carry out its PMC mandate. Indeed, eventually, in October 1935 and on the eve of Lugard's stepping down from the PMC, he confessed to being continually dumbstruck by an administration such as New Zealand's, which did not seem to do much else other than report unrest. He contended that the New Zealanders were simply out of their depth in this respect and that hopefully at some point soon an administrator 'with experience of native races' would be appointed in Western Samoa.[39]

Perham, for her part, remained convinced of the essential failings of New Zealand's colonial administration in Western Samoa, echoing the view held by Lugard and the PMC generally. In her usual perspicacious way she inter- viewed a number of the officials involved, especially General George Sir Stafford Richardson, Resident Administrator of Western Samoa from 1923 to 1928, whose military career and overbearing style were deemed to have been largely responsible for the breakout and expansion of the Mau.[40] On the whole, these experiences confirmed her view – shared with Lugard – that what was required in Western Samoa and, by extension, everywhere else in the Empire, was a fully professional cadre of colonial officers capable of understanding local conditions and acting appropriately so as to, at the very least, blunt the sharp edge of rebellion before it had the opportunity and time to foment. Such a view would only solidify in the months to come and be given expression, in part, in a pair of articles she wrote – the first of many such pieces to come – for *The Times*, entitled 'White Rule in Samoa' and published in April 1930.

The remainder of Perham's time in the South Pacific took her to New Zealand itself, which despite her harsh estimation of its administrative handling of Western Samoa, she praised as a 'beautiful country', and to Australia, which, owing to the harsh treatment meted out to its aboriginal people and to what she regarded as the social vulgarities of its 'mate' culture, she did not.[41] Regardless, her prelude in the Pacific now over, she sailed off to Africa from Perth at the end of September thanks again to the White Star Line and, this time, the S.S. *Demosthenes*, a rather small 10,000 ton ship but, importantly to Perham, captained and crewed by Englishmen! As she neared Africa some three weeks later she seems to have sensed that her arrival there portended something highly significant in her life: 'I brace myself physically and mentally for a longer and deeper encounter with the problems of race than any I have encountered in this almost frantic rush across America, the Polynesian Pacific and the dominions of New Zealand and Australia. For me this will be the really serious part of my journey round the world and probably the most serious subject of my future work'.[42]

Margery Perham's first glimpse of South Africa came off Durban on 19 October 1929. The capital of Natal province and established in 1824 on land given to an English adventurer, Henry Francis Fynn, by the great Zulu king, Shaka, Durban had grown exponentially in the years that followed. Much of its more recent prosperity was owing to large-scale sugar cane production in the fields worked by imported and indentured Indian labourers – it was here that Mohandas Gandhi had begun his politicization with the Natal Indian Congress, founded in 1894 to represent the interests of an Indian population that had swelled by then to some 75,000. Perham stayed only a couple of days before steaming down the coast to Cape Town. But her brief stay in Durban nevertheless had left a significant impact on the nature of her mission. To the unsettling dockside shouts of 'nigger' and 'kaffir' Perham was reintroduced to racism in Africa, and it left her feeling 'faint'. The enormity of endeavouring to study such a large and amorphous thing as race relations across the continent of Africa overwhelmed her: 'I wanted to lock myself in my cabin, hide under the blankets. Understand this? Study it? Report on it? I felt I dared not face this ridiculous enterprise, could hardly dare to step off the ship on to the docks, in order to begin it'.[43]

South Africa in 1929 was then almost a generation into its modern iteration as a union of the four old colonies, two British (Natal and the Cape) and two Boer (Transvaal and Orange River), that had fought for the last time at the turn-of-the-century and then following the 1902 Treaty of Vereeniging had settled into a reasonably amicable relationship that had yielded the Union of South Africa in 1910. The country's political, social, and economic reality was a complex amalgam, however, which only a much later generation would see as virtuous and advantageous, and its Boer political leadership was travelling rather quickly along a road that would pave the way for government by the racist National Party in 1948 and the enunciation of apartheid as its foundational organizing principle. Indeed, the political mythology that would lead to apartheid had already begun to take hold in the form of debates over the symbols of so-called oppressive British imperialism during the premiership of J.B.M. Hertzog. A national flag and anthem – exclusive of the Union Jack and *God Save the King* – therefore became the grounds upon which a bitterly divisive debate was carried out. Arriving when she did meant that Perham had sailed into the midst of these rumblings.[44]

Still, the beauty of the country, including Cape Town itself, impressed her right away. The racial diversity of the city's people, its stunning geography, dominated by Table Mountain, the 'thoroughness' of its bilingualism in the form of English and Afrikaans, all had an immediate impact on Perham, as did the hospitality and wealth of her initial hosts who lived near Groote Schuur, once the grand hillside estate of Cecil Rhodes. But South African politics, dominated by the ex-military man, General Hertzog, she came quickly to loathe. 'The Afrikaners' domestic architecture was one of the few good things they brought to the sub-continent', she wrote grudgingly shortly after her arrival. And in light of Hertzog's clear anti-African, pro-Boer politics – a marked departure from those of his much more liberal-minded predecessors, Louis Botha and Jan Christian Smuts – she set herself on a course of determining what a future of retaining any vestige of racial equality might have in South Africa.[45] To do so she began a rather systematic progress through the 'British element', as she called the range of administrators, churchmen, and academics she encountered over the course of about two weeks spent in Cape Town.[46] But these conversations, as pleasant or as pugnacious as they sometimes were, counted as a mere 'curtain-raiser' in her desire to probe as deeply as possible the nature of the race question in the country. And that meant meeting Africans and, if possible, Afrikaners too. For the first group she went initially to the longtime primary school for Africans founded by the Glasgow Missionary Society in 1824, Lovedale, and its contiguous and more recently founded higher education analogue, the University College of Fort Hare.

On 12 November 1929 Perham boarded a train in Cape Town for the 400-mile journey to Alice in the Eastern Cape, where the school and university were located. She crossed rich agricultural country, then just at the outset of its transformation into one of the world's great wine-growing regions that it is today. Once arrived in Alice she was met by the Principals of both Lovedale and Fort Hare. Perham's visit began with the then putative university. Fort Hare had a student population of about 100, mostly men. They wore threadbare suits, she noted, but after prayers and the daily Bible lesson, they went off smartly to class exhibiting a joy that belied their humble circumstances. She admired their apparent religious conviction and their commitment to learning, but 'wondered whether Christianity could and would enable these people to exercise the almost unimaginable restraint that will increasingly be demanded of them'. These were the first African students Perham had had the occasion to meet, and she was impressed immediately with their attitude and bearing: 'These people are not cowed; they *seem* free and lusty'.[47]

At the time of Perham's visit Fort Hare still had a long way to go in what would become a journey mirroring the rise of African nationalism itself throughout the continent. A list of its alumni reads like a roll call of the worthies of the independence period to come, and beyond: Julius Nyerere, Joshua Nkomo, Seretse Khama, Oliver Tambo, Kenneth Kaunda, and Nelson Mandela. For Perham, much later, these names, and others, would populate her intellectual universe, and one of them, Khama, would become a close friend. For now, however, she was interested in determining what was on the minds of this first generation of Africans exposed to higher education on the Western model. What she found, somewhat to her surprise, was essentially reminiscent of 'talking to a group of students at home'. Of course, as they were ethnically Basuto, Zulu, Xhosa, and Fingo, they were spectacularly different from contemporary Oxford undergraduates. But they brought with them the same intellectual keenness as their British peers, an eagerness born of South Africa's extremely difficult racial and political position. Even then Perham sympathized greatly with the jejeune nature of modern African politics and the enormous responsibility that she could see rested upon this first real generation of African university students. Her approach was conservative, yet robust. As she spoke she reminded them – now rapt with attention and, as she tells it, hanging on her every word – that a grave duty lay upon them to raise up their people and to 'win and use your rights'. Violence and simple agitation must be eschewed in favour of working with those white people – as few as there might seem to be – whose commitment was to a multi-racial state and society. In a head to head battle with most of the whites of South Africa, they would be crushed easily, she warned them. The way forward, therefore, was education and engagement and patience!

In a sense, Perham's understanding of the lot of black Africans at this point in their history – of the tiny educated elite: 'these few to whom we have given this terrible gift of intellectual training' – would be a fixed star in her apprehension of the dilemma faced by the educated, nationalist African for the next forty years. Perham was acutely conscious of the rarefied air she was breathing at Fort Hare, of the almost surreal atmosphere of debate and discussion, black with white, that belied the segregated life the students lived off-campus where blacks 'may not sit in the same railway carriage, or eat at the same table, but must live under a different law, in a semi-servile state. Hertzog and even Smuts refer to the blacks as barbarians'.[48] Perham despised such retrograde thinking – 'I think I shall have hard work to keep my emotions in order while in this country' – and as her journey through South Africa continued her sense of injustice became ever more acute. A thorough visit to Lovedale followed, one-half of 'Scotland's gift to Africa', and then it was off to the Transkei, a so-called black 'homeland', to observe the domestic situation even more closely.[49]

Arriving early in November, Perham's introduction to the Transkei confirmed to her its importance to the position of blacks in South Africa. Carved out of the Eastern Cape in the last quarter of the nineteenth century as a kind of territorial reserve initially for the Xhosa, it would later – during the apartheid era as a 'bantustan' – become a byword for state illegitimacy at the hands of the Afrikaner government. In Perham's day, however, the vestiges of the Transkei's creation by the relatively liberal British of the Cape continued to yield a limited amount of local, shared control over its affairs, which the Hertzog government was now at pains to bring to an end.[50] Unmet at the railway station at Umtata, the Transkei's capital – an unusual experience for her – Perham took herself off to a local hotel and then the next day plunged into her usual round of encounter, discussion, and observation. The land continued to impress her with its abundance and its beauty, and by the degree to which it had been tamed by African and colonialist alike. She was also impressed by the constant missionary presence, how longstanding it was, and also, by contrast, how new was that of the State. Her view of missionaries – whether the Presbyterians of Fort Hare and Lovedale, or the High Church Anglicans of St. Cuthbert's in the Transkei, which she visited, or anyone else – was not, however, uncritical. The missionary presence may have been deep and, in her view, mostly welcome, but she complained of its rigidity and of its almost complete lack of imagination in the establishment and maintenance of the mission station, that cornerstone of all contemporary missionary endeavour. 'It is impossible not to feel', she opined, 'that the missionary too often gives just what is ready in his hand to give, without more careful adaptation to the needs of the native'.[51]

Arguably, the same thing could be said of the State – perhaps even with greater force. Certainly, Perham left the Transkei deeply pessimistic about the future of the *Bunga*, or council, that body which strove to enable some measure of multi-racial local government in the face of Pretoria's steady attempts to take it away. But with the alacrity of movement that was a hallmark of her journey she moved on from the Transkei later in November to Basutoland.

Established in 1868 as a High Commission Territory and made a crown colony fifteen years later, Basutoland occupied a rather romantic place in the minds of the British as both a wild mountain kingdom, and as a bulwark against both Zulu and Boer regional hegemony. The colony's history was a colourful one, laced with the outsized personality of the Sotho king, Moshoeshoe, and his towering citadel, Thaba Bosiu, and of the later interventions of Cecil Rhodes and General Charles Gordon. By the time of Perham's arrival, Basutoland's governance was centred on Maseru, the capital, and, as usual, she greeted the prospect of probing the workings of the colonial state there with some degree of trepidation: 'I always have a sinking feeling when I first encounter a new enterprise ...'.[52] Nonetheless, she was in Basutoland to see for herself a British Protectorate in Africa *in situ* and therefore, after alighting from the train onto an empty platform save for her greeting at the hands of the Assistant Commissioner of Maseru District, Captain Hugh Ashton, she got right down to work pouring through documents at the courthouse. To the degree that Perham had by now developed a *modus operandi* for her visits to colonial capitals, it consisted of anchoring them in the reading of documents and the acquisition of information, on top of which would come a layer of impressions topped off by conversation and discussion with the leading officials, which almost always included the Governor.

Basutoland made an immediate favourable impression on Perham, partly because of the courtesy with which she had been treated upon her arrival by Ashton, but more generally because she agreed with the British understanding that Basutoland was the 'Switzerland of Africa'.[53] Despite its postage stamp size within the vastness of southern Africa, and regardless of the fact that there was much remaining to see and do on this protracted journey, Basutoland made an indelible impression on Perham. She spent the better part of a month there, much of it centred on a two-week pony trek into the highlands that was reminiscent of her Somaliland experience. In her diary she raves about the colony's beauty and the excitement she felt on the eve of the trek, which had been arranged by the Resident Commissioner, John Sturrock.[54] An old Africa hand who had begun his career as a tutor at the court of the Kabaka of Buganda, Sturrock impressed Perham immediately with, in her view, a kind of saintliness: he is 'quiet, modest, simple, earnest, sympathetic, thoughtful ... beloved and respected'.[55] High praise, indeed, and we can see here Perham's predilection to be rather star-struck by the members of the Colonial Service or their equivalent. In any event, mounted on a horse with the unpromising name of 'Stumpy', she set off for what proved to be an idyllic two-weeks in the saddle that took her into the heart of Basutoland guided by Captain Ashton. Perham's recounting of this trip leaves room to conjecture as to the degree of attraction that existed between herself and Ashton. He was married with a pair of young sons, and there was no hint of sexual impropriety between them. Yet it strains credulity to think that a man with whom Perham spent a fortnight on trek and described as being fair, slender and over six feet tall, would fail to stir her romantically. Indeed, while Perham never made it clear whether or not she fell in love with Ashton, he certainly fell hard for her – as his letters to her show – in what amounted to an unrequited affair.

The fortnight in Basutoland's backcountry left Perham with a lifetime's impressions of wild Africa, remote and beautiful, and largely untouched by modernity. Camping out under the stars, carefully navigating her horse along a windswept plateau at 9,000-feet, and, exultantly, bathing in mountain streams: 'I stooped under water gushing from the rocks as if the nymph of the stream were pouring from a jug … . I sat on a smooth shelf of rock and let it rush over me while I looked up at the deep blue sky above the rocky heights and gave thanks to God, Cecil Rhodes, Barbara Gwyer, and the A.C.'[56] Alas, the trek was not all about watery idylls. The riding was hard in places, and the sight of impoverished and, often, leprosy-ridden Sotho was a reminder of the social and political reality of Basutoland. Indeed, as dreamy as her account of trekking through the Protectorate can be, she never loses sight of the fact of colonial rule, about which she remains clear-eyed and convinced of its necessity in order to improve the lives of the local people.[57]

Perham's memorable time in Basutoland, the vividness of which was maintained by a stream of letters from Hugh Ashton that would begin in January of 1930 – 'I sat with my eyes closed and thought about you' – was followed by a grim but enlightening visit to the Rand and to the Afrikaner-dominated city of Johannesburg that stretched through the Christmas season of 1929. Initially, she could do little more than to comment that 'I hate this city'.[58] Reproving herself for her hasty judgement, however, she nevertheless saw little but a regrettable materialism and a pervasive racism in the heart of Afrikanerdom, a view reinforced by an old South African friend from Oxford who now lectured at the local University of Witwatersrand, Margaret Hodgson. Liberal in outlook, Hodgson had been born in Scotland but moved as a child to South Africa. Educated there and at Somerville College, Oxford, she had returned to what she regarded as her home to teach history. Hodgson would be in the vanguard of white liberal opinion in South Africa in the mid-twentieth century, and she did much to reinforce Perham's own crystallizing views on the range of problems that beset native Africans there. Indeed, it was Hodgson who took Perham to her first mass meeting designed to spur agitation against Afrikaner rule. Later, Hodgson – by then known as Margaret Ballinger after marrying the trade union activist, William Ballinger – would be elected to the Cape Parliament as one of only three white representatives for the native African population, and during an extraordinary period of political activism that coincided with the rise of the National Party and apartheid would emerge as 'Queen of the Blacks' and the first president of the South African Liberal Party.[59]

Perham's experience in Johannesburg awakened her to the weakening influence on South African society of the old liberal British view of native Africans. Such a view, represented by the existence of the Cape native franchise, for example, had always obviated the harsher racial line taken by the Afrikaner leadership. For this weakening she blamed the British themselves, however, a process begun by the magnanimous terms (toward the beaten Boers) of the Treaty of Vereeniging that had ended the South African War in 1902. Magnanimous in the eyes of the British the treaty may have been, but from the vantage point of 1929, Perham began to think that the British may have been guilty of 'a betrayal of the native', a betrayal whose reversal was now increasingly unlikely in light of Hertzog's continuing campaign to reinforce Afrikaner paramountcy within the Union.[60]

Christmas day arrived, but as far as Perham could tell, the commemoration of Christ's birth was simply an excuse for Johannesburg to let off steam. 'The streets were impassable. Thousands of hooligans, fifty per cent of them drunk', she complained in her journal. 'I could not help relating it to my main subject – all these leering, drunken, degenerate looking people, to claim such absolute and eternal right over the native and to have the power to enforce their claim'. She asked with high incredulity: 'these men have the vote?' In this way a 'beastly' Christmas was passed and before the New Year arrived she happily departed for Pretoria.[61] But if leaving the Rand was a relief, 1 January 1930 would find her in the political capital of Afrikanerdom and confronted still by the aggressive ethnic nationalism of the Boer.

Perham's critical view of Afrikaners was reinforced immediately in Pretoria as she decried the ornate architecture of the central part of the city built by Paul Kruger, the legendary former president of the Transvaal, 'with', as she observed coolly, 'the gold looted from the Uitlanders on the Reef'.[62] She may have been a little too sympathetic to the Uitlanders' – so-called foreigners, but mostly British, living in the Transvaal in the years leading up to the South African War – given their own checkered history. They were not, after all, the most liberal and well-disposed of people toward either black or Boer. But clearly she was tiring of what she saw as the systematic aggrandizement of Afrikanerdom at the expense of what she believed was the essentially progressive nature of the British tradition in recent South African politics. At least, she pointed out, the glorious Union buildings designed by Sir Herbert Baker, the doyen of Imperial architects, witnessed

to the much more equitable racial aspirations of the architects of the Union
of South Africa between 1902 and 1910.[63]

The end of 1929 and the advent of the New Year had brought with it
a rather hurried conclusion to Perham's time in South Africa before heading north to take in Bechuanaland, the Congo, and the Rhodesias. At
Government House in Pretoria she visited the Governor-General, the Earl
of Athlone, who had likewise ridden into the backcountry of Basutoland
(on the same horse as Perham, Stumpy, she was amused to learn!) and was
similarly impressed with Ashton, the charming and knowledgeable Assistant
Commissioner. Perham was momentarily nonplussed morally, however,
when she explained that her party had consisted of *just* the AC and herself.
But Athlone did not seem to notice and immediately took the conversation
off in the direction of native policy and then, more or less separately, the
degree to which he despised Hertzog. Perham left disappointed, however,
for as much as Athlone was loud in his dislike of Hertzog and of Afrikaners
generally, he was not about to court severe political strain by opposing the
incremental Afrikanerization of South Africa. But on this subject, Perham
had already said enough, she decided. 'I expect it would be dangerous politically for more liberal views to be declared at Government House'.[64]

Throughout January of 1930 Perham made a series of flying visits, the
first of which was a return to Cape Town, where she attended the opening
of Parliament. A depressing affair, was her view of the event, made so by
the fact that the Hertzog government's moves to end the native franchise in
the Cape were approaching fruition. 'Racially', observed Perham ruefully
but with prescience, 'South Africa is now set on the downward path'. The
other impression left on her by the pomp and circumstance of that day at
Cape Town's Parliament House, was the pronounced physical presence of
Afrikaners who, among other things, either ignored the Governor General
entirely, or chatted throughout his speech from the throne when given in
English, but sat up smartly when it was read out in Afrikaans. Worse still,
noted Perham in a characteristic observation, was the way they looked. The
Afrikaners, in her unflattering view, were 'big, lean, stringy men, some with
shrewd but none with intellectual faces. One or two looked almost sub-
normal'. To top it off, she lamented, their wives were equally appalling:
'Mostly big, fat, red, hard women, they were bursting out of their party
clothes and tight gloves. Their true dignity would be on the farm'.[65]

During this especially hurried period of her journey Perham also managed
to have an interview, in Kimberley, with Sol Plaatje. Earlier, in 1912, he had
been one of the founders of the South African Native National Congress
(which had become the African National Congress in 1923). Plaatje was an

accomplished man of letters as well as an activist and a devout Christian, and Perham came away from their brief meeting thoroughly impressed with his strength of mind and with the unwavering devotion he displayed to his fellow black South Africans. Sadly, Plaatje died of pneumonia just two years later, but ever since he has been a revered figure in the annals of the ANC. (The house where he lived in Kimberley, and at which their meeting took place, for example, was declared a National Monument in 1992 during the Presidency of Nelson Mandela.)

The time had now come for Perham to leave South Africa. But, inspired in part by her conversation with Plaatje, it would not come before taking in something that would give her a more direct window into the lives of native Africans. In order to do that, she returned to Natal, to Zululand, where she went on a motoring tour under the auspices of the Native Affairs Department. En route she passed by some of the great historic sites connected with both Natal's and South Africa's history, including Ulundi, where in the summer of 1879 British forces had smashed the ferocious Zulu *impis*, which, several months before, had done the same thing to them at Isandhlwana. She visited villages and schools, clinics and hospitals, industrial sites and coal mines, all of which spoke to immense poverty, political disenfranchisement, and relentless despair. 'What does this Church [Dutch Reformed]', she asked plaintively of the mission school connected with one of the mines, 'educate the Africans *for*?'[66]

In revisiting Natal Perham had come full circle in her tour of South Africa. Durban once again offered up memorable experiences, especially the evening she attended a raucous and potentially dangerous Industrial and Commercial Union rally that featured George Champion, its leader in Natal, a commanding and charismatic Zulu, who pressed Perham on a number of points before enjoining her to 'tell England' of the wrongs inflicted upon him and his people now for generations. 'We want our capacities recognized', he thundered, in an age-old lament. 'There is nothing an African cannot do if he is given a chance'. Perham was asked to speak to the gathered trade unionists and acceded somewhat reluctantly, but once having begun she spoke with increasing confidence and force. She distanced herself from the radical nature of Champion's politics, however, pointing out that she was in Africa to learn only, and reiterating the message that education was the key to progress. But her words – and even more, her presence – were received extremely well by those present. Her colleague from the Native Affairs Department had warned her of the potential danger in going, which had given Perham pause long enough to leave a note at her hotel saying that should she not be back by 11:00 p.m. something had likely gone wrong and would therefore need to be 'fetched'. But the evening – including a wildly entertaining and rather erotic mass male dance: 'naked but for a thong round the loins' – went off without a hitch, even the fact that she did not return to the hotel until 11:30.[67]

The sort of rally witnessed by Perham would become standard fare in many locations across the continent over the next three decades, when economic demands fused with those of a political and social nature created the phenomenon of African mass nationalism. But in 1930 in Durban, Perham was certainly in the minority of Europeans to have experienced it and the event did much to shape her views as to what the African future might hold.

Still, feeling a bit 'battered' and 'shocked' by the experience Perham left Durban by train bound for Johannesburg and then north to Bechuanaland (modern Botswana). Claimed by the British in 1885, its status as a Protectorate was affirmed by the Colonial Office a decade later. The leading ethnic tribe in the territory was the Bamangwato, presided over by the Khama political dynasty, currently under the regency of Tshekedi, uncle of the heir to the throne, Seretse, then a minor.[68] Perham was keen to visit this Oxford-educated African leader in his home at Serowe after having run into him – almost literally – at the office of the Imperial Secretary in Cape Town some months before. Tshekedi did not disappoint. 'The best educated chief in Southern Africa', praised Perham, and admirable adversary against the current move to put Bechuanaland under South African control, as well as to resist the blandishments of the ever present British South Africa Company, Rhodes's old mining syndicate, which was intent on exploiting the Protectorate's mineral resources. 'Give my people a chance to develop a little further', is how Perham transcribed Tshekedi's main message in this regard, 'before you push this industrialism upon us. The gold will keep'.[69]

Bechuanaland and the Khamas would, as we shall see in a subsequent chapter, continue to be important to Perham, something that is unsurprising given that she recorded her visit to the Protectorate in the following way: 'I think that the time I spent talking to Tshekedi in his house was, in political interest, the high-water mark of my visit to South Africa'.[70] Nevertheless, in her usual haste she departed for the Congo, where she briefly witnessed Belgian colonialism. She found the Belgians to be every bit as impervious to her reasoned position in favour of education and development for native Africans as were the Afrikaners: 'Is it always I who raises the native question? I don't know, but it inevitably crops up'. And it invariably becomes controversial, she might have added, for 'I suppose I question the first contemptuous reference to "the nigger"'.[71]

Circumstances were scarcely better when Perham pushed on to Northern Rhodesia on 15 February. Colonized just a generation earlier in one of the great set pieces of British extroversion, the mining of lead, zinc, and copper now required the labour of thousands of native Africans, while systematic farming had begun to develop also. The prevailing view of the native African's intellectual capacity, Perham found, was a little better than in the Congo, but only just. Perham arrived by train in Broken Hill (modern Kabwe), located roughly in the middle of the colony, and was treated to the usual official welcome. From there she proceeded south to Livingstone, the colonial capital hard by the Zambesi River and Victoria Falls. 'Government House luxury' awaited her, as did the Governor, Sir James Maxwell, trained as a medical doctor and in Africa since his first posting as assistant colonial surgeon in Sierra Leone in 1897, together with his, apparently, rotund wife. Incapable, it seems, of resisting a pen portrait, Perham described her rather evocatively, if ungenerously, as resembling 'a large, splendid cabbage rose just tumbling over its prime'. In any event, Perham proceeded to engage in her usual round of discussions and a perusal of government documents, but these sometime mundane activities quickly took second place to a river cruise up to the mighty Falls. Cabbage rose-like or not, Lady Maxwell arranged this tour for Perham and like everyone else who has ever visited Victoria Falls, the mad, rushing water proved to be an overwhelming sensory experience for her. Ultimately, she concluded, their 'beauty and terror reach depths of you where interpretation becomes beyond your power or wish'.[72]

Despite Perham's enjoyable time socially and scenically in Livingstone her discussions about colonial policy with Governor Maxwell were testy and unfruitful. To her dismay, she found him essentially to parrot Hertzog in his views of political differentiation and social segregation – early polite terms for apartheid – and she was frustrated that he could not see that urban, increasingly de-tribalized native Africans were pushing for equal political status, and would not stop until they had achieved it. Forget, she argued, the obviating influence of the missions, as valuable as they were as social and religious agencies. Participatory politics, justice, enfranchisement, these clear marks of temporal power were what modernizing Africans were after and the British, from the gubernatorial class on down, she maintained, had to recognize this reality if the colonial project was going to both carry on and do any good in the long term.[73]

Having taken a last glimpse at the Falls from the spectacular bridge that spans the thundering cataract downriver from its base – 'surely the most dramatic bridge in the world' – she was off across the Zambesi and into

Southern Rhodesia.[74] A monument to Rhodes's gargantuan ambition in southern Africa, Southern Rhodesia had been administered by the British South Africa Company until 1923 when it became a self-governing Crown Colony. Arriving in Bulawayo, she met with Native Affairs officials, visited the courthouse, stopped at one of the stations of the London Missionary Society and then capped her stay with a visit to the Matopos Hills and Rhodes's simple but dramatically located gravesite. Once again, she engaged in close conversation with the Governor, Sir Cecil Rodwell, an archetypal senior colonial official educated at Eton and Cambridge, who had begun his career in South Africa under the tutelage of Sir Alfred Milner. And once again, she encountered views about native Africans that clashed with her own. Happily for Perham, she also found views more consistent with hers in the person of the Prime Minister, H.W. Moffatt, the grandson of the famous missionary, Robert Moffatt, founder of LMS operations in southern Africa and David Livingstone's father-in-law. Moffatt, in Perham's estimation, was 'humane and liberal' and as such heartened her as she departed for East Africa and what would be the final part of her first African progress.

In doing so Perham was hoping to make contact soon with Sir Donald Cameron, Governor of Tanganyika, and known similarly as progressive on matters of colonial policy. But before that would take place she passed through Portuguese Mozambique – where she seems to have contracted malaria – and then spent a brief spell in Uganda in the company of the Governor, Sir William Gowers, who was then coming to the end of a long career of colonial service in Africa that had started in 1899 with the British South Africa Company. Perham's tour round Uganda did not make a great impression on her, however, and she was keen to move on to Tanganyika and Kenya where the question of white settlers and native administration was much more acute. More pressing too was the movement for Closer Union, a kind of pan-East African administrative plan to bind the three regional British dependencies together in what would amount to a policy of white settler paramountcy. Perham, needless to say, was against the plan.

In the meantime, however, and in ways that would make clear both her professional intentions and bring about an immediate change in her itinerary, Perham resolved to 'devote myself entirely to the study of the government of 'native' races, especially in the African regions administered by Britain'.[75] Almost concurrent with that solemn resolution was an offer by the Rhodes Trust to extend her fellowship by a year. Impressed by her industry and reportage of the tour thus far, they proposed an extension. Since 1 July 1929 Perham, as noted earlier, had been collecting £100 per month. A further £1200 would be provided, they said, in order to have the tour continue until mid-1931. As Philip Kerr (later Lord Lothian), Chairman of the Rhodes Trust, would confirm shortly, it was thought 'well worthwhile to enable you to complete your researches thoroughly'.[76] This meant that she would have to give up her fellowship at St. Hugh's – no mean thing for an unmarried don without independent wealth. But so enamoured was she of the prospect of spending another year in the field she happily sacrificed the job in order, as she saw it, to have a career. 'Accept' she said to the Trust, and 'resign' she notified St. Hugh's, and with that question settled she plunged into East Africa.

Perham's first glimpse of Kenya came at the Lake Victoria port of Kisumu on 5 April 1930. The terminus of the Uganda Railway, the so-called 'Lunatic Line' built at surpassingly uneconomic cost by the British government some thirty years earlier to link Mombasa with the African interior, Kisumu was the colony's third-largest city. She did not stay long in 'mud-bound' (it was the season of the long rains) Kisumu, however, but was soon off to Nairobi, the colonial capital located some 200 miles to the east. Nairobi was the creature of the same railway line, but given its location on the other side of the Highlands was destined to emerge as the colony's financial and governmental centre. Not a particularly attractive town, its cheap buildings were mostly wood and sheet metal and the red dust of the plains would occasionally be churned up into a choking miasma. Not that the settlers and colonial officials seemed to mind, however. To them, Nairobi was the height of cosmopolitan life in Africa. Its various hotels and clubs, especially the Norfolk Hotel and the Muthaiga Country Club, both known for their social hi-jinks and for being generative of a free-flowing morality, had led to the inevitable question for which the colony was acquiring a reputation: 'Are you married, or do you live in Kenya?'

At the time of Perham's visit Nairobi may have had a population of 30,000 – no one was really sure – and its politics and social life were still dominated by the first generation of settlers led by Lord Delamere. Red-faced and domineering, Delamere was doctrinaire in his position advocating white settler paramountcy, dead-set against the position taken by the British government earlier in 1925 that native African interests would have to take precedence over those of the settlers. The fight over the future of the colony was now reaching a crescendo – and indeed determining which direction the colony would go was destined to be at the centre of affairs for the next thirty years. Perham's policy interests and her entrée into the highest of colonial circles meant that she had an ideal vantage point from which to witness the early stirrings of white resistance to African nationalism and Britain's response to it.

Like others before her nothing about Nairobi initially impressed Perham. 'Unpalatable,' 'disappointing,' 'inefficient,' and her list of derogatory terms for the place goes on. 'It is one of the shabbiest and shoddiest towns I have seen in my travels, which is saying a great deal ... . Most government offices are tumbledown tin shacks: the Supreme Court is like an abandoned warehouse'.[77] She was being, it might be suggested, a little hard on Nairobi, however. After all, most colonial towns in their infancy had left much to be desired. From Calgary to Khartoum, no one was going to mistake frontier towns for sophisticated burghs. Undesirable or no, Perham quickly got down to business. Having arrived in Nairobi on the morning of 7 April she checked into the New Stanley Hotel – inevitably it was 'dirty and ... rowdy groups were always drinking and hanging about the entrance-hall' – and went immediately to attend a sitting of the Legislative Council.[78] This session would be her introduction to Kenyan politics, and it was the one thing about the place initially that did not disappoint her. Indeed, the dominant issue of settler versus native rights was being debated that very day. The Governor, Sir Edward Grigg, presided over a raucous assemblage of representatives, including its most famous member, the Rev'd Canon Louis Leakey, Church of England missionary, patriarch of the future family dynasty, and leading advocate for the native African. That morning's Council meeting would inaugurate nine months in East Africa for Perham during which she would make two circuits through Kenya and Tanganyika, taking in everything from safaris to native African dance *ngomas* to gubernatorial lunches. She would remain in Africa until the end of December 1930, leaving for home with a stack of notes on the issues of the day and a lifetime's worth of vivid memories; of these, a handful standout in sharp relief.

A few months into her stay in Kenya Perham met Baron Bror von Blixen, the (in)famous Swedish expatriate aristocrat who had come out to East Africa in 1913. Initially planning to be a cattle farmer he had opted instead for coffee – 'I did not come to Africa to sit with silly cows!' – and using money supplied by his wife Karen Dinesen's family, invested in a 6,000-acre coffee farm. Sadly, the farm was never a success, and in 1930 with his marriage in tatters and the farm virtually bankrupt he was living a precarious financial existence. In the meantime, however, he had gained fame, if not a lot of money, as one of East Africa's 'Great White Hunters', who later would so impress Ernest Hemingway that he wrote a story – 'The Short Happy Life of Francis Macomber' – on them using Blixen as his singular model.[79] Always a charmer and lothario, he had married Karen in Mombasa in January 1914 before they set up house together just outside Nairobi at the foot of the Ngong Hills. For Baroness von Blixen – as the marriage made her – the seventeen years she would spend in Africa would be the fulcrum of her life and not long after her defeated return home to Denmark she would pen an evocative pastoral account of her time in Kenya – the coffee farm, the native Africans, the early white settlers, and her dead British lover, Denys Finch Hatton. As the author of *Out of Africa* (1937), as she named her account, Karen Blixen of course would become world-renowned as the writer Isak Dinesen. In his own time, Bror was certainly well-known in Kenya, as hunting guide to visiting royalty including the Prince of Wales, American plutocrats, and European aristocrats, and as an inveterate womanizer whose affairs with many of the colony's society women was an open secret. Indeed, the author of his biography none too subtly chose to call it, *The Man whom Women Loved*.[80]

As Perham acknowledged pithily, in Kenya 'there is a fair amount of matrimonial rearrangement'. And she certainly was aware of Blixen's reputation as a roué before accepting an invitation to lunch with him at the home he had established after Karen Blixen had demanded that he move out of the Ngong farmhouse some years earlier, followed by their divorce in 1925.[81] Blixen had remarried in 1928, but adultery clung to him like a wet shirt and doubtless some in his social circle may have thought that Perham – just thirty-four years of age, tall, attractive, and adventurous – might prove to be an irresistible target for his evident charms. Of course, none of Blixen's social circle, which included aristocratic wastrels such as Joss Erroll, Idina Sackville, and Alice de Janze, known as the 'Happy Valley' set, had any knowledge of Perham's character and personality, for whom an affair with Bror Blixen was unlikely in the extreme. Still, what proved to be a convivial lunch, turned into an invitation to hunt buffalo in nearby Tanganyika and the prospect of it proved too alluring for Perham to reject, whatever the potential risk to her virtue: 'In the end I threw everything to the winds. I am terribly excited tonight.'[82] Calling on her Somaliland experience and taking three shots with a rifle for practice, she quickly entered into the spirit of big-game hunting: 'I was absolutely terrified and enjoyed it'. In the end Perham did not fell one of the enormous, shaggy beasts known for their aggressive nature and great horned heads. She shot, but the bullet missed its mark. Nevertheless, the whole experience was elemental in its impact and she was, indeed, quite charmed by Blixen even though she could not have disagreed with him more over his settlers-first view of Kenya with which he and a few of his other hunting mates regaled her around the campfire.[83] On this point there was more to come when Perham would again meet with Blixen, this time over lunch in Nairobi and in the presence of Delamere. But both before and after that meeting she would spend time considering the same

issue with two men unlike Bror Blixen in almost every way, Cameron and
Grigg, the colonial governors of Tanganyika and Kenya respectively.

Throughout her stay in East Africa she saw both of these men regularly.
Whether it was over lunch or dinner, during legislative sessions, while staying at Government House, or out walking in the garden, she came to know
both of them rather well. Cameron she came to idolize as a 'Great Man
and above all the one I want to study'. He was on the right side of the
native versus settler question, in her view, but what really impressed Perham
about him was that his 'self-confidence is sublime … His brain works with
amazing quickness and sureness: he has an immediate answer to every
problem'.[84] Grigg, on the other hand, was less impressive intellectually, but
temperamentally evenhanded and gracious and came with an impeccable
personal pedigree. His father had been in the Indian Civil Service and the
son was a Wykehamist and then a scholar at New College, Oxford. Grigg
had also married into the aristocracy. Perham admired the fact that he did
not choose to run down any of his gubernatorial colleagues, something the
voluble Cameron did all the time. The gentlemanly Grigg also had the more
difficult task of the two governors because white settlement was an issue of
considerably greater force and import in Kenya than it was in Tanganyika.
Nevertheless, she would state later that Grigg 'was, I think, a disaster …
Trust the settlers was his idea'. On this score she had already written to
Philip Kerr complaining, 'must we assume that these minorities [the white
settlers], selected by divine right of race, govern the black populations?' In
this regard, she observed, 'Kenya seems to be a pathological study'.[85]

The question of white settlement and colonial governance remained constant during her stay in Kenya. In 1929, the Parliamentary Hilton Young
Commission report had weighed into the debate but did not, to the dismay
of Cameron, deal directly and positively with the idea of separate development of the races. To have done so, he argued vehemently to Perham, would
have been to see the situation clearly: settler local control and nothing more.
'Kenya settlers ask for self-government. Give it to them!' he thundered.
'That has nothing to do with governing other people … . I am all for self-
government of the settlers, but let it be local government.' To Perham, such
a position made perfect sense: 'I was much excited to find that his views
about the future exactly coincided with mine about the only solution – to
separate the areas'.[86]

The problem in this view, however, was that partial self-government,
really just a name for local government, was unacceptable to the settlers
and, in time, would be criticized ferociously by native Africans. At lunch
with Bror Blixen and Lord Delamere at Nairobi's New Stanley Hotel in July

Perham received a stiff dose of the settlers' medicine. As charming as Blixen was, Delamere – in Perham's estimation – was the exact opposite. As usual, she sized him up physically: 'he has long white hair yet just fails to look venerable. I can imagine an enemy likening him to a vulture and a friend to a bishop – not the most spiritual!' The lunch was testy. Blixen, for his part ever the sportsmen, sat back and enjoyed the contest of wills. Delamere accused Perham of being a 'sentimentalist' about native Africans. 'Well', he stated scornfully, 'we all were once'. But real progress demands much more than what the native can achieve, he continued. Perham interjected that self-government as opposed to governing other people might allow for both the settlers and the Africans to develop in a mutually rewarding way. Delamere regarded this position as little more than the cant typical of a cloistered academic, and exploded, arguing that a period of aristocratic government has always been necessary to any society's advancement wherever one looks in history. Accordingly, he concluded, 'I and my friends mean to rule', practically yelling now. 'And very soon'.

On that belligerent note the lunch came to an end. Despite being harangued in this way Perham held a grudging respect for Delamere, however, for his over thirty years in Kenya and for his complete commitment to the settlers' cause. He would, as it happened, die the following year, but his cause would run on after him for a full generation. As for Blixen, this meeting would be Perham's last with him during her visit to Kenya. After lunch, they took a drive out to the Muthaiga Club – the epicentre of settler, as opposed to, official social life since opening in 1913 – and then toured around Nairobi. 'I like him', she concluded simply, and then Bror Blixen drove off in his big Buick and perhaps out of her life forever.[87]

For Perham, the nine months in East Africa brought her close to native African life too. She toured Maasai territory, trekked the backcountry, and at the invitation of one of the senior Kikuyu chiefs, Waruhiu, slept in a hut in the midst of his people as an expression of understanding and solidarity. The request was made of Perham during an ongoing crisis over the native African practice of female circumcision, or clitoridectomy, against which the missionary community in Kenya had taken a strong stand. She agreed to do it without telling any Europeans. 'I don't think I slept at all', she wrote, and given the fact that in January a group of enraged Kikuyu had killed an elderly female African Inland Mission worker, having tried to circumcise her first, a sleepless night comes as no surprise. The case of the mutilated and murdered missionary was deeply disturbing to many, including of course many Africans, with the settler community especially enraged. The issue of female circumcision would continue to arouse great controversy long after

Perham's visit. As for her attempt at inspiring trust by sleeping in a hut on a hilltop, she was never sure 'whether this event had any of the significance which Waruhiu, in his deep gratitude, assigned to it'.[88]

By December 1930 Perham had been out of England for about a year and half. Her globetrotting, to use a term coined by Kipling – a 'general sort of toning up,' as she later recalled Philip Kerr describing it jocularly – from North America to the South Pacific and Australasia to Africa was nearly over, at least for now. She was ready to go home, where, given the generous provision of the Rhodes Trust, and her own frugality, she would be able to examine and write up her findings in the comfort of St. Hugh's College. Thanks to its principal, Barbara Gwyer, she became a non-stipendiary research fellow, although being without a regular income would present problems soon enough. And so for Perham it was back to England enlivened by a clearly enunciated purpose and still savouring the 'wonderful gift of time' that the Trust had given her.[89]

5

JOURNEY TO WEST AFRICA AND BECOMING AN AFRICANIST

Margery Perham arrived back in England from Africa in March 1931 after an extended voyage that stopped in a number of colonial ports, especially Italian, on the way. In Perham's view, owing to the fact that her steamer was full of Italian colonial officers returning from Africa, she had, as she put it baldly, 'an instructive, if not very congenial, voyage'.[1] The passage also included a visit to Cairo. But at last home was reached. She was thirty-five years old, superbly-educated, well-travelled, forthright, in all ways accomplished, really, a modern woman – but out of a job! Of course, this predicament did not take her by surprise. Indeed, she had been the author of it, even if the starkness of unemployment had to be experienced to be fully understood. It was not as if she were penniless, however. The fellowship from the Rhodes Trust would continue to yield her £100 per month for awhile longer, and this amount of money combined with £500 received from the estate of her deceased parents – Marion Perham having died in 1929 – kept body and soul together and allowed her, along with Ethel and Harry Rayne, to purchase a rural property – Ponds Farm at Shere, near Guildford in Surrey.[2] For the next five years or so this farm would be her home, and that of the Raynes who had now returned permanently from Africa. Still, from the moment in October 1930 when she had resigned her official fellowship at St. Hugh's, she was on her own financially. St. Hugh's, as noted earlier, had been quick to make her a non-stipendiary research fellow, in the first instance for the academic year 1930–31 – something that later would be extended through to 1939. And the college was intensely proud of its intrepid don. As Principal Gwyer put it in the 1929–30 edition of the *St. Hugh's College Chronicle*: 'There can be no doubt that Miss Perham is utilising to the full the extraordinary opportunities provided by her Fellowship … . More power to her elbow, and hearty acknowledgement to Cecil Rhodes!'[3] But in becoming a willing servant to her chosen subject of native administration in Africa she would have to be able to piece together a living wage. And, though never easy, eventually she was able to do so.

Once settled back in England Perham spent much of the remainder of 1931 in deepening her academic knowledge of African peoples and societies, something she realized was necessary if the ways and means of British colonial administration were to be understood and relayed effectively. Gaining such knowledge took the form principally of a period of study at the London School of Economics. In those days anthropology was in its infancy as a discipline, but had begun to throw up its leading lights, especially Bronisław Malinowski, the brilliant Polish-born ethnographer. His stated goal was 'to grasp the native's point of view, his relation to life, to realize *his* vision of *his* world.' In so doing he helped to develop structural functionalist sociology, which was just beginning to influence the field when Perham had started to read Malinowski's work while in Kenya in the summer of 1930. Once back home she began to study under him systematically at the LSE in anticipation of a return to Africa in the autumn of 1931. Under lecture headings such as 'Patterns of Culture', 'The Science of Customs', and 'Human Traits', she took copious notes in the spring and summer of that year while simultaneously battling through occasional attacks of malaria, latent in her system from her African travels.[4] Meanwhile, the International Institute of African Languages and Cultures in London – founded just a few years earlier in 1926 – had taken a clear interest in Perham. Her byline had begun to appear in the pages of *The Times*, something that readers would come to expect over the next forty years. Indeed, on the 13th, 14th, and 15th of August under the heading, 'The Future of East Africa', she had spelled out in close detail why the settler interest there simply could not prevail over that of the native Africans. Unsurprisingly, her decisive and uncompromising words provoked a backlash, notably so in her erstwhile gubernatorial friend from Kenya, Sir Edward Grigg. He complained to Kerr that 'I think it very desirable to make our people in Africa understand that the Rhodes Trust is not becoming associated with propaganda against the ideals for which Rhodes and Milner spent their lives'. Kerr wrote off Grigg's protest as 'absurd', but Perham's penchant for ruffling the feathers of some within the colonial establishment was becoming clear.[5]

Despite Grigg's overwrought criticism, Perham had many admirers in high places nonetheless, chief among them Lord Lugard. The IIALC was chaired by him and run by the well known missionary-ecumenist, Dr. Joseph Houldsworth Oldham, and in October it awarded her a fellowship. As she wrote happily to Kerr, the day after receiving the news: 'it enables me to continue those studies which their [the Rhodes Trustees] generosity allowed me to begin'.[6] And so barely seven months after returning from Africa she set off for it again, only this time she would spend her time in the western part of the continent, centred on Nigeria.

Perham's first port of call in Africa was the Gold Coast (modern Ghana). She went ashore at Takoradi on 17 November, amazed by its deep-water harbour constructed recently under the governorship of Sir Gordon Guggisberg, the Canadian-born empire builder who had served in the Gold Coast for most of the 1920s.[7] The colony occupied a prominent place in Britain's West African empire dating from the protracted defeat of the Ashanti people beginning under General Wolseley and his celebrated Ring of military colleagues back in the 1870s and, more recently, because of its cocoa crop. The economy of the Gold Coast revolved around the monoculture of cocoa and that fact, in Perham's view, made the construction of the grand harbour at Takoradi both an amazing feat and one of questionable economics. Quickly, however, she moved a brief distance along the coast to Sekondi, stopping to take in a few sights along the way. The November 'heat was painful', and refuge had to be taken at a hotel bar where the local lager was readily drunk before catching a ship, the S.S. *Adda*, bound for Accra, the colony's capital, and a meeting to come with a pair of officials from Native Affairs. Once there Perham was as unimpressed with both of them – the Secretary she described as being 'a fat man with glassy eyes' – as they were with her, apparently, and after a short meeting in the debilitating heat of the Administrative building she feigned going upcountry to Achimota and instead headed back to her ship for the 250 mile Gulf of Guinea coastal run to Lagos.[8] Her reintroduction to Africa by way of the Gold Coast had been less than stirring, but the prospect of Nigeria – the place where she anticipated spending the better part of the next six months and, in British administrative terms, a monument to Lugard – filled her with great anticipation.

Today, Lagos is a burgeoning conurbation of some 16-million people, one of the largest cities in the world and second in Africa only to Cairo. In mid-November 1931, however, when Perham disembarked at Lagos Lagoon, the city had a population of just 170,000 people spread over its two main islands, small by modern standards but sizeable for the day. The short rainy season was coming to an end and the air was hot and damp. She did not much like the place, at first blush, and was concerned also that the person she most wanted to see, Sir Donald Cameron, the recently-appointed Governor fresh from Tanganyika, had had to attend to business up-country and therefore she might be left to her own devices, at least for a time. Based on her East African experience, Cameron was the ideal British colonial governor, 'the real thing', she had said of him, 'what one was really coming to see. Because here was an administration that was trying to do something, which had some sort of philosophy behind it'.[9] Happily, Cameron had not forgotten about her for just as she began to encounter difficulties with an intransigent police officer who perhaps understandably looked askance at her claim that she was in Nigeria as a 'guest of the Governor', along came a representative of Cameron's Chief Secretary together with 'a beautiful six-seater Humber … . I felt like the heroine exalted from rags to riches as we sailed past the police and the customs'.[10]

Over the next few days Perham ensconced herself at the Secretariat, 'the most handsome building of its kind I had yet seen in British Africa', undertaking her usual practice of delving into papers and documents, 'trying at close quarters', she noted in her diary, 'to understand Nigeria'. Given that thirty-seven years later in 1968 she would fly out to Lagos from London in an attempt to more fully understand the Biafran conflict that had ruptured the Nigerian federation, the task of making sense of Nigeria for Perham had only just begun.[11]

In the history of British colonial administration in Africa no country is of greater importance than Nigeria. Its sheer size, especially after the unification of the North and South in 1914, was matched by the equally ambitious way in which the British chose to govern it. In the person of the curiously named Scottish explorer Mungo Park in the late eighteenth and early nineteenth centuries, British interest began to be exercised in the region. Attempts by them to suppress the slave trade led to the establishment of a base at Lagos in 1851. By the 1880s the palm-oil trade had yielded the creation of the Royal Niger Company under the control of Sir George Goldie and when its lands passed to the Crown in 1900 British protectorates were declared over Southern and Northern Nigeria respectively.[12] A railway was undertaken later to join the two territories together, constructed largely under the direction of Canadian railway builder turned British colonial governor, Sir Percy Girouard, and in 1914, they were unified as a single colony.[13] Throughout this latter period the British – mainly through the inimitable character of Lugard – developed the system of indirect rule by which it exercised government across a wide landscape and upon a disparate population. In Perham's time, and indeed right up until Nigerian independence in 1960, indirect rule dominated the understanding of British colonial governance in Africa and elsewhere. Consequently, it was this form of governance, of course, that Perham now sought to view and understand *in situ*.

By the time of Perham's visit to Nigeria in 1931 indirect rule had been in place for some thirty years. In essence, IR – as it came to be known, especially by those in the field – employed the traditional local power structure within the superstructure of British colonial administration. As a policy it was not unique to Nigeria; indeed, a form of it had long been practiced by the East India Company, which was continued by the Raj after Company rule ended in India in 1858. But owing to Lugard's careful and well-publicized elaboration of its principles, and to its subsequent elevation to near-unassailable status as both philosophy and policy in his book, *The Dual Mandate in British Tropical Africa* (1922), indirect rule was usually seen as his personal creation.[14] Not without its critics, either then or now, indirect rule was usually praised as properly gradual in readying colonial peoples for their eventual independence – or sometimes denounced as a stultifying form of social and political control whose chief effect was to stunt local development. Both of these understandings of indirect rule shall be examined subsequently in chapter seven. For Perham, though, as she gazed out at Lagos Lagoon on that steamy November afternoon in 1931, she was certainly of the opinion that Lugard was a great man and a superb colonial administrator and among the things she was planning to observe while in Nigeria was evidence of his good handiwork.[15]

Despite the fact that Perham was not enamoured of Lagos, she nonetheless was highly impressed with the Nigerians she encountered there. They were, in her view, a 'proud, assertive people … . Compared with East Africans these people struck me as being confident …'. She had noticed immediately too the varied religious streams, 'pagan, Christian and Muslim', evident in the colony and the complexion this fact would give to her travels.[16] Shortly, she employed a local youth, Bakari, as her assistant, or, in the continuing parlance of the day, her 'boy', who would be invaluable for the duration of her stay. About ten days after arriving in Lagos Perham set out to see the colony in its entirety, beginning with the city of Ibadan and the Yoruba people. The journey there was short, about 120 miles, but it carried her away from the coast and into the heart of the Nigerian south. Perham was now entering a land where there were very few Europeans, but where evidence of their outsized impact was being readily felt in religion, government, and market relations. Immediately upon arrival she admired the flowing dress of the people and the preponderance of the colour blue, as she noted that most Yoruba households had their own indigo plants, and settled into the British Club for a short stay. In what had become both a personal habit and a financial necessity Perham moved quickly, if no impediments stood in her way. Alas, in Ibadan, she was sent to bed by the recurrence of fever, but within a couple of days had rallied and pushed onto Oyo, the home of the King or *Alafin* of the Yoruba. She was met there by the Resident, that trustworthy Oxbridge (usually) man who was responsible for administering the province. At Oyo, the Resident was H.L. Ward-Price, and at the moment of Perham's arrival he happened to be reading *Twelfth Night*, in itself a marvelous vignette of colonial juxtaposition. Her Sheffield playwright days being not so far behind her, Perham commenced on a conversation about the Bard before being shown to the guesthouse and being introduced to a pair of Oxford Colonial Service cadets, the product of the one-year course that had been established at Oxford and Cambridge for their training in 1926 and with which Perham would soon be intimately involved.

Perham's recurring fever was made worse, alas, by the fact that the guest-house was shared with 'rats, lizards, bats and a mist of mosquitoes'.[17] Uncharacteristically, she exhibited considerable trepidation at this point on her journey but as it continued, the less troubling were these hallmarks of contemporary African travel and the more they became part of the physical and mental furniture of the adventure. She was granted an audience with the Alafin – reputed to have five hundred wives. He would not deign to shake the hand of a (white) woman, however, and so received from the self-possessed Perham a curt bow in response. She then moved on to the houses and huts of some of the 60,000 ordinary inhabitants of the city. In poking her head into these 'warrens of red mud with trickling open drains' she was given a quick introduction to the Yoruba *Orishas*, or gods, who numbered some four hundred, many of which were on display. Her visit concluded with – at her request – a tour of the city's prison, which was run by the Native Administration. A grim and ghastly place, she observed the 'dejected' prisoners, especially the one who was serving the longest sentence: six years for cutting open a living child and eating its heart in order to symbolically imbibe its best attributes. 'The sentence seemed light', she remarked pithily, noting that traditionally each Alafin was required to eat the heart of his predecessor so 'after forty generations the present ruler must have a formidable accumulation of qualities'.[18]

Coming face to face with such apparent savagery seemed not to phase Perham much, although her visit to Oyo combined with her feverish condition and the size and complexity of Nigeria were beginning to have a depressive effect on her. Nonetheless, she was able to cut through this growing fog in two ways. First, once back in Ibadan, she engaged in a wide-ranging conversation with a group of African students – 'How were Africans treated in South Africa? Really! Then why did the British Government allow it?' – studying to be teachers at the Church Missionary Society Training

College. Chatting with them was a tonic: 'If only administrative officers and missionaries would let me talk to the Africans alone! It is most difficult to achieve this'.[19] Second, she got up on horseback and rode round the town, partly to observe closely the people of Ibadan at work and otherwise, and partly to enjoy a bit of exercise and clear her mind. Beginning essentially in Somaliland riding had become a necessary pastime for Perham, and one that she would continue to do whenever possible for most of the rest of her life.[20]

Perham's visit to Ibadan, Oyo, and a little later, Ife, occupied her until early in December. None of these places seemed to really capture her imagination, however: 'Why has this country – so far – no charm for me?' But Ife, with its recently discovered elaborate religious shrine, hitherto hidden from Western eyes, complete with fetish priests and terracotta heads enlivened her.[21] Unfortunately, however, she took ill again and had to return to Lagos to recuperate. The balance of December, including Christmas was spent in this way at Government House. The sudden attack of malarial fever had necessitated a change in her itinerary too so her scheduled trip to the Cameroons, under French control, was put off, and, once sufficiently recovered, she decided to strike out instead for Northern Nigeria, the essential Lugardian laboratory for indirect rule and, importantly, a much drier and therefore a much healthier environment than the swampy south.

Accordingly, on the morning of 28 December Perham left Lagos by train bound for the northern cities of Kaduna and Kano. Both would take her into that part of Nigeria where Islam held sway. Kano, in particular, was a place of exotic mythic grandeur to most Europeans, a walled city whose baked red mud had been visited first by Heinrich Barth, the great German explorer of Africa who had traversed the continent between 1849 and 1855 during which time he was also a sometime representative of the British Foreign Office.[22] Later, in 1903, Kano had been conquered by the British under Lugard as part of the subjugation of its surrounding empire, the Sokoto Caliphate. He then had named it the capital city of the new Protectorate of Northern Nigeria.

The conquest of Sokoto had brought with it the attendant problem of how it was to be governed. As we shall see when we look at Lugard in greater detail in chapter seven, the existence of a centuries-old Islamic society in Northern Nigeria presented a myriad of challenges to the British, not the least of which was that it spread itself over a region extending over some 200,000 square miles. Perham's understanding of the complexities of the North, thus far, had been shaped by reading and conversation – including that with Lugard himself – but in readying herself for 'going north' she understood that she would be encountering a delicate situation. In the first instance, as a woman – especially in an official capacity – she would be instantly unwelcome. As true as that was for the Emirs – who, she noted, required that 'dogs and women' be kept out of the way – it was true also for their British overlords, the Residents, who did their utmost to keep the Emirs unperturbed. Having Perham arrive to gain a keener insight into the workings of indirect rule therefore was, *a priori*, objectionable to them. Secondly, Sir Donald Cameron, who had spent many of his formative colonial service years in Nigeria, had returned as Governor intent on ensuring that the amalgamation of North and South carried out by Lugard in 1914 was as thoroughgoing as possible; that is to say, as Governor, he meant to be at the crux of British rule in all of Nigeria, not simply in the South.[23]

Exhibiting a wistful nod to the comforts and conveniences of Government House, Perham departed Lagos and reached Kaduna on 30 December. The administrative centre of British rule in the North, she remained there for about a week experiencing in its outlying districts, as she called it, 'basic Africa. Here was the real bush village, each poor little hut built to immemorial pattern – extended family groups; naked people bent over their tasks; the women crushing grain with grinding-stones; little patterns of white pebbles between the huts marking the graves of their fathers'.[24] Kaduna was situated roughly in the middle of Nigeria and in that way was populated mainly by neither Christian nor Muslim but by pagan, a term, as Perham notes, used by the government much more in a social than in a religious sense.

Perham celebrated the New Year 1932 in Kaduna, and then a few days later, thanks to the use of a hospitalized Resident's unused car, she drove on to Zaria, one of the North's original Hausa city-states. Today, Zaria is home to over a million people and to Ahmadu Bello University, Nigeria's largest. Lugard's conquest of the North had included the city in 1901. Bouncing along on the road into Zaria Perham was surprised and amazed at the level of agricultural cultivation around the city, and with the help of the now-recovered Resident and a couple of administrative officers, one of whom was the brother of a student at St Hugh's College – 'How pervasive Oxford is!' – proceeded both to do her usual reading of government documents and to explore as much of Zaria and its surrounding countryside as she could in the next few days.[25] As her time in Nigeria continued – now approaching two months – she was becoming much more at ease with the vagaries of local travel and with those of the administrative officers she was meeting and upon whom the practicalities of her journey depended. At the top of this administrative pyramid sat the imposing figure of Governor Cameron, who Perham would always respect greatly and admire. To her, Cameron continued to be 'an extraordinary character – great, long, lean, leathery faced man, absolutely brutally efficient and didn't care a bit what he did to people so long as they did what he wanted'. And it was those very characteristics that had enabled her to go north in the first place. For, as she recalled years later, 'up there in the north it was a sort of he-man's country with hard-bitten, polo-playing types who didn't want any reform … no wives were allowed. They didn't want me to go up there … . But Cameron insisted and overrode them …'.[26] At the same time, as grateful as she was for Cameron's dogged support, she realized also that his clarity, decisiveness, and outspokenness – which had clearly marked his years in Tanganyika – were perhaps too blunt instruments for the highly complex and stratified environment of Nigeria.

Visits to court and treasury – 'I am always impressed by seeing Africans handling local government finance partly because I know nothing of accountancy and have never kept the simplest accounts' – to the markets where the distinctive colourful robes of the Hausa were sold, to the Agricultural Station for the North, all were part of Perham's round.[27] And then, in haste, it was off about a hundred miles directly north to Kano.

Kano did not disappoint. The *harmattan*, the hazy wind of the region, obscured the approach to the city, but then suddenly there stood its famous red wall. Perham passed through it, the oldest part of which dates from the eleventh century, and proceeded to the Residency located in the Sabon Gari, the foreign quarter. There she was received by a phalanx of colonial officials, led by the Resident, H.O. Lindsell – another ubiquitous Oxford man. Perham seems to have been overawed by this 'formidable reception party', but did her best to play up to its apparent gravity, all the while remembering that she was now in the 'most important and historic state in Northern Nigeria, perhaps in all 'British' Africa'.[28]

Perham spent almost two weeks in Kano. She found its history captivating, from its seventh-century foundations to its British conquest thirteen hundred years later. In between had come all manner of invasions, wars, and famines. At the beginning of the nineteenth century the Fulani Islamic leader, Usman dan Fodio, led a jihad, the result of which was the emergence of the Sokoto Caliphate, a slave-based Muslim empire that would long defy the British outlawing of the Atlantic Slave Trade in 1833.[29] Her fortnight in the storied city included attending a meeting of the Kano Council. Such meetings took place on a regular basis between the Resident and the Emir, together with assorted lesser officials on both sides. Etiquette – as Lugard had made clear years earlier – ruled these encounters, with the seating plan of highest importance and provisions for a sort of purdah enforced. As Perham noted, with a hint of incredulity: 'until lately political officers on public occasions veiled their own wives in deference to Muslim custom;

in the past net curtains have been hung over the gallery holding European women at public events'.

The ceremonial nature of the Kano Council went a considerable distance in masking the exercise of British power, which Perham was quick to recognize. Having read extensively about it, she was now in the presence of indirect rule in its clearest form, which she described as being a kind of 'constitutional trick that we have learned in England'. In going on to elaborate her meaning, Perham articulated one of the best explanations that one is likely to find anywhere of how indirect rule in Northern Nigeria actually worked:

> The autocratic Emir retains nearly all his powers in theory while in practice, behind the curtain, he is checked and propelled, not by a ministry, still less by a democracy, but by an unobtrusive, kindly, middle-aged Englishman who derives his authority from the military power and wealth of Great Britain. That power and wealth is not what it was in the days when the first Resident came in with a walking-stick … . One wonders what would happen if they called our bluff, India, perhaps, having shown the way. The policy now is at once to reform and modernize … .[30]

In addition to the Council Perham took in shops, schools, hospitals – 'It is astonishing what Africa can do to do the human body in the extent and variety of her injuries' – the court and the prison. At the latter, she was again taken aback by the crudeness of what she saw: 'naked men were turning big wheels to grind corn. Their sweating black bodies caught all the light that came in and their silent, rhythmic exertion suggested a scene from the *Inferno*'. The prison visit caused her to wax philosophical, asking whether or not the kind of power Britain exercised in Nigeria or anywhere else in the Empire was justified. On the other hand, and in relation directly to the prison, she recalled reading a report from Kano written by Lugard in 1903 in which he detailed that one of the local methods of capital punishment ended by the paramount British 'was to throw victims up against the ceiling until they died'.[31]

Perham's round of official visitations was spiked by lunches and dinners, occasional tennis matches, and by introductions to all sorts of people, official and unofficial, Nigerian and European. One of the most notable of the latter type was Walter Crocker, a brilliant Oxford-educated Australian Colonial Service cadet. Having recently joined the Service and come out to Nigeria, he quickly loathed both and would leave it in 1934 for what proved to be a starry career in academe and diplomacy. For Perham at the time, however, she was simply happy to meet someone with an academic mind who therefore 'talks one's own language ... . I felt more vividly than ever before the meaning of the spirit of Oxford'. And with that bit of rejuvenation she ended her visit to Kano, packed up for a short reconnaissance of nearby Bichi district, which fed its wealth into the city, downed 'a strong gin, [and] went on alone northward for the next state, Katsina'.[32]

Perham was now approaching the mid-way point of her West African journey. She set out for Katsina on 23 January. Located just south of the border with French colonial territory (modern Niger), Perham would soon leave Northern Nigeria and experience firsthand a comparative (and competitive) form of European rule in the region. Before doing so, however, she continued with her usual round of reading government documents and making visits to schools – 'a very new and exceptional institution in this conservative part of Africa' – and courthouses and treasuries. So, too, did she continue to ride on horseback. The vast expanses of Northern Nigeria were magnificent horse country, whether that meant the District Officer – such as Harry Rudbeck in Joyce Cary's superbly evocative novel of the period, *Mister Johnson* (1939) – heading out for a long tour on his sturdy pony or the colourful Hausa horsemen who 'make quite dazzling pictures' with their 'fold upon fold of cloth, metallic blue or red and white' and their sleek mounts with plaited manes. Africa, for Perham, remained yet a place of surpassing romance and this journey still an adventure into the realm of new experience, if not any longer into the unknown.[33]

At the end of January Perham began to falter, however, owing to illness, both a recurrence of malaria and what she later learned was sleeping sickness, probably in the chronic form in which it was usually found in West Africa. Though Perham does not mention it in her diary, she likely would have been treated by Suramin, an arsenic-based drug developed in Germany in 1916 that would be a mainstay in the fight against the ravages of the tsetse fly for the following half-century. Her hectic pace of course did not help her health either, and so once again she had to alter her plans and rest, if only briefly. To do so, and in search of better medical care, she went south to Enugu. Once reasonably well-recovered there it was back up to Jos, the great mid-Nigerian plateau where enormous deposits of tin were now being mined. From there she hired a car – a big, battered Chevrolet – and driver, and together with Bakari set off for the north-eastern province of Bornu. This colourfully historic region of Nigeria had been fought over constantly, with the most recent series of wars being those undertaken by Fulani invaders and Sudanese slavers in the late-nineteenth century, and Perham was eager to travel through it as a preparation for crossing into the French territories of the Cameroons and Chad located along Nigeria's northeastern border.

Such was the plan, but as often happens on any journey – perhaps especially in Africa in the 1930s – plans go awry. Perham had made a bad choice in her driver, alas, as he was no mechanic, knew nothing about Northern Nigeria, and was disinclined to talk, a singularly unfortunate attribute in a long-distance driving partner. 'He is' – Bassey was his name – 'the first African ever to make me see red', she wrote in utter exasperation a few days into their journey.[34] Meanwhile, the old Chevrolet limped along in scorching heat over unspeakably bad roads, only to give out completely at various times. Lunches consisted of a bit of stringy chicken and warm beer. Along the way welcome refuge was taken at the stations of District Officers – who from Somaliland ever after would be heroic figures for Perham. Maiduguri, the provincial capital, at last was reached, and then Dikwa. The latter was home to Captain P.E. Lewis, District Officer, decorated in the First World War, who had come out to Northern Nigeria right after it ended. And a fine, upstanding man he was too, although on the day of Perham's arrival he was falling-down drunk having just returned from a parched six weeks on tour in the bush. He was not expecting Perham for at least another day! Alas, she arrived in the midst of his temporary dishevelment, but she liked him right away nonetheless. And he quickly proved his worth. Lewis put Perham up happily and then accompanied her to Lake Chad and on to its southern effluent that marked the border between the French Cameroons and Nigeria. And then, as he watched, she 'went forward on to French soil'.[35]

The political geography of the region was such that Perham would simply pass through the northern tip of the French Cameroons before entering Chad. A little later in her journey she would spend time in the Cameroons, a large pie-shaped slice of territory running south all the way down to the Gulf of Guinea that had formerly been under German rule but which the provisions of the Paris Peace Conference had divided and turned over to the British and French as mandate trust territories.[36] She, Bakari, and Bassey motored into Chad on 20 February and quickly made the Chari River, across which lay the mandate's capital, Fort Lamy (the modern capital city of N'Djamena). The French roads were smooth and impressive compared to those in Nigeria and keeping up 'a level fifty without a jar, after what I have lately endured, strained my patriotism', Perham remarked phlegmatically. No bridge crossed the river, however, and after an open-ended wait for some kind of assistance the car was duly left behind and the river crossed in a makeshift canoe, all the while trying not to drop their clothes and other belongings into the swirling Chari.

This unpropitious beginning did not improve upon presenting herself at Government House in Fort Lamy. In reasonable French she introduced herself to the Governor's wife, Madame de Coppet. The Governor was away, Perham was told, and there was no room in Government House for her so it was off into town where she was shown to a 'filthy and dilapidated' house with a dirt floor and a heap of old clothes as a mattress. One might surmise that such accommodation was offered to Perham with a Gallic shrug by the French official who had walked her there. Meanwhile, Bassey had gone to ground and Bakari, who had become separated from her, turned up frantic an hour or so later only to set about feverishly trying to clean the place up, an almost impossible task without so much as a broom to hand. In any event, such was Perham's welcome to French colonialism on the African frontier.

In the days that followed – Perham would stay in Fort Lamy for almost a week – not much improvement was experienced. The house, it turned out to Bakari's horror especially, was shared by a white man and a Fulani woman. If at first Bakari's report that they were 'eating chop' together reduced the suspicion that this hovel was a sometime bawdy house, then the fact that the couple were 'noisy and kept me awake far into the night' confirmed one of its functions to Perham. Indeed, the place seemed to be a kind of community centre with all sorts of people coming by to beg or trade. The only relief from it to be had was the meals she enjoyed with Madame de Coppet, 'blessed' interludes, as Perham awaited the expected return of the Governor. Alas, there were no government documents to read, which amazed her; indeed, she was told that in all of French Equatorial Africa no official published documents of any kind were sent to Paris. So, consequently, there she was 'with nothing to read and nothing to do'. Exasperated and bored she was of a mind to cut this frustrating excursion short and return to Bornu and the comparative comforts of the British district station at Dikwa. Instead, she did what she could to understand how the French governed their West African colonies. Off to the local school she went, therefore, so too the market, and then to a visit with the local missionary, the latter, remarkably, a Protestant New Zealander. Unaffiliated with any missionary society, mostly despised locally, but doggedly at work for the previous twelve years in anthropological study, he had learned the local language and then translated the Bible: 'I felt a great respect for him', she wrote, awestruck by the level of his thankless commitment.[37]

Finally, on the fifth day of her stay the Governor, Jules Marcel de Coppet, returned. The fact that he was 'most strikingly handsome' meant that Perham was well-disposed to him immediately.[38] Over the next twenty-four hours she engaged him in an intense conversation about French colonial practices, the cardinal feature of which was their system of direct as opposed to the British indirect system of rule. How had this come to be, she asked de Coppet? Partly, came the answer in Perham's paraphrase, it could be attributed to the lingering dislike of local government in modern France, 'a hangover from strong feudal power and an obstacle to centralization'. In addition, the French experience in Africa had been, from the start, more about military and imperial control than anything else, objectives backed up by the dominant French colonial paradigm to the north, represented by Algeria. At times, Perham's strong belief in indirect rule came up against de Coppet's diametrically opposed position in the starkest of terms. 'No native', stated the Governor flatly, 'is fit to conduct a court of justice. The natives know that and they prefer our justice'. Still, despite their contrasting views, she was highly impressed with him and at the end of their spirited conversation wondered if the difference between French and British colonialism was not merely 'a difference of manners rather than morals?'[39]

On 25 February a nonetheless relieved Perham left Fort Lamy intending initially to head south to Bongor and then west into the French Cameroons via Marua and from there back to Nigeria. But instead, she wrote, 'today I think for the first time in any of this African travel I changed a programme from sheer cowardice'. She was tired, a bit fearful of car trouble and the likely scarcity of petrol and, perhaps most strongly, she yearned 'longingly for British soil'. And so, along with Bakari and Bassey, she was back in Dikwa by that afternoon, welcomed warmly by the trustworthy Captain Lewis, who, she noted approvingly, was 'quite sober this time'.[40]

The balance of February and into March Perham spent travelling down the eastern flank of Nigeria along the border with the French Cameroons and then, briefly, the British Cameroons. Perham and her party then turned north in the direction of Jos. Despite having employed a driver, she usually did most of the driving herself, and this stretch of road was no exception. She did not much trust Bassey behind the wheel, but out of sheer exhaustion she would, from time to time, turn the car over to him. One of those times was in the final run-up to Bauchi, the last stop in the protracted loop that would take her back to Jos. 'It proved to be an almost fatal act', she wrote. For some reason Bassey lost control of the car while driving at forty miles per hour 'along a perfectly straight road', Perham wrote with evident incredulity. The heavily-laden Chevrolet spun around twice, narrowly avoiding an open pit and then carrying on with considerable velocity smashed through a wall before coming to rest against an overgrown tree. Remarkably, no one was injured, although the car's steering was essentially broken. In stunned silence – 'I said nothing. What was there to say even if I had adequate African language in which to say it?' – the shaky trio got the half-wrecked car back onto the empty road and inched along to Bauchi.[41]

A couple of days later Perham left Bauchi behind, as well as the unfortunate Bassey himself and his rented heap of a car, fired up an old lorry provided by the District Officer, and at the grand speed of twelve miles per hour slowly made her way to Jos where she spent two days in close observation of life on the spectacular plateau. She took in the tin mines – then suffering under the collapse of world minerals prices – and a series of local villages before setting out on 12 March directly south for Makurdi on the banks of the great Benue River. She stayed there for about a week and then moved further south still to the previously visited Enugu and finally to Port Harcourt in the Niger River delta. The 1st of April found her on board a German ship anchored off Fernando Po (modern Bioko, part of Equatorial Guinea), a Spanish island colony where Sir Richard Burton had gone as British Consul in 1861 following his acrimonious search for the headwaters of the Nile with John Speke a few years earlier.

Perham spent the following two weeks in an eye-opening tour of the French Cameroons. After seeing round Fernando Po for a day, she went across to Douala on the Cameroonian coast and then inland to the capital of Yaounde. Her visit was the second installment in her two-part study of French tropical African colonialism. Just as in her stay in Chad of five weeks earlier, Perham was impressed by the roads and physical infrastructure provided by the French. She met with the High Commissioner, Theodore-Paul Marchand, and asked him a series of questions designed to elicit the similarities and differences between French and British colonial rule. 'They are children!', he expostulated in answer to Perham's probing of the French attitude to Africans.[42] Shortly thereafter she was felled by fever again and had to take to her bed for a couple of days before heading up country for the last week of her tour, complete with a government car and the otherwise gentlemanly Marchand's chauffeur. The tour confirmed for Perham the key to the superiority of French colonial infrastructure, and at least in part the reason for it. As suspected at the time when she had been driving smoothly across to Chad, the use of forced labour (*prestation*) made all the difference in this respect. During her interview with the High Commissioner she had pressed him on this point, especially as it regarded women, and he had denied that women were *prestataires*. Alas, 'rounding a corner I came upon a gang of forty women working in line under a policeman armed with a heavy whip'. For a moment the situation became sticky, with the chauffeur obviously uncomfortable in having his chief caught out so blatantly, especially when the policeman answered Perham's question about whether or not he was allowed to put women to work in this way by stating matter-of-factly: 'When the men run away we take the women'. Her point made, Perham took a photograph of the scene for evidence and bid the chagrined chauffeur to drive away.[43]

Her stay winding down, on 16 April, and thanks to Sir Donald Cameron's launch, the *Dayspring*, Perham crossed from Douala to Victoria in the British Cameroons. From there she travelled a short distance to Buea located on the picturesque 4100-foot high Cameroon Mountain and the local Resident's headquarters: 'I blush ... to confess how my heart leapt because I was back on British territory'.[44] She got on splendidly with the Resident, G.S. Browne, formerly Lugard's Private Secretary when he was Nigeria's Governor General, and relaxed for a day with an 'exhilarating' game of golf, and the next morning a ride on horseback. Having arrived 'jaded' from the French Cameroons, especially her encounter with the *prestataires*, this brief respite in the clouds was just what was required before a return to Lagos and then to England. Perham arrived home in May 1932. After almost six months her West African passage was over.

Perham's homecoming marked, in a sense, the conclusion of her formation as an Africanist. In the previous three years she had traversed the continent rather thoroughly, at times almost in the style of a Victorian explorer. Together with her time in British Somaliland in 1921 her first-hand experience of Africa was as comprehensive as any of her academic contemporaries and combined with her book-knowledge she was clearly in the vanguard of the emergent field of African studies; indeed, in her chosen specialization of native administration in Africa only Lugard was her superior. All she needed now was time to begin to exercise that knowledge, and an institutional home in which to do so.

Time, she had, while a permanent institutional home would have to wait for another three years. St. Hugh's, of course, was happy to keep her on the books as a research fellow, but this was hardly the same as holding a stipendiary post. Perham's fortitude at this point in her life, of remaining committed to her subject in the face of limited financial resources and – as the next few years would show – some degree of compromised health, is impressive. Certainly she had her champions, including the International Institute of African Languages and Cultures who, in the autumn of 1932, informed Perham that they would be granting her an annual studentship of £250.[45] In the meantime, she retired to Ponds Farm where Harry Rayne 'turned the cowshed into a library for me' and began to collate her stacks of notes and files from which would emerge the first of her many studies on native administration.[46] Out of this welter of material came, too, the news-paper pieces on contemporary Africa that would become as much a part of her public signature as the weightier tomes on the continent's history and its colonial administration.

The early to mid-1930s for Perham became a kind of forcing-ground for the creation of a career and the texturing of a persona. London teemed with all kinds of societies that concentrated their efforts on Africa. In addition to the IIALC there were the Royal African Society, the Imperial Institute's Africa Circle, the Royal Institute of International Affairs (Chatham House), and others. She became well known to them all, as supporter, lecturer, expert; indeed, one writer captures the almost-frantic activity of these years by observing that 'Miss Perham moved between Oxford and Whitehall, Chatham House and Fleet Street'.[47] Her 'extraordinary feeling about Africa', as she later called the powerful attachment she had to it, drove her to delve deeply into a myriad of debates about the continent's past, present, and future. There was nothing new in this, of course. From Wilberforce's public, medallion-wearing campaigns against the Atlantic Slave Trade –'Am I not a slave and a brother' – to Livingstone's impassioned speeches to Oxbridge undergraduates enjoining them to give a care for Africa: 'Do you carry on the work which I have begun. I Leave It With You!', to, in our own day, Bob Geldof's Live Aid concerts, Africa in the last two hundred years has called forth an endless stream of ways and means to make it something other than what it is.[48] The key difference with Perham's engagement with Africa was that, unlike the celebrity-driven attachment that dominates its pub-lic understanding today, hers was essentially academic, governed by hard-headed historical understanding and expansive policy prescription. There was, of course, as we have seen, room for emotion in this comprehensive attachment, but unlike the media's current fascination with Africa Perham's attachment to it did not remain principally emotional.

The first piece of writing to emerge from Perham's active pen after her return from Africa came in late-December 1932. A three-part series entitled 'Nigeria Today', it was published in *The Times* from the 28th to the 30th and was met with considerable approbation by the widening circle of Africanists of which she was now a significant part, as well as beyond. The paper's editor, Geoffrey Dawson, formerly assistant private secretary to Colonial Secretary Joseph Chamberlain and a member of Milner's 'Kindergarten' – but who would disgrace himself publicly as an advocate of appeasement later in the 1930s – wrote effusively to commend her efforts: 'The Nigeria series has been first rate … . What is your plan now? … . I would like to know – both for the sake of 'The Times' & all of those Rhodes Trustees [of which he was one] who launched you on your African adventures! Every good wish to you this coming year, whether you spend it among the Emirs or among the aspirant administrators at Oxford'.[49]

During the year that followed, 1933, Perham would begin to answer these questions in a number of ways. After battling early through a debilitating flu – 'I do hope that you are rapidly recovering' – wrote a paternal Lugard in February, she turned her attention to writing additional newspaper pieces.[50] That year saw another two of them published, and there were more to come in 1934 and 1935. Perham's clearly enunciated position championing native Africans against settlers drew her into a public debate with Lionel Curtis, the former Beit Lecturer in Colonial History at Oxford and a leading Commonwealth publicist. They clashed specifically over the attempt by South Africa to have the High Commission Territories, including Bechuanaland, transferred to its control. The attempt to do so was being made over the vociferous objections of Tshekedi Khama, the territory's regent, who Perham had so enjoyed meeting and with whom she had become friends during her visit to Africa in 1930. She went on the offensive in *The Times* arguing against the transfer. Curtis took the opposite position and the battle was joined. 'Trust the settler, trust the white man – if you trust him then he behaves well', was the way she recalled his position in this debate years later.[51] The words of a gentleman, of course, and the battle indeed was chivalrous, with mutual compliments the order of the day, the result of this cordiality being their joint publication of Perham's first academic book, *The Protectorates of South Africa*.[52] As for the debate itself, she was hailed as the clear winner, even if by then Curtis was widely considered to be one of the grand old men of empire.[53] As for Bechuanaland and the other High Commission Territories themselves, they remained out of the hands of South Africa – at least for the time being.

Just as the Curtis episode was winding down in mid-1935 Perham received the kind of news that would put an end to the uncertainties of her professional life. Oxford had chosen to appoint her Research Lecturer in Colonial Administration. The post was a University one only and therefore did not carry with it a College fellowship. But it was clear recognition of her status in the field all the same and a confirmation that she should be at its centre. Again it was the Rhodes Trustees, with Philip Kerr continuing as General Secretary, that had done Perham a good turn, campaigning for the post's creation and for her to fill it, especially as the trustees saw Rhodes House, their recently completed project, as being the natural home in Oxford of research on Africa and the Empire-Commonwealth.[54] This timely appointment meant that Margery Perham was now on her way.

6

OXFORD, NUFFIELD, AND THE COLONIAL SERVICE: *AFRICA IPSISSIMA*

Perham's appointment to Oxford's newly-created Research Lectureship in Colonial Administration came with a welcome annual stipend of £300.[1] The appointment was for five years and took effect from October 1935, shortly after her fortieth birthday. The eighteen years since she had first gone to Sheffield had been a long period of personal and professional formation, the confirmation of which was this appointment that not only gave her a firm footing back in Oxford but also gave her subject a similar imprimatur. Perham's main residence continued to be Ponds Farm, but soon she began to rent a flat in Oxford, at 72 High Street, which she used as both a home for herself during term and as an office for the Lectureship. The flat was located at the bottom of The High between the Examination Schools and Magdalen College. From its rooftop a good view of the spires of central Oxford could be had. Nearby was the Cherwell River, full of languid punts in the summer, and to the south lay the verdant expanse of Christ Church meadow. She would remain in the flat until after the war – occasionally doing lookout duty from the roof of the building as German bombers flew overhead on their way to Coventry without once dropping their deadly payload on Oxford.[2]

As was referred to in chapter four, Imperial history was now a well-established discipline at Oxford with Professor Reginald Coupland remaining in the Beit Chair. In that sense Perham had a considerable tradition upon which to draw, although colonial administration was a sub-field that few scholars at Oxford, or indeed anywhere else, had spent much time considering. The tenor of the University at large in the mid-1930s was a mixture of the pacifism exemplified by the Oxford Union debate of February

1933, where, by a vote of 275 to 153, it was declared 'that this House will
in no circumstances fight for its King and Country', and an increasingly
resolute abhorrence of Hitler's thuggish Nazi regime and what its export
might mean for Europe and the world.[3] Slowly, and especially after Neville
Chamberlain's failed attempt to avert war signified by the empty Munich
Agreement of 1938, the University – like the country – was taken up by
preparations for a war that most now thought inevitable. In this atmosphere,
Imperial issues found themselves of lesser public importance than had hitherto been true, but in most other ways those things that Perham had been
studying intensely for a decade had not lost their practical insistence.

Within a year after taking up her new post Perham had published another
book, *Ten Africans*, an edited work, in which the life stories of two African
women and eight African men are told in their own words.[4] In 1936, the
year the book came out, a reviewer still thought it necessary to remind
readers that its subjects were not wholly exotic specimens from the back
of beyond, but rather, 'Africans are flesh and blood like ourselves'.[5] Still,
Perham had gathered the stories on her travels and lightly edited they made
for one of the early texts in which the African voice was heard clearly. Of
course, to anyone who had spent time in Africa, especially someone like
the writer Joyce Cary who had been a District Officer in Northern Nigeria
at the time of the First World War and whose fictional representation of
the experience would be published as the aforementioned *Mister Johnson*
just a few years later in 1939, Perham's clearly developed understanding of
the continent accorded well with their own. 'I've just finished your book',
he wrote to her admiringly in September, '& I liked every bit of it. The
character drawing could not be equaled by any novelist and what characters
to draw'.

Ten Africans was released in the midst of Perham's intensive work on what
would be the major publication of her early career, *Native Administration
in Nigeria* (1937).[6] The book grew out of a plan for a general study of
British colonial administration in Africa and was the culmination of some
five years of exhaustive collation and hard thinking. Its publication served to
confirm her growing reputation as the modern voice of British indirect rule
in Africa. Throughout this period various professional appointments continued apace. In 1936, the International Institute of African Languages and
Cultures, her ongoing patron, made her a Research Fellow just before she
set out in August on a partially underwritten eight-month return journey to
East Africa and the Sudan, her first time back to the continent since 1932.
She began also to serve as a research consultant on an enormous African survey initiated by the Royal Institute of International Affairs that would come

under the direction of Sir Malcolm Hailey, the career Indian Civil Servant and former Governor of the Punjab. Produced as *An African Survey* (1938), Hailey's influence on the direction of British colonial policy in Africa during and after the Second World War would be strong, but it was Perham who pushed him to take into account more directly the realities of West Africa rather than the assumed-to-be importance of settler-dominated East Africa. Her book on Nigeria made plain the importance she placed on the colony for the foundations of British policy, and its enthusiastic reception of it by her peers cemented Perham's reputation in the field. Chief among them was Lugard, who wrote the highly favourable foreword after he had finished, as he informed her good naturedly, 'tearing your book to pieces – a task I find extremely difficult'.[7]

Not all reactions to the book were positive, however. Walter Crocker, her Australian friend from Northern Nigeria who had given up on the Colonial Service two years after meeting Perham in Kano in 1932, was now serving with the International Labour Organization in Geneva. Still bitter over his Nigerian experience, he wrote: 'My dear Gentle Margery, ... My main criticisms are two: 1) your persistence in accepting officials' views and official announcements at their own value, and 2) naivete. In both cases there is really no excuse for you, because you know the country well ...'.[8]

In essence, the book was a detailed exposition of the theory and application of indirect rule in Nigeria. In chapter seven much more will be said about indirect rule and Lugard. Here it is enough to note that for Perham the book gave her an opportunity to make clear her understanding of it as a moral force for good. 'One thing is certain', she declared near the end of the book, 'it is both our duty and our interest to assist the Africans of Nigeria to build up a sound united state'.[9]

For Perham, requests to lecture or give talks, to write newspaper pieces or to sit on committees now began to arrive thick and fast. She continued to be a regular contributor to *The Times* and in 1937 was an observer on the De La Warr Commission on colonial education in East Africa and the Sudan during which she visited Makerere College in Uganda and Gordon College in Khartoum. Indeed, the proofs of her Nigeria book were checked on the fly in Uganda and Kenya. One of the new calls on her time was the creation of the Summer School on Colonial Administration, held at Oxford in consecutive years, 1937 and 1938. Inaugurated by Oxford's Social Studies Research Committee, and in the spirit of the Tropical African Service (Colonial Administrative Service after 1933) course for Colonial Service cadets held since 1926, the two Summer Schools brought together a couple of hundred administrative officers for an intensive session with their peers and with the senior members of the Service. Chaired by Professor Coupland, its Vice-Chair and prime mover was Perham. This pair of Summer Schools put her in front of the full panoply of colonial worthies, from the Colonial Secretary (William Ormsby-Gore and Malcolm MacDonald respectively) to Assistant District Officers and 'there could be little doubt …', as Tony Kirk-Greene notes, 'about who, next to Lord Lugard, really was the expert on colonial administration – and hence on the Colonial Service'.[10]

From the moment of Perham's infatuation with Harry Rayne as the lone British sentinel in the backcountry of Somaliland in 1921, to her later tours of Africa, to her expositions of indirect rule, her imagination was captured forever by the work of the men of the Colonial (Administrative) Service. To her, they were the embodiment of Britain's moral project in Africa and the Summer Schools – no less than the courses for cadets – provided an opportunity to engage closely and personally with those who were serving on the frontiers of empire. Over the next generation her book on Nigeria would become standard reading for Colonial Service probationers in advance of going out to the colony to which they had been posted, as well as once in harness on the ground.

But it was for more than her book alone that Perham became, as Kirk-Greene puts it, 'godmother to the Service during the last thirty years of colonial rule'.[11] Hers was a constant – critics might say ubiquitous – presence at the various courses and summer schools devoted to the training and professional development of colonial officers, she was known to all those in positions of authority at the Colonial Office, her frequent tours of Africa – those that came prior to the Second World War and then essentially yearly after it until her retirement in 1963 – made her a regular presence at Government House and, sometimes, up-country. From her base at Oxford – which indeed had achieved Rhodes's desire to see it become an Imperial university – Perham was able to insert herself into most of the main questions of how the Empire was governed in Africa, how things might be done better in this regard, and where it was thought the Empire was headed.[12]

As war with Germany approached during the waning days of 1938 and into the following year Perham remained as focused as ever on the tasks at hand. One of these was her continuing engagement with writing for newspapers and magazines. Naturally, with the onset of war in September of 1939 her mind turned expressly to the conflict and what its impact might be on the Empire. In a piece entitled, 'War and the Colonies', published in *The Spectator* on 6 October, she noted that one of the clearest dangers in wartime was that Britain's colonies would simply become neglected as the nation narrowed its attention to the requirements of fighting the war. 'It is not possible', she pointed out, however, 'to devise a sort of colonial moratorium for the duration of the war'. Events would arise in the colonies and the British government must be alert to them and respond well to their demands, she advised. Moreover, the war, even with all its attendant dangers and responsibilities, should not be allowed to make the government less inclined to initiate colonial policy and carry out reform. Colonial maturation demanded that the government 'press on' in the areas of education and economic development 'and to enlarge in every practicable way the sphere of cooperation with them'. Such a view would be a recurring theme for Perham, especially after the fall of Hong Kong and Singapore in 1942 to the Japanese and with these defeats the recognition of the Empire's contraction, diminution, and vulnerability.[13]

The year 1939 also brought some significant changes to Perham's professional position and status. The previous four years as Research Lecturer had convinced Oxford University that she should be elevated to a 'Readership' – a step down from the ultimate professorial rank but recognition that both she and her field were important and that her designation needed to reflect as much. At virtually the same time she was also approached as to her interest in becoming a fellow of Nuffield, a new foundation on its way to becoming a full-fledged college. A couple of years earlier in the summer of 1937, William Morris, Lord Nuffield, the celebrated maker of the Morris Minor whose First World War era car-works at Cowley had done much to transform Oxford into an industrial city thereby winning him both scorn and admiration, offered the University approximately £1 million to found a college of 'engineering and accountancy'. In the end, and after considerable debate, Nuffield College was founded as a post-graduate institution that would concentrate on the social sciences. Nuffield himself, apparently, was not pleased with this development, but by 1939 the lineaments of its structure were being put in place, which, of course, included the composition of its fellowship.[14] Margery Perham would be its first member.

In May she was informed by Douglas Veale, University Registrar and a former colleague of hers at St. Hugh's where he had been Chair of College Council, that she had been appointed Faculty Fellow of Nuffield. Perham's reply was typically gracious, and she certainly found the appointment to be 'a very great honour' but the fact that – at least for the time being – it came with no remuneration was a significant problem. Despite the Lectureship of the previous four years her personal finances continued to be a worry, she wrote to Veale. The University would have to do better. In the meantime, the Readership in Colonial Administration was finalized and thus it was that in July Veale could write to Perham with the happy news that her Readership – which had been announced in the Oxford University *Gazette* in June – would come with an annual stipend of £400, which, when combined now with £300 annually from Nuffield and a further £100 yearly for travelling expenses from the University Chest, would give her the tidy sum of £800 per annum.[15] Her renewable appointment would be for seven years from that October and with that she settled gratefully into her new position and into what was still a virtual college.

Perham's Nuffield fellowship brought with it the end of her fifteen year formal relationship with St. Hugh's. Her resignation from the college that autumn marked the end of an era for her, but also for Barbara Gwyer, ever Perham's champion and still principal until her retirement in 1946. She wrote warmly in November to wish Perham well personally with her new fellowship and readership and to offer congratulations on behalf of the St. Hugh's College Council.[16] Perham's allegiance and energies would be focused now on Nuffield, and as its first Official Fellow (from October 1939) she would have a considerable impact on its growth and development until her own retirement twenty-four years later. As David Fieldhouse, who would spend fifteen years as a Fellow of Nuffield beginning in 1966, remarked retrospectively, 'the College was built around her'.[17] At first, of course, there was nothing to build. The 'college' was located in a house at 151 Woodstock Road, as it happens just a little way beyond St. Hugh's in North Oxford. Construction on its present site in New Road across from the medieval Oxford Castle would not begin until after the war in 1949, a process that would take thirteen years to complete.

Even though the Nazi menace had been unleashed in the closing months of 1939, the so-called Phoney War meant that the British public was largely at one remove from the German onslaught until the spring of 1940. For Perham, like most others who had survived the First World War but had seen loved ones perish in it, the prospect of another conflagration on an epic scale filled her with both foreboding and anguish. Meanwhile, and conversely in professional terms, her life had now unfolded in such a way as to bring great satisfaction. Her renewed Oxford career was the most obvious and lasting recognition of her achievements, but in the form of her being awarded the Royal African Society's Silver Medal, the announcement of which came at the end of June 1939, her eminence in the field was confirmed.[18] The decade to follow would only deepen and broaden that standing.

In the first instance Perham now began to teach again in a way that she had not done since her days at St. Hugh's in the mid- to late-1920s. Her lectures on British Imperial history, on Africa, and on colonial administration fell within Oxford's Modern History faculty. But her focus was sharpest in the early 1940s on producing another book, which became the briefly controversial *Africans and British Rule*.[19] Published in 1941, the book was a kind of primer on British Africa, designed for Africans themselves, and limited in scope and detail. The publisher, Oxford University Press, asked Perham for a book of 15,000 words suitable for an undemanding readership. Its focus – which fit squarely with her own as exemplified by her early wartime newspaper articles cited earlier – was to be the need for Britain not to lose sight of its African colonies during a time of extreme national stress. As Perham put it, the book was to remind Britons that their African colonies 'were a stern test of our high claims' to govern there.[20] As instructed by OUP the book was written in simple language and accordingly Perham offered a straightforward interpretation of African history, why and how the British came to rule much of the continent in the late nineteenth century, how such rule was justified, and the way forward in race relations and the development of self-government.

In the end, *Africans and British Rule* came in at over twice the prescribed length and, perhaps for an academic book, was of unusual clarity. Given the parameters within which it was written, however, it has never been seen as one of Perham's significant works. Still – and for the very reason of its commissioning – the book reveals clearly Perham's state of understanding of British Africa in the last years before the drive to independence by many African colonies would commence. Roland Oliver has argued persuasively that there were 'two' Margery Perhams, the second of whom emerged during the Second World War.[21] If this is so then *Africans and British Rule*, with its somewhat patronizing discussion of African 'backwardness' and her Whiggish interpretation of Britain's own history being an instructive guide to what Africans must necessarily go through to achieve political independence and economic development, is the last clear enunciation of the 'first' Perham.

The irony of the book, however, is that even though its anti-colonial critics saw it in the terms expressed above, it produced another set of critics who, for a short time, were successful in having the book banned in that most tetchy of contemporary colonial societies, Kenya. In the summer of 1942 OUP informed Perham that *Africans and British Rule* had been banned there. The book's banning had resulted from local complaints about its alleged anti-settler tone and content. Perham's views advocating greater African political representation and development were described as 'fanatically theoretical' in a Nairobi newspaper, and in the heightened wartime context of Japan's march through Southeast Asia and what that might mean potentially for East Africa banning came almost naturally to the Kenyan government. As Michael Twaddle shows in a brief and sinewy article on the episode, Perham was enraged by the news and immediately set out to have the book un-banned, which indeed was to happen shortly thereafter.[22] To achieve that end, however, she enlisted the help of a few key people, particularly Arthur Creech Jones, the future Labour Colonial Secretary with whom Perham would come to have a very close working relationship. His pointed question in the House of Commons in July brought the issue to the attention of the public, but his private query of a few days earlier to a junior minister at the Colonial Office, the future Tory prime minister, Harold Macmillan, had set in motion the book's almost immediate unbanning by the rather timid Governor of Kenya, Sir Henry Monck-Mason Moore, who would leave Africa shortly thereafter to finish his undistinguished gubernatorial career in post-war Ceylon.

By the time *Africans and British Rule* was back on store shelves in Nairobi in the autumn of 1942 Perham's next book was already in print. *African Discovery: an Anthology of Exploration* was co-edited with Jack Simmons.[23] A Christ Church pupil of Reginald Coupland's, Simmons impressed both him and Perham as a budding Imperial historian. Together – with Perham in the role of mentor – she and Simmons put together a list of the most prominent European explorers of Africa – Mungo Park, David Livingstone, Heinrich Barth, and a number of others – and related their exploits through publishing extracts from their journals. The book was an instant success, going through a number of reprints as well as a second edition. In 1946, at just thirty-one years of age, Simmons left Oxford and went to University College, Leicester (later the University of Leicester), as its first Professor of History. There he would have a long and productive career, especially as a leading historian of railways and empire.

The war of course cut off travel to Africa for Perham, but together with her teaching and writing she began to collect a number of committee appointments that occupied much of her time, time that she might have otherwise spent going on journeys. For the entire duration of the war, for example, she was a member of the Colonial Office Advisory Committee on Education in the Colonies. In 1943, she sat on the Asquith Committee on Higher Education in the Colonies and the next year served in a similar capacity on the Irvine Commission on Higher Education in the West Indies. She had also advised both the Colonial Office and the Foreign Office on Ethiopia, it having been invaded in 1936 by Italy. As busy as she became professionally in this period, however, other much more personal matters began to disrupt her life.

Perham's living arrangements had never been conventional. Since returning from Africa in 1932 her home base when not in Oxford, as noted earlier, had been the Surrey property, Ponds Farm. Originally it had been a
ramshackle place, about six miles east of Guildford near the quaint village
of Shere. But its location, in the Tillingbourne Valley, nestled between the
Downs and the Surrey Hills, was cozily beautiful and remains so today in
the form of a riding school. Once renovated in the early 1930s, however, the
farm became an earthy home for Perham and for Ethel and Harry Rayne,
and their four children – Wilfrid, Robert, John, and 'Little' Margery – when
visiting from school and university. Ponds Farm was also very near to the
country home of Lord Lugard and, as will be elaborated in chapter seven,
therefore made for easy contact between the two of them, which would be
a central feature of Perham's life in the mid-late 1930s. Located only about
seventy-miles from Oxford, and as quiescent as life at the farm usually was –
'war seems impossible – the farm so peaceful … wisteria heavy with hanging
blooms' – Perham's domestic arrangements broke down mid-way through
the war when Harry Rayne's infidelity with the hired maid wrecked his
marriage and caused a severe family crisis. For Ethel, a situation in which
Harry was willingly complicit was made worse by the fact that she could
not avoid constantly seeing the woman whom she regarded as the destroyer
of her marriage and home, especially since the infidelity resulted in a preg-
nancy. As she lamented to her sister in Oxford in May of 1941: 'Ran into
Monica, bold as brass. I just can't allow such a position to continue. I just
can't endure it.' Accordingly, she did not endure it for much longer and
the end result of this sad irruption was that Perham and Ethel would live
together for the rest of their lives.

Harry had a long way to fall in Perham's eyes. When she had first met him
as her sister's dashing District Commissioner husband in Somaliland she had
probably, as noted earlier, fallen in love with him.[24] The heroic Major Dane
as a fictional representation of Rayne was clear. But now that was all over
and once the dust had settled, the farm was sold, Harry went shamefacedly
to live in London – 'this that I have done is DONE, irrevocable … . What
a bloody mess!' – and, eventually, the sisters would live together in various
Oxford locations, including Nuffield College. Despite Harry's acknowledgement that he was to blame – 'to call myself a fool is simply to commiserate
my infidelity' – Perham naturally harboured a great deal of animus toward
him for his treatment of Ethel during this period, and she would maintain it
for a long time after the break-up.[25]

Exacerbating this domestic falling-out was the continued strain of the
war, most clearly represented by the death of Wilfrid Rayne, killed while

serving at sea off Malta in March of 1942, and by Robert, who spent time in a German POW camp, but survived. Meanwhile, 'Little' Margery was abroad too serving in the Ministry of Information in Eritrea.[26] Indeed, the war would prove to be the most psychologically stressful period of Perham's life since her breakdown twenty years earlier at Sheffield. For most of those intervening years her formative High Anglican religiosity had been in abeyance. At one point of severe introspection she had even accused herself of having 'no religion and no principles' whatsoever. On another, she articulated her philosophy as being comprised simply of 'myself. That is my God'.[27] Her apparently dormant faith was revivified decisively, however, when she chanced upon hearing an installment of Dorothy Sayers's radio production, *The Man Born to be King: A Play-Cycle on the Life of our Lord and Saviour Jesus Christ*. Sayers, the renowned crime writer and Christian humanist, wrote the play in a contemporary manner, with unvarnished speech and heavy dramatization. The BBC Home Service then broadcast it on Sunday evenings every four weeks beginning in December 1941 and ending in October 1942. The play produced a storm of reaction. Some argued that it was Christian propaganda; others that its modern style was blasphemous. But controversy over its broadcast did what controversy usually does: increase its popularity, and the play was both a critical and a commercial success.

Perham heard at least one of the twelve parts of the cycle, probably the first one, on Sunday evening, 21 December, while on a brief Christmas holiday in the Cotswolds. And it had a powerful impact on her. Her private papers do not detail whether or not she tuned in for the complete cycle, but given the interest it piqued and the faith it rekindled, plus her own enjoyable experiences in her younger days as a sometime playwright, it would seem likely that she did. Once having revived her Christian faith it remained a lively part of her being ever after. Her revivified mode of practice, anglo-catholicism, militated against anything that might be construed as proselytizing, although in the years that followed a robust Christianity certainly informed her view of Britain's responsibilities in Africa. In personal terms, however, she wore her faith lightly. But as in all things she committed herself to she was firm about it nonetheless. Such firmness occasionally extended itself to some of her friends who did not share her beliefs and she would, therefore, from time to time lament that a similar Christian faith was lacking in their lives.[28]

The Sayers' play and Perham's return to faith coincided roughly in time with the collapse of British power in Hong Kong, and then shortly there after in Malaya and Singapore. These startling events signaled an Imperial crisis that was essentially terminal. Singapore's fall in particular – the 'Gibraltar of the East' – caused Perham to realize that the old verities about the British Empire in Asia had come to an end. The Japanese overran Singapore from 8–15 February 1942, causing the single largest surrender of a British-led military force in history. Some 80,000 British, Australian, and Indian troops were taken prisoner while about 2,000 were killed and 5,000 lay wounded. The invasion saw the wanton slaughter too – many by bayonet – of approximately 600 patients and staff at the Alexandra Barracks Hospital, a particularly heinous act that caused immediate outrage once reports of it were published in Britain.[29]

Perham's response to the crisis was swift. Just a few weeks after the events in Singapore had taken place she published a pair of thoughtful and wide-ranging articles in *The Times*, both of which suggest the degree to which her thinking about the Empire had changed in those critical intervening days. Roland Oliver, as noted above, sees these events rightly as genera-tive of the 'second Miss Perham'.[30] The articles, especially the first of them, 'The Colonial Empire: The need for Stocktaking and Review', published on 13 March, impressed upon her readers that 'our colonial administration needs adjustment to the new conditions of our world'. If anything, Oliver is too sure of Singapore's impact on Perham, as certainly her thinking about Kenya, for example, had, a decade earlier, pushed her to consider much more deeply the merits of developing a genuine pluralistic society in the face of the multiplicity of divisions caused by Imperial rule and 'the steel frame of its imported state system'. Indeed, she was just then about to enter into a lengthy correspondence with Elspeth Huxley, the most eloquent defender of Kenya's white settlers and about which we shall turn in chapter eight. In light of the potential reality of the Japanese fleet arriving off Mombasa harbour, Perham asked, 'how would the 'plural society' of Kenya respond? The small settler community would know very well what they were fighting for … . Would the Kikuyu, still unsatisfied about their land and with some of the leaders of their political societies in prison, give the wholehearted cooperation that would be needed?'[31]

As expressed in these articles, Perham did begin to ask some hard and probing questions about the basis of imperial power, the reason for its exer-cise, and, most importantly, the nature of its end. Her answers were for the British to deliver more economic development, greater political responsibil-ity, and wider educational opportunities, all of which, she argued, are gifts that the British could give to those in their dependent empire. Moreover, she added pointedly, 'we should start in real earnest to lift from the colo-nial peoples the vast dead-weight of female ignorance and backwardness'.[32]

In light of Perham's later stance on independence and decolonization her response to the fall of Singapore marks, if not the precise moment that her thinking on the future proper exercise of British Imperial power changed, certainly signifies the time at which she began to enjoin the British public to think seriously about the colonies as something substantially more than mere appendages to the greater British state.

This same period, the early to mid-1940s, was when Perham became ever more closely allied to the Colonial Service, building on the experience of the pre-war Summer Schools. Her relationship with the Service during these years was mediated mainly – though not exclusively – through the prominent figure of the Director of Recruitment at the Colonial Office, Sir Ralph Furse. A spare, leonine figure, Furse had emerged as the godfather of the Service, presiding over an effective though idiosyncratic cadet recruitment process. Educated at Eton and Oxford, and steeped in the ethos of the Colonial Office since before the First World War, Furse did more than anyone else to create the modern, unified (after 1931) Colonial Service, populating it largely with Oxbridge graduates.[33]

Evidence that Perham had been thinking of the ideas that she had expressed in her March 1942 pieces for *The Times* is readily seen in discussions that she had had with Furse in January of that year. He had already begun to think of a new, second-stage course for Colonial Service veterans. This new course would offer an intensive learning experience whereby the best and brightest – the 'rising rockets', as Furse called them – of the Colonial Service would be plucked from the field and brought to Oxford, preferably, for what the modern age would call professional development.[34] They agreed that the world had changed and that the Empire must respond appropriately. Perham got right to work on the idea, corresponding with the University Registrar, her old friend, Douglas Veale, to see how Oxford might accommodate this aspiration. Over the next two years progress toward their shared goal was made, the most important feature of it being the Devonshire Committee meetings, chaired by the Duke of Devonshire, Undersecretary of State at the Colonial Office, which worked out the precise nature of the courses that would be implemented. In 1946, the Committee made its report. The new 'Devonshire Courses' would be offered at three universities: Oxford, Cambridge, and London, with the first one commencing in the autumn of 1946.[35] The post-war Empire was going to be a different place, they believed, and those who were responsible for administering it must change along with it. Of this fact, Perham was sure.

In the midst of the meetings and discussions that led to the establishment of the Devonshire Courses, Perham took on the role of Director of the

Institute of Colonial Studies at Oxford. The Institute had really grown out of her work as first Lecturer and then Reader in Colonial Administration, and in practical terms had outstripped the means she had to house it in her High Street flat. Of more pressing import, however, was the death in April 1945 of her longtime mentor and friend, Lord Lugard. The fact of his passing, and the eventual undertaking by Perham of Lugard's official biography, would be central to her life for the next fifteen years, as the following chapter will demonstrate. In the meantime, Perham, like millions of her compatriots, was overjoyed by the dawn of peace in Europe on 8 May and, approaching the age of fifty, was ready to embark on the final phase of her professional career.

Perham's post-war life would prove to be just as busy and productive as that of the previous six years, with the welcome addition to it of travel, after its suspension (especially to Africa) for the duration of the conflict. One of the places that Perham came to know well in this period, and to which she would come to experience a deep attachment, was the Sudan, visited first back in 1937. Her journey there at that time had been as an addendum to an itinerary that began with her departure from England in August 1936 and was focused on East Africa. That tour had been sponsored by the International Institute for African Languages and Cultures through a grant from the Rockefeller Foundation, a travelling fellowship hitherto left unused owing to bouts of ill-health and unpropitious timing since 1932. And that visit did not begin auspiciously, however. Sudan is 'an abysm of backwardness' she noted upon her arrival in the south of the country in February 1937.[36] For the previous thirty-eight years Sudan had been governed as an Anglo-Egyptian Condominium, put into effect following the reconquest of the Sudan led by Lord Kitchener. His overwhelming victory at Omdurman in 1898 had brought an end to the Mahdiya, a period of Islamic rule won through the vanquishing of General Charles Gordon and his Anglo-Egyptian garrison by the Mahdi at Khartoum in January of 1885.[37] Like most people of her time Perham was well-versed in the Gordon epic, but it was not top of mind either in February or later that year when she travelled again to the Sudan – this time through Egypt – and in the service of the aforementioned De La Warr Commission on Higher Education in the Colonies.

At this point in Perham's life it is not too harsh to say that she loathed Egypt and regarded its role in the Condominium as an unfortunate twist of history. Much of this dislike was based on the obvious discomfort that Egyptian officials had in dealing with a woman, but it came also from what she viewed as the chaotic and duplicitous way in which the Egyptians held up their end of the Condominium arrangement, not to mention that everything in which they had a hand in their own country was 'dirty', at least according to her. Such 'sordidness, dirt, unspeakable lavatories and dishevelled and indifferent officials' contrasted sharply, she observed with great pride, with the 'efficiency, intelligent paternalism and cleanliness which marks the Sudan'. These features of preponderant British rule she saw simply, if narrowly, as evidence of superior colonial administration. Very quickly into her second stay in the Sudan – which lasted until nearly the end of March 1938 – Perham became wholly impressed with how the British ran it, in stark contrast to what she had experienced in Egypt.[38]

Most impressive of all to Perham was one of the Sudan's provincial governors, Douglas Newbold. When she first met him in January 1938 he was in his mid-forties and had served either in Khartoum or up-country since joining the Sudan Political Service in 1920. Educated in the classics at Oxford he had seen military service in the Middle East during the First World War. The first decade of his time in the SPS had been spent as a District Officer until in 1932 he was made Governor of the province of Kordofan, the position he held still when Perham arrived in Khartoum. The SPS had been created in 1899 following the reconquest and put under the control of the Foreign Office. Beginning two years later it began to recruit direct-entry candidates, mainly from Oxbridge. One of the distinguishing features of the SPS was the high number of its members who had won Blues for their athletic prowess while competing in the Varsity Match in a given sport for either Oxford or Cambridge. As the contemporary line put it, Sudan was 'the Land of Blacks ruled by Blues'.[39] While Newbold was not an athlete – at least not as measured by Oxford's Blues Committee – he was nonetheless a sterling example of the type of scholar-hearty who had made the SPS, in the words of Lord Vansittart, Permanent Under Secretary at the Foreign Office, 'the finest body in the world … . They were all picked men, scholars and athletes'.[40]

Perham would come to echo Vansittart's estimation of the SPS, and it was through the lens of Newbold that she did so. Her attraction to the unmarried governor was instant, and over the ensuing two months she spent a great deal of time in conversation with him, in horseback riding together, and in playing tennis. Like her infatuation with Harry Rayne, and then with Hugh Ashton a decade later, her encounter with Newbold left her both personally excited and in great admiration of his work on the Imperial frontier. Not long after Perham returned to Oxford in the spring of 1938 Newbold was made Civil Secretary, the highest ranking British official in the Sudan, a position that he would hold through his being made KBE in 1944 and his untimely death the following year when he was thrown from a horse. In the meantime during Perham's visit, Newbold gave her unfettered access to Sudanese government official papers and was happy to stay up into the wee hours of the night with her discussing their content.

The attraction was mutual, as Newbold's following ditty on Perham shows. Employing the sometime nickname of 'Pro' given to Perham by her family, he wrote and gave his little poetical offering to her on the day she left the Sudan in March 1938:

> ODE to the 'PRO'
> Margery P. lives on weak tea,
> Refuses to eat pies or red meat.
> But *she'd* travel miles, to devour old files.
> Like Oliver Twist, to her mill all is grist,
> And shouts Hip! Hooray! When she tastes some N.A.[41]

The problem for Perham as the attraction to Newbold deepened was that unknown to her at the time was that he was gay. The so-called 'unspeakable vice of the Greeks', as the Victorians would have it, was not something that one of Perham's generation and background would have assumed was behind Newbold's apparent romantic reticence. 'I would have married him if he had asked me', she wrote in a letter at the time of his death.[42] Alas, of course he did not ask and thus another one of her cyclical romantic interludes failed to yield a firm relationship, much less marriage.

Perham's professional admiration of Newbold's work, however, was unimpaired by whatever thwarted romantic attraction she may have had – Patricia Pugh, the archivist who catalogued the Perham Papers and knows their contents better than anyone, finds only a 'hint of love' in her feelings for Newbold.[43] Regardless, Perham's posthumous monument to Newbold would come in 1953 in her admiring introduction – 'the humanizing of administration came to him almost unconsciously' – in K.D.D. Anderson's *The Making of the Modern Sudan: The Life and Letters of Sir Douglas Newbold*.[44] Apart from her own personal attraction to Newbold, she greatly admired his desire to somehow bridge the gap that existed in the Sudan between the Arab and Islamic North and the Black and heavily Christian and animistic South, a problem that would continue to be evident at the time of Sudanese independence in 1956 and today still remains the war-torn country's principal cleavage.

Like Lugard's death in 1945, Newbold's in the same year came as a severe blow to Perham, all the more in the latter case because it was unexpected and therefore shocking. Her continuing weight of work, however, did much to assuage the grief she felt at the passing of both of these formidable men in her life. In 1946, she was appointed to the Executive Committee of the Inter-University Council for Higher Education in the Colonies, as well as to the Council of Makarere College in Kampala, Uganda. These two bodies would occupy a great deal of her time and energy in the years that followed, including many trips to Africa where she, as Mary Bull remembers, 'tried to advance the university education of women'. Shortly thereafter too, she would begin a seventeen-year span as a special speaker at the Summer Schools on African Administration run by the Colonial Office at Cambridge, as well as her ongoing commitment to those in Oxford. All of these varied involvements meant that Perham lived her life at speed. Her domestic arrangements with sister Ethel meant that she had virtually no responsibilities at home and, being without either a husband or children, she could make enormous amounts of time almost exclusively her own. Consequently, she worked at a prodigious rate. She was 'very busy, always', comments Bull, and had 'a vast energy for work'.[45] Her research assistants, as they later came to be employed, also performed the function of gatekeepers so as to control the number of people and the amount of correspondence that came her way. As Isabel Roberts recalls, 'the requirement was that I protected her from the outside world ... . Her life was WORK on a superhuman scale'.[46] Perhaps such devotion to work was the redirection of a multifarious psycho-sexual drive into a complete devotion to Africa. At least that is what David Fieldhouse, in what he calls an expression of her 'feminine energy', thinks.[47] In any case she was a whirlwind to be around, but a benevolent one. 'She pretty well owned me,' observed Roberts, 'but at the time I was quite happy to be so in thrall'.[48]

The later 1940s would see increased public recognition of Perham's longstanding interest in and expertise on Africa. In 1948, she was made a Companion of the British Empire. The CBE was the highest honour that had yet been bestowed upon her and it came, it seemed, with a number of new responsibilities. The Attlee Labour government, in office since the end of the war, was committed to probing the workings of the colonial empire thoroughly with a view to speeding up the eventuality of responsible government in a number of colonies. Arthur Creech Jones remained as Colonial Secretary and was involved closely with the file. As MP from 1935 Creech Jones had specialized in colonial questions, especially those pertaining to Africa. His views on the settler question in Kenya, for example, accorded with Perham's own, and once in office he had to handle a number of controversial issues including ending the British mandate over Palestine in 1948. Only the year before India and Pakistan had become independent, and their example cast a long shadow over the remaining dependent empire. In particular, Creech Jones presided over the granting of dominion status (and therefore effective independence) to Ceylon. It was in this context that Perham began to serve in 1948 and 1949 on a number of committees charged with examining various features of colonial rule. One of these had to do with the political significance of colonial students in Britain; while another, for example, dealt with constitutional development in the smaller colonial territories. Meanwhile, her engagement with the Sudan continued when she was asked to advise on the potential creation of a School of Administration in Khartoum. Shortly thereafter, Creech Jones would lose his seat at the 1950 general election, and would never hold office again. But he continued to be a leading figure in colonial debates, nonetheless, especially through his work with the Fabian Colonial Bureau. In this way he and Perham would share much in common throughout the 1950s, as we shall see in chapter eight.

In this same period, Perham began to scale back her teaching and administrative responsibilities at Oxford in order to delve more deeply and deliberately into research, writing, and travel. Apart from the book co-written with Elspeth Huxley in 1944, *Race and Politics in Kenya* – which shall be looked at separately in chapter eight – Perham's only book-length publication between the relatively slight *African Discovery* in 1942 and the first volume of the Lugard biography in 1956 was *The Government of Ethiopia* in 1948.[49] Written at the British government's request as it wrestled with the possibility of assuming at least some degree of responsibility for the ravaged country in the post-war world, it did not reflect her leading interests and, in conjunction with the many other calls on her time, deflected her from ever writing a thorough study of the Sudan. Long gone was the 'gift of time' that she had enjoyed back in 1929–30 as she journeyed round the world, and to that end she relinquished the Readership in Colonial Administration in favour of an undemanding Fellowship in Imperial Government at Nuffield College. She also stepped down from her three years as Director of the Institute of Colonial Studies. If not exactly a free agent in 1948 she was considerably less encumbered than before.

Later that year she travelled to Nigeria and the Sudan, both of which were rapidly approaching independence, even though that swift eventuality was neither known nor expected by Perham or anyone else. The post-war world was unkind to conventional imperialism; that is, to the kind long practiced by Britain. Despite its support for Britain during the war the United States was firmly against the British Empire's prolongation and in the first period of imperial liquidation, as defined by Wm. Roger Louis as occurring from 1945–51, the downward trajectory of British Imperialism became clear.[50] The Attlee government, as noted above, set in motion the final run-up to Indian independence in 1947, and with it was inaugurated the method by which Britain would pursue decolonization: by seeking to control the transfer of power. The key to this approach was to get out in advance of the nationalist wave and from that frontal position control the process, working to 'secure the collaboration of moderate nationalists', as Louis describes it, 'by yielding control before the initiative passed to irreconcilibles'.[51]

As would become clear over the next twenty years the British plan did not often match the reality, although the record is not as blemished as is sometimes thought. The world of colonial nationalism and its independence corollary was not a readily accessible world for Perham to enter. But in the early 1950s she began gingerly to experience its first stirrings. At all events, she maintained throughout the three periods of imperial liquidation as described by Louis, that the clock was ticking too fast, everything was 'too hurried'.[52] The British had not had adequate time to prepare its colonies, she believed – especially those in Africa – to be thrust into the modern world on their own as sovereign states. If this was old style paternalism at work – after all, Perham's own academic subject of native administration was now in peril – it was nonetheless a position held honestly and sincerely from a person whose knowledge of pre-war British colonial Africa was probably without equal. If Churchill's truculent 1942 wartime comment that he had not become the King's first minister to preside over the liquidation of the British Empire put the case for hanging on too bluntly, then Perham's softer post-war line was not wholly out of step with the Prime Minister's sentiments.

Meanwhile, by the early 1950s Perham's living arrangements had settled comfortably into a new pattern. The High Street flat had been let go, succeeded by rental housing in North Oxford, which, in those days before the explosion in housing prices and Oxford's inclusion in the London commuter belt, was still very much a suburban home for college dons that it had always been. She and Ethel now lived together at 10 Bardwell Road, near her old college of St. Hugh's and an easy walk or bicycle ride along the Woodstock Road into central Oxford. Nuffield College had just gotten under construction, a process that owing to post-war restrictions on building materials would take until 1962 to complete. Later, the two women would transfer their residence to a suite of rooms in the college. But in the meantime North Oxford was home, as too was the cottage they purchased at Farnborough located at the foot of the Berkshire Downs in the Vale of the White Horse. An easy fifteen-mile drive southwest of Oxford, the cottage proved to be a lovely respite from the usual hurly-burly of Perham's life in town.

This period of time would see Perham drawn into a number of colonial controversies, the first of them involving her old Bechuanaland friend, Tshekedi Khama, which shall be examined in chapter eight. The other major episode of the early 1950s that drew sharp intervention from Perham was the British government's proposal to unify Northern Rhodesia, Southern Rhodesia, and Nyasaland. Negotiations to effect this federation began under the Attlee government in November 1950 and would continue until the Central African Federation was declared in August 1953. The impetus for it sprang mainly from the aspirations of the minority European population of Southern Rhodesia (modern Zimbabwe) to consolidate their political position in the region in the face of growing African nationalism and what were expected to be concomitant demands for independence. Desirous too, in economic terms, were the enormous copper deposits found in Northern Rhodesia's aptly named Copperbelt region.[53]

The Colonial Secretary at the time was Jim Griffiths, successor to Arthur Creech Jones, who would himself be succeeded by Oliver Lyttleton upon the general election victory by Churchill's Tories in October of 1951. The constant figure throughout most of the negotiations, however, was Sir Andrew Cohen, Colonial Office Undersecretary for African Affairs. Born into a distinguished Anglo-Jewish family, Cohen was a graduate of Trinity College, Cambridge. Though he was no racist himself, he estimated that the racism of the National Party in South Africa – in power since 1948 – was easily exportable northwards and therefore capable of establishing apartheid in the Rhodesias. To ward off such an eventuality he argued that 'white ascendancy' was preferable to 'white supremacy' and this position became cardinal for him over the course of the almost three-year negotiations, the last year of which saw him removed from their execution owing to his appointment as Governor of Uganda.[54]

From the beginning, Perham opposed the federation, which in its earliest form was proposed as a full amalgamation by its strongest advocate, Sir Godfrey Martin Huggins, Prime Minister of Southern Rhodesia. Working in concert with likeminded critics, such as the Fabian Colonial Bureau and Creech Jones, Perham criticized the proposal for its privileging of the settlers' position and its blinkered non-recognition of the claims of the vast black majority of all three colonies. In a series of published letters and essays beginning in 1951 she struck hard at the working assumptions of those engaged in the negotiations. While not yet ready to countenance African independence, neither was she willing to subject millions of Africans to the rule of a comparatively small number of whites: 'It is just because the Africans are politically unready', she wrote in a letter published in *The Times* on 26 February 1953, 'that power over them should not be transferred to a group of people who, however high their individual merit, together represent a small racial minority of employers and large landowners'. As trenchant as was her argument it did not, however, win the day, and the Central African Federation was established in August of that year and would run on until its dissolution at the end of 1963.

Culminating in 1956 the independence of the Sudan was another major episode in which Perham exercised a close, though similarly disappointing, involvement. The shift in her thinking about the future of British colonial rule made clear by the fall of Singapore in 1942 made her view British responsibility in the Sudan in a different light. British rule there must be replaced by 'helping and advising', she wrote in 1946. And for the next ten years she never wavered from this position although the end result of such helping and advising was not what she had envisaged at the time she wrote these words.

A decade earlier, in 1936, the two controlling powers in the Sudan had signed the Anglo-Egyptian Treaty, which called for the withdrawal of all British troops from Egypt except for those (some 10,000) required for the protection of the Suez Canal Zone. Now, in October 1946, the treaty was opened up at the insistence of the Egyptian Prime Minister, Sidky Pasha, who demanded, among other things, that henceforth Egypt and the Sudan would share a common Egyptian crown. To do so went against the provisions of the 1899 Anglo-Egyptian Condominium Agreement, however. Nonetheless, in order to move the negotiations along, the Foreign Secretary, Ernest Bevin, agreed. Immediately, protests ensued, both by Sudanese nationalists and by members of the Sudan Political Service who believed themselves to have been betrayed and their mandate to ready the Sudan for a self-determined future undermined. This is the point at which Perham entered the scene directly.[55]

The Civil Secretary in the Sudan at that time was James Robertson. He was the lately-deceased Sir Douglas Newbold's successor, and once the Anglo-Egyptian negotiations had yielded the proposal for the latter's effective control of the Sudan he got in touch with Perham. Like so many of his SPS compatriots he was an Oxford man and a Blue, and his sense of fair-play, one can only assume, was severely offended by what he took to be a diplomatic sell-out by the Foreign Office.[56] Aware of what he believed to be the impropriety of writing directly to Perham in this way, he told her

nonetheless that Khartoum had erupted in rioting over the provisions of the
new agreement and that Sudanese security was in peril. He implored her to
rouse 'your many influential friends' to take up the cause and make Britons
back home aware of what was surely the coming betrayal of Sudan's right
to self-determination, which, earlier, the British had pledged to uphold.[57]
Suitably outraged, Perham got right on it, including writing a letter to
The Times that came out in early December. Lamenting the fact that the
Sudanese were being kept in 'feverish suspense' about their fate she asked a
series of pointed rhetorical questions designed to make clear that the British
must not carry out any agreement with Egypt that violated the promise –
made by Bevin – of the Sudanese determining their own political future.[58]
As it happened, the crisis passed in the face of intense protests made by the
Sudanese themselves. But progress toward Sudanese independence did not
pass, and it would occupy a prominent place in her mind until it came to
pass ten years later.

During those intervening years she visited the Sudan on three occasions,
thought much about the future of Sudanese administration once the British
were gone, considered the implications of the impending end of British
Imperial rule worldwide – her recurring fear being that even though such an
end was inevitable, in most places independence would come too soon. She
recognized the irony of this position, however, in that the alacrity of its ces-
sion was necessary lest colonial impatience yield up extremists rather than
those moderates best placed to govern post-imperially. During a period of
time when she gave herself over fully to the research and writing of Lugard's
biography, as we shall see in the next chapter, Perham nevertheless 'followed
constitutional events in the Sudan with almost breathless interest', she wrote
to Robertson.[59] She was especially dismayed by the repudiation by Egypt
in 1951 of the terms of the 1899 Condominium. Then a year later, the
Egyptian revolution led by General Mohammed Neguib, made it part of the
new order to allow the Sudan to determine its own future. For Perham, such
an allowance would play right into the hands of the Foreign Office who, in
her view, cared nothing for the welfare of the Sudan but would use it as a
bargaining chip in its negotiations over the future of the Canal Zone.[60]

As events would show, Perham was right. The Foreign Office was impa-
tient to have Sudan gain its independence as soon as possible. In February
1953, the Anglo-Egyptian Agreement on the Sudan was finalized, setting out
a schedule that would see self-determination achieved by the end of 1955,
to be followed by independence soon thereafter. The Foreign Office wanted
out, with little by way of ceremony and without even the opportunity for
a grand goodbye as had been the case in India. 'Would not a Mountbatten

help', she had asked Robertson earlier when contemplating the possibility of an independent Sudan becoming a member of the Commonwealth. At the last, as the clock wound down on the Anglo-Egyptian condominium, Perham felt acutely for the members of the Sudan Political Service – 'the salt of the earth – or at least of our imperial world' – who were about to find their careers brought to an abrupt end and, in the bitter words of one of their number, 'the work of fifty years in the Sudan ... thrown away in the hope that Egypt might toe the line over the Suez Canal issue'.[61]

In December 1955, the Sudan duly declared its independence sparking a civil war between North and South that would last – in its first iteration – until 1972. She was saddened, of course, by the outbreak of war and the 'appalling personal and professional loss', as she wrote during that month in a letter published in the *Manchester Guardian*.[62] But her displeasure at the hurried and, in her opinion, ignoble way in which the Foreign Office had handled the affair was uppermost in her mind. To the Sudanese themselves, she welcomed the chance they had now of building an independent country, even though she believed that in some respects they had been abandoned to their fate. Still, the lessons of the loss of British power and of colonial independence were piling up: first there was Singapore; then India; and now the Sudan. 'Strange, that nothing short of the final act of transfer ever satisfies the nationalist', she had written a couple of years earlier.[63] And of that – as we shall see – there was much more to come.

Altogether, the 1950s – marked too by the Uganda crisis, 1953–55, over the deposition and reinstallation of Kabaka Mutesa II, which had been occasioned by the debate around the Central African Federation – for Perham proved to be a prefatory period to the nationalist push that would see so much of British Africa achieve its independence by the early 1960s. In 1955–56 she was awarded a sabbatical by Oxford – her first – and used it to travel and to write. Though now sixty-years-old there was no hint of her slowing down, although she would from time to time admit to being somewhat out of touch and out of sympathy with the emergent strident tone of African nationalism, so readily embodied, for example, by Kwame Nkrumah and the Convention Peoples' Party in the Gold Coast. Certainly the Colonial Office remained open to her opinion, and Alan Lennox-Boyd, Colonial Secretary from 1954–59, had, in the view of Kenneth Robinson, Perham's successor in 1948 in the Readership (of Commonwealth Government, as the position was henceforth called) at Oxford, a 'special relationship' with her.[64] But the intrepid Perham of earlier times had been replaced by the senior academic, an eminence grise of the field and in that way was not in nearly as close touch with the dynamism of contemporary African societies as she had been twenty-five years before. And nothing spoke more loudly of that eminence (and perhaps remoteness from contemporary Africa) than did Perham's earlier close relationship with Lugard and the six volumes of material devoted to his long life and eventful record that she produced between 1956 and 1963, to which we shall now turn.

7

LUGARD'S FRIEND AND BIOGRAPHER

Of all the British proconsuls at work in nineteenth- and twentieth-century Africa no one remains as well known, as influential, or perhaps as controversial as Frederick John Dealtry Lugard, 1ˢᵗ Baron Lugard. A 'mercenary of Empire', James Morris called him bluntly, if accurately.[1] He was also, for about twenty years, Margery Perham's friend, mentor, and muse, and, for a further eighteen years after his death, the focus of her chief scholarly preoccupation. The result of these labours was an exhaustive two-volume biography and a comprehensive four-volume edition of his African diaries, which laid bare the man along with the times in which he lived. They also sealed Perham's reputation as the foremost authority on how the British had governed their African empire, even as contemporaneously that empire was collapsing. Indeed, as her former Oxford colleague, David Fieldhouse, put it: 'her subject died before she did'.[2] In a sense that is true, of course. If there was no empire then there need not be any administrators. But it is the business of historians – of which Perham was a leading one – to probe the dead past regardless of what the present day offers, and that, ultimately, is what she was doing with her protracted project on Lugard.

Perham first met Lugard briefly, as noted in chapter four, in 1927. She the young history don at Oxford; he the aging but still vigorous lion of empire, now engaged mainly as the British delegate to the Permanent Mandates Commission of the League of Nations in Geneva. The career for which he had become justly – to his contemporaries, if not to succeeding generations – as famous as Rhodes, was now firmly in the past. But to Perham, just then on the cusp of making the British Empire in Africa her life's work, no meeting could have been more fortuitous. And for the duration of that career the fixed star in her Imperial firmament was the wiry and indefatigable Lugard.

Staring out from any number of period photographs, Lugard's small, piercing eyes, receding hairline, and handlebar moustache, give him the hard visage of someone used to issuing orders and having them obeyed. That certainly was the Lugard of maturity. But that Lugard was formed over a number of years and a series of mostly African experiences. The young Lugard, on the other hand, the boy who became a man on the frontiers of the Empire, was the son of the parsonage, a sometimes hard but usually humane environment in which to grow up. Born in an auspicious year for the British Empire – 1858, the year following the Indian Mutiny – at what would shortly be the former East India Company Presidency of Madras – Lugard's father, the Rev'd Frederick Grueber Lugard, was the senior chaplain at Fort St. George. His mother, Mary Jane, was a Church of England missionary and his father's third wife. Together, they suffered the heat and privations of life in South India and in 1863 – when Lugard was five-years-old – they returned to England, to York, initially, and then eventually to Worcester where the Rev'd Lugard had secured a living and where the young Frederick would spend most of his remaining formative years. Sadly, Lugard's mother died within two years of the family's return from India. Just seven years of age when this unhappy event occurred, Lugard's character, as Perham suggests in the opening chapters of her biography of him in a kind of Jesuit-like paraphrase, 'was now, in all essentials, formed'.[3]

For the next six years until he went off to the Rossall School located along the Lancashire coast, Worcester was home to Lugard and his 'blended' family of four sisters and a brother. The eldest child, Lugard's half-sister Lucy, soon became *in loco parentis* to him and to the other motherless children. In the event, Lugard's primary education suffered. He spent a year locally in a small establishment run by 'two old ladies', not necessarily a recipe for disaster but in this case it apparently was so. He then was sent to a school run by the Moravian brotherhood near Manchester. Equally unsuccessful there, it was not until Lugard went to Rossall in 1871, a Church of England school founded in the 1840s for boys from the north of the country, that he became settled and began to achieve both the academic record and the social maturation that his native talents and character suggested were there to be developed. But such growth was slow in coming. Lugard was not especially studious or athletic – in an age when the Arnoldian model had taken hold of the public schools – and he was reprimanded regularly for general sloth. Accordingly, canings, the means of punishment meted out with too much relish, it seems clear, by occasionally sadistic Victorian schoolmasters, were threatened. 'Fancy the disgrace to be thrashed like a dog', Lugard opined to his favourite sister, Emma, on one such occasion.[4] But in the last of his six years at Rossall the school got a new headmaster, Dr. H.A. James, whose inspiring sermons in chapel and general charisma throughout the school helped to transform Lugard. He worked harder academically, with his grades improving as a consequence. And in his essays of the time, written for the headmaster himself, can even be found a glimpse of the future servant of empire: 'We may select as an example of the different brands of courage combined', wrote the seventeen-year-old Lugard while ruminating on the nature of the subject, 'England's missionary explorer, Livingstone … . Justly we may regard him as a pattern of British courage and we shall not disparage England's other heroes by selecting him as the greatest among them'.[5]

Despite Lugard's improved performance at Rossall his future remained unclear until 1877, his final year at the school. Earlier in life, he had thought about following in his father's footsteps and taking Holy Orders in the Church of England. But this aspiration was not sustaining and he considered the Indian Civil Service instead. A place among the so-called 'Heaven Born' had a naturalness to it, at least given his Anglo-Indian early childhood, but failure at the entrance examination, attributed to bad coaching from Rossall masters who knew little of its form and less of its content, left Lugard adrift. However, at this point his uncle, General Sir Edward Lugard, his father's younger brother and just then Permanent Under-Secretary of State at the War Office, stepped in propitiously and upon his advice Lugard changed course and took the army examinations at the end of 1877. Great success followed – he ranked an astonishing sixth out of about a thousand candidates – and in February of the following year he entered the Royal Military College Sandhurst. Lugard's life as a career soldier had now begun.

His period of training at Sandhurst was brief, however, owing to strategic exigencies in India. Just eight weeks were spent in gaining the rudiments of Victorian military practice before Lugard was hastily commissioned into the 9th Regiment, East Norfolk, and shipped out to India later that year as a member of the 2nd Battalion, which was stationed at the critical North West Frontier post of Peshawar. And that is where the barely twenty-one-year-old subaltern would spend the better part of 1878–79. The post offered the usual forms of excitement for young officers – polo; pig-sticking; horsemanship of all kinds – together with the ever-present threat of disease, unremitting heat, and boredom. And just as he was reaching the end of his patience with such latter irritations, the Norfolks were called – as long anticipated – into action and marched their way off to that timeless graveyard of empires, Afghanistan. Lugard, though ill with 'Peshawar fever' – some sort of gastrointestinal complaint – could not have been happier as he passed through the Khyber Pass in the fall of 1879. He was now at the heart of the 'Great

Game', the crossroads where the leading international powers of the day –
especially Britain and Russia – had chosen to engage one another in a geo-
strategic dance that defined the era.

For Britain at the time, the vulnerability of the North West Frontier to
potential incursions from Russia was constant. Under Disraeli's authority
since 1874, the British government and the Raj had both worked to keep
the Russian Bear at bay, mainly through its propping up of the Afghan
government. This attempt reached a crescendo in 1880 when the second of
what would eventually be three Afghan Wars was fought. For Lugard, too
sick to fight however, the war nonetheless was his first exposure to being on
campaign. But stricken with illness, he passed the months from December
1879 until the summer of 1880 in the toppled Amir's palace in Kabul, after
which he was invalided home to England. A year later, fully recovered and
itching to reinvigorate his aborted military career, he returned to India.

Over the next decade Lugard would forge an impressive military record,
followed by personal catastrophe, and then by redemption in Africa. The
first five years of the 1880s were spent in India. Lugard used this time almost
as an extended period of professional improvement, mastering Hindustani
and Urdu, as well as indulging in his continuing passion of pig sticking;
that is, hunting wild boar on horseback. As he described it to his younger
brother, Edward (Ned): 'An old boar will not run far but when pressed at
once shows great fight, so I thought nothing but a breakneck pace, besides
the prize was so great!'[6]

In 1884, Lugard went on secondment to the military transport service.
The money was better – a recurring theme in the life of someone with no
private wealth – and the position exposed him to imperial administration in
a way not yet encountered, something that would prove highly useful in the
future. The following year, as the Scramble for Africa formally got under-
way in the aftermath of the Berlin Conference on West Africa and as the
symbolic impact of Gordon's last stand in Khartoum was felt throughout
the Empire, Lugard was sent along with his battalion to the Sudan. It was
his first visit to the continent that would become the locus of his imperial
service, and in classic soldierly style the visit ended with a lot of fighting. In
Kitchener's campaign to dislodge Osman Digna and break the slave trade in
the eastern Sudan, Lugard was a keen participant. Then it was off to Burma
for Lugard in 1886 following the deposition of King Thibaw and the next
year the awarding of the DSO for his services rendered to the crown thus
far. All seemed well.

Lugard's steady rise was about to be reversed, however. His Burmese days
had carried a stinger in the tail in the form of a woman named Francis

Catherine Gambier, a rather disreputable divorcee who, to the romantically gullible Lugard, was known simply as 'C'. In July 1887, when his posting in Burma was almost over, a telegram arrived from Catherine then in Lucknow, informing him that she was near death as a result of a recent carriage accident. The previous year while in India Lugard and Catherine had engaged in a passionate love affair. She was stunningly beautiful and an accomplished horsewoman and Lugard had fallen hard for her. Now, in her apparent hour of need, he rushed to India to be by her side. By the time he arrived, however, Catherine had enjoyed a too-speedy recovery and had departed promptly for England, without so much as a word to the panicked Lugard. Frantic now, he sailed for home and eventually caught up to Catherine in London, only to discover that despite his intense ardour and clear devotion he had become not much more than an afterthought to her. In Perham's chaste words used later to describe the scene, he arrived breathlessly at Catherine's address only to find her 'at that very moment engaged in bestowing her affections elsewhere'.[7] Devastated by this turn of events, he resigned his commission (which was refused) and sought all manner of ways, including volunteering for the manifestly dangerous work of a being member of the London fire brigade, to assuage his wounded pride and cauterize his broken heart. Finally, placed by the army on medical leave, he determined to get as far away from Catherine as possible (inexplicably, she continued to pester him with letters for years) by going back to Africa. At first, this meant Zanzibar, but then in a peripatetic progress Lugard moved on to Abyssinia, the port of Aden, and then finally to Mozambique. There, in the employ of the African Lakes Company, he was hired to hunt elephant. It was now 1888 and Lugard was only thirty-years-old, but his career seemed over.

In later years, Lugard would recognize the 'C' episode – which had pushed him as far as to entertain thoughts of suicide – as the turning point in his life. 'The real key to the story of a life', he wrote, 'lies in the knowledge of the emotions and passions which have sometimes disfigured, sometimes built up character, and in every case influenced the actions recorded. Of these the sexual instinct is recognized as the most potent for good or ill and it has certainly been so in my life'.[8] Regardless of the psychological cost of this lost romance, it had the fortuitous impact for Lugard of sending him back to Africa. And far from his career being over when he landed in Mozambique, it was really just beginning.

For the first year or so in the service of the African Lakes Company Lugard hunted big game – 'the man who hunts lions with his bare hands' – his admiring bearers called him, and took action against the Arab slave traders who infested both the coast and the interior. In one gun battle with them he was wounded: 'They've got me!' he shouted, before crawling off in the direction of the trading post's doctor expecting to die.[9] Instead, he was only temporarily paralyzed, and shortly plunged back into the fray. Working at the rank of captain, Lugard quickly became an indispensable presence for the company and soon his anti-slavery exploits, which among other things saved from destruction its trading compound at Karonga at the head of Lake Nyasa (in modern Malawi), brought him to the attention of Cecil Rhodes and, more important, William Mackinnon. The latter was the founder of the Imperial British East Africa Company and he hired Lugard promptly to blaze a new route from Mombasa on the East African coast to the interior of the continent. Ultimately, the interior for Lugard meant Uganda, which is where he based himself from 1890 until 1894.

During those years Uganda was at the centre of a stormy debate in London over whether or not it should be annexed to the British Empire. The territory's recent history, especially the killing of a group of young Christian converts – the 'Uganda Martyrs' – by the native king, the *Kabaka* Mwanga II, from 1885 to 1887, had generated a strong missionary lobby at home to have Uganda named a British protectorate. The aging Liberal prime minister, William Gladstone, suspicious of the kind of imperial acquisition that Uganda potentially represented, resisted adding it to a growing list of British African territories, all of which, he had argued earlier, spoke merely of no greater national aspiration than an unjustifiable 'earth hunger'.[10] But his government was split on the issue and ultimately in 1894 he lost the battle against the so-called Liberal Imperialists. Lord Rosebery, their leader, won the day, Gladstone resigned, and Uganda was made a protectorate. The approaches to the headwaters of the mighty Nile, in the grand strategic plan of the British in which the Suez Canal and India lay at the centre, now seemed safe.

In this protracted political fight Lugard had played a key role by negotiating a series of treaties with local native rulers, stoutly supporting the missionary and anti-slavery lobby, and writing a book in which he expounded his views, *The Rise of our East African Empire* (1893).[11] He thought, as a result of these actions, a senior government appointment in the new Ugandan protectorate might be his, but he was mistaken. His impassioned and highly-partisan support for protectorate status had in some respects worked against him, and he was passed over. Deeply disappointed – 'I feel very sorry to find that I am to be excluded from going on with my work in East Africa' – he now struck out for West Africa instead, where Sir George Goldie, the founder of the Royal Niger Company, wanted Lugard to entrench the company's trading interests in the region.[12] In an area of Africa first traversed by a European over a hundred years earlier in the person of Mungo Park, the Royal Niger Company now beat the French (and to a lesser extent the Germans) to the minerals and resources – notably rubber – of the rich Niger basin.

In the spring of 1895, however, and after successful service to the RNC, Lugard found himself at loose ends once again. He had hoped that his success over the previous year might convince the now-faltering Rosebery government (it fell in June) to grant him an appointment. But once again he was disappointed – although being created a Companion of the Order of the Bath provided a small balm – and as a consequence ventured south into Bechuanaland to accept a position with yet another trading company. This time it was the British West Charterland Company and Lugard was charged with leading a mineral transport that involved a 700-mile trek across the blistering Kalahari Desert. To do so in a 'motor car', Lugard deadpanned of the new-to-market form of transport, would have been 'just the thing'.[13] As it was, his sun-baked job completed by the summer of 1896, Lugard now had once again to wait in hopes of a government appointment, 'some deed of noble note', as he called it.[14] The interminable wait lasted for almost a year, however, but finally in August of 1897 he was asked to return to the Niger region. The Conservative government of Lord Salisbury, in office since 1895, thought it prudent to resist attempted French expansion in the region. To perform this task of resistance, said Colonial Secretary Joseph Chamberlain in a secret message to Lugard, the government had him in mind. Lugard was to be given a dual charge: Her Majesty's Commissioner for the Nigerian hinterland, and Commandant of what was swiftly going to become the local sword of empire, the 2,000-man West African Frontier Force. Initially, Lugard was not keen on the idea of a return to the Niger. His first choice for deployment was East Africa and, besides, in West Africa the French loathed him as the man who had checked their expansion two years before. But it was a government appointment at last, which he was not really about to turn down. 'How can I decline?' he wondered. Accordingly, he accepted the government's offer and in April of 1898 he went back to West Africa.

Lugard would spend sixteen of the next twenty-one years in Nigeria, as the region had begun to be called the previous year. In 1900, after he had pushed hard to extend and consolidate the British presence in the area, the Salisbury government declared a protectorate over Northern and Southern Nigeria, the Royal Niger Company's charter was terminated, and Lugard was made High Commissioner of the Northern protectorate. 'We drink to

the success of Northern Nigeria ...', he said to a small group of administrators and soldiers gathered at the proclamation of the new protectorate at
Lokoja, its capital, on 1 January 1900. 'It is in the hands of each one of us; it
is we who are selected to mould the young beginnings, to set the precedents
and set the tone and, in short, to make or mar this work'.[15]

From then until 1906 Sir Frederick Lugard – knighted in the first year
of his high commissionership – led a lean but determined regime that
brought all of the Islamic protectorate's kingdoms under British control.
Unsurprisingly, military action came just as easily as diplomacy to Lugard,
and despite constant Colonial Office objections to his armed operations, he
was committed to 'pacifying' Northern Nigeria. In practice, this meant the
forced adoption of indirect rule, the system, as we saw in previous chapters, with which Lugard would become synonymous. Even though he did
not create it – its basic principles stretch back as least as far as the Roman
Empire – he refined it for British purposes, especially through his later
writings: *Political Memoranda* (1919) and, as was noted earlier, *The Dual
Mandate in British Tropical Africa* (1922). As he said in the latter book,
a lengthy disquisition on the combined moral and administrative responsibilities of the British Empire in Africa: 'The task of the administrative
officer is to clothe his principles in the garb of evolution, not of revolution;
to make it apparent alike to the educated native, the conservative Moslem
[sic], and the primitive pagan, each in his own degree, that the policy of the
Government is not antagonistic but progressive ...'.[16]

In 1906, fed up with what he took to be endless Colonial Office med-
dling in Nigerian affairs, and now happily married – to the former Flora
Shaw, sometime colonial editor of *The Times* during which she had coined
the name 'Nigeria' for the RNC's West African territories – he submitted
his resignation. He was not out of work for long, however. The next year
he was named governor of Hong Kong, a post he held until 1912. Lugard's
governorship there was something that never quite suited him, however, and
apart from founding the University of Hong Kong he left no indelible mark.
Africa was his self-proclaimed 'destiny', and so it was back to Nigeria in the
autumn of 1912, this time to draw up a plan to implement the British government's desire to create an amalgamated Nigerian colony. And on New
Year's Day 1914, the unitary Nigeria was duly proclaimed, with Lugard as
its Governor-General.

The next four years until his final resignation in 1918 were Lugard's
culminating period in Africa. He presided over Nigeria in wartime, which
brought considerable military action to the colony's eastern region adjacent
to German Cameroon (Kameroun). There were also internal disturbances

over the nature and implementation of indirect rule, including one uprising in the city of Abeokuta where over 500 people were killed. Meanwhile, Lugard also ensured that a railway was built in order to link the North and South. But by the end of the war he was sixty-years-old and exhausted and in November of 1918 he retired, returning to England for good.

In the years that followed Lugard remained nearly as busy and productive as he had been during his gubernatorial service. As noted above, he undertook serious writing projects, he also travelled, and in 1922 began what stretched into a fourteen-year period representing Britain on the Permanent Mandates Commission in Geneva. He served on the governing body at the School of Oriental (and later African) Studies in London, as well as continuing to work with J.H. Oldham and the International Institute of African Languages and Cultures, as well as with corporate boards. Lugard's remarkable capacity for work was based on an iron constitution making this level of activity possible. His country property, Little Parkhurst near Abinger, Surrey, was the headquarters for his varied pursuits. His wife Flora had begun their association with this sylvan area of Leith Hill in 1883 when she rented had a room in what was then a cottage at Little Parkhurst. Once they had married in 1902, the cottage was remodelled and a second one added, and together the expanded Little Parkhurst would remain the Lugards' home and retreat for the rest of their lives.[17]

Like so many other men of standing in his day, Lugard was a member of a West End club, in his case the Athenaeum. Located on Waterloo Place at Pall Mall, it was generally considered to be a club at the very pinnacle of the social pyramid, anchoring what was a kind of local club 'triptych', including the more intimate Travellers Club next door and beyond it, the enormous Reform Club. The Athenaeum was the place where – it will be recalled – Margery Perham had first met Lugard formally in the spring of 1929 in a rather physically uncomfortable encounter sitting side-by-side in the Ladies' Annexe – a 'cubby hole' she later called it – overlooking Carlton Gardens.[18] Famously un-accepting of distaff members, it now seems sweetly ironic that the Athenaeum provided for Perham's entrée into the highly masculine world of colonial administration as embodied by Lugard, its most important male theorist and former practitioner.

Their meeting came not long in advance of Perham's departure on her round the world trip compliments of the Rhodes Trust. Upon her return from both of her early trips to Africa, and the subsequent purchase of Ponds Farm with the Raynes in 1932, Lugard became her neighbour. By then, Lord Lugard – he was elevated to the peerage as Baron Lugard of Abinger in 1928 – was a widower. The light that Flora had been to him was

extinguished upon her death in 1929, just a few months before his meeting with Perham at the Athenaeum. He stayed on in the cavernous Little
Parkhurst, however, where Flora was memorialized by her former bed-
sitting room remaining forever untouched.

The proximity that Perham had to Lugard contributed much to his
becoming her mentor and friend and the early- to mid-1930s were years
in which the almost seven-mile horsepath between Ponds Farm and Little
Parkhurst was well-trod by her. Often she would ride over to converse
on some topic of African or imperial affairs – just then, for example, the
issue of Closer Union in East Africa was raging, to which they both were
opposed – while sitting in front of the blazing brick fireplace in the drawing
room. Lugard would also entertain a series of government officials, visiting
Nigerians, and cultural figures such as Rudyard Kipling and Robert Louis
Stevenson. Having met him only when he was a relatively old man – 'with
the experience and prestige of his long achievement, while I was the student' – Perham would always retain a high level of respect and esteem for
Lugard, both personally and as his biographer.[19] This fact did not mean,
however, that she could not look at various aspects of his career with an
arched eyebrow and ask penetrating questions about events past, policies
made, or assumptions held. In the beginning, however, all was somewhat
Socratic, with Lugard the repository of colonial knowledge and experience
and Perham – to some extent at least – the colonial ingénue.

During Perham's initial period of international travel she corresponded
regularly with Lugard, he warning her on one occasion in 1932, for example, to stay clear of a restive Liberia: 'it is not safe, and this is not the time'.[20]
Accordingly, she did not go there. Many of their letters have a jaunty quality
to them, but from time to time would also become rather serious as on the
July day in 1931, in the midst of her anthropological studies in London,
when Perham wrote to Lugard in deep admiration: 'I hardly like to say
how much it has meant to me to know you and to work beside you for the
same object'.[21] Due formality in address would remain until the next year
when 'Dear Lord Lugard' and 'Dear Miss Perham' were replaced with first
names. 'My dear Margery', wrote Lugard in November 1932, you see that I
am taking you at your word! I hope you will do the same to me. My name
is Fred'.[22] This degree of informality coincided with their close neighbour-
hood proximity and the friendship that had now blossomed. There is no
hint of romance in any of their extensive correspondence, but the degree to
which Perham had always thrived under paternal influence was confirmed
and extended by her relationship with the sexagenarian Lugard. 'It was
extremely nice of you to know of my birthday and send me good wishes', he

wrote to her on 22 January 1934, the day he turned seventy-six and three days before marking five years since the death of his beloved Flora. 'It is a <u>very</u> sad anniversary for me'.[23]

In hindsight, Perham becoming Lugard's biographer seems obvious, but at the time it was not so. Initially, in 1926, Flora Lugard had approached Reginald Coupland at Oxford to consider writing her husband's life story.[24] Just then in the midst of both his responsibilities as Beit Chair in Colonial History and as biographer of Sir John Kirk, the great Scottish explorer of Africa and medical doctor on Livingstone's Zambezi expedition in the early 1860s, he cited overwork and declined the offer.[25] Then, when his desk had been cleared somewhat a few years later and after Flora's death, Coupland contacted Lugard himself about taking up the life. Lugard had never liked the idea of a biography – notwithstanding Flora's desire to see one written – and Coupland's renewed interest to undertake the job seems to have been met with indifference by him. However, by the mid-1930s – and with the advent of his friendship with and mentorship of Perham – he grudgingly admitted that perhaps his life story should be written, but if so only Perham would be able to do it in the way that Flora would have wished it to be done. Lugard's admiring younger brother Ned was committed to the idea of Perham writing it too. But she was not so sure, and in any event Perham certainly would not do it while Lugard was alive: 'I do not believe that biographies should appear in the lifetime of the subject'. But by 1938 Ned was happy to report to his elder brother that Perham was 'keen' to do it; that it would be a 'privilege' and a 'noble task' to do so, and would constitute the 'best work of her life. Long after her books on 'Native Administration' etc. are out of date and forgotten, the Biography will remain *a classic*'.[26] Time, it would seem, has proven the devoted Ned right.

Between 1938 and Lugard's death in 1945 Perham continued to see him, although not as frequently as earlier when she had been living mainly at Ponds Farm, and of course exchange numerous letters. He had praised her highly upon the publication of *Native Administration in Nigeria* in 1937, making clear to her that 'I hand over to you the torch' of their chosen subject, and that with Perham it would 'be in hands so much more capable than mine'.[27] She was humbled by this sort of effusive language about their shared discipline of colonial administration but at the same time was happy to be the repository of such faith. During this time too Lugard contemplated what to do with his enormous archive, settling eventually on Rhodes House as the right place for it. Still fairly spry and whole of mind, Lugard was nonetheless over eighty years of age during the Second World War and its impact – from the profound shock he felt at the 'atrocities in Hong Kong' in

1942 to the 'flying-bombs' that turned his 700-year-old parish church into 'a mass of rubble' in 1944 – left him acutely aware of the destructiveness of the war, and that his own life was drawing to an end.[28] There is a plaintive note to his mild wish expressed in 1941 to talk more frequently with Perham and the fact that, in his view, he 'had lost touch' with what she was doing. But these were the understandable complaints of an old, and increasingly, lonely man. Lugard also expressed some degree of dissatisfaction with Perham's series of letters to *The Times* in March 1942 in the aftermath of the fall of Singapore, arguing that her call for a 'New Order' in colonial affairs was mistaken. 'I believe', he stated flatly, 'that our Colonial policy is the best in the world. Of course, it has weak spots and can be improved, as it has been steadily in the past … . I shall as I said look forward to a talk over divergent standpoints when next we meet.'[29] They did meet, of course, but such meetings became infrequent – 'you seem as far distant in Oxford as you would be in Australia!'[30] Lugard's last letter to her was sent from Little Parkhurst, on 1 April 1945. As a valedictory missive, it could not have been better. Remarking on the affectionate nature of so many of Perham's letters of late, Lugard was deeply touched by the fact that she would choose to mention him in her prayers: 'I wish I were worthy of affection so sacred and so moving'.[31] Just twenty-four hours later he slipped into unconsciousness and on 11 April, having remained in a coma throughout the intervening nine days, Lord Lugard died.

The personal loss for Perham was great – in the persuasive view of Patricia Pugh, she was the daughter Lugard never had; the public loss, meanwhile, was marked by a service of remembrance at Westminster Abbey a few weeks later on 26 April.[32] Lugard the man had moved irrevocably into the territory of myth and it was within that realm that Perham now began to think seriously about how she would capture both features of his life in the impending biography. Ned Lugard was hopeful that something might be quickly put into the hands of the reading public. At first, she thought writing a short life of Lugard indeed might suffice, with a full biography to come when time and thorough research allowed. However, as she plunged more deeply into Lugard's papers a short life seemed possible only as a distillation of an exhaustively-written biography. There simply was too much to understand, too much context surrounding the partition of Africa, for example, to extract Lugard thinly from the full run of the times in which he lived. Indeed, his actions could be made intelligible only by making clear the comprehensive Imperial picture of Africa in the closing years of the nineteenth century and the early ones of the twentieth. By 1947, she had reached this conclusion. By then she was also considering a two-volume biography, in part to try and meet the impatience of Ned who wished to see at least part of his brother's life in print before his own death, which, given that he was then eighty-two years old, was assumed could not be too far off. Perham did not agree with this proposal for some time, but when she finally did in a sense it met some of the requirements of a short biography because it truncated Lugard's life into two parts: 1858–98 and 1898–1945. All along, despite questions as to its format, Perham never lost sight of her sense of duty in writing it. As well, however, and more importantly, was her keen desire to do it. I want to write this book, she had told Ned, shortly after Lugard's death in April 1945, 'more than I want to do any other piece of work'.[33]

The problem for Perham, in the late 1940s, was that she had become stretched rather thinly over a large number of commitments. As we saw in the previous chapter, in 1948 in recognition of this fact she had begun to pare back some of these commitments, particularly related to teaching. Regardless, however, she researched and wrote the Lugard biography during, as Mary Bull observes, 'the busiest fifteen years of her life'.[34] In so doing she first had to deal with the issue of limited access to what Lugard himself, and now also Ned, regarded as the most sensitive of the biographical material, the so-called 'secret diary' that detailed events like the protracted romance and its aftermath with 'C'. Lugard had left strict instructions that this material was to be read only by Ned who was empowered to extract bits of it for Perham's eyes alone, after which all of it was to be burnt. The system was never satisfactory, however, even though Ned read a copious number of his deceased brother's letters turning over some of their contents to Perham. Her own sense of propriety, however, together with publishing in an age that did not yet regard purely personal details – especially those of a sexual nature – as essential pieces of biographical writing, meant that the finished product is not as probing of character and personal minutiae as would be the case now. Moreover, the main challenge for Perham was that she was writing about someone whose friendship had been long and deep and nuanced. 'I do not approach Lugard as a scientist', she told those gathered at one of the weekly meetings of the Oxford Imperial history seminar in 1950, 'nor even as an historian, but as a friend'.[35]

Despite these handicaps, the work continued apace through the early 1950s. To help out with the enormous task of research Perham began to employ assistants, one of the first of whom was Mary Bull, who had joined her fiancé, Hedley Bull, in Oxford in March of 1954. He was then reading for a B.Phil. in politics, the prelude to a celebrated academic career in the UK, as well as in his native Australia, as a theorist in international affairs. Perham hired her that summer and 'this provided not only an interesting occupation, but a reasonable salary', recalls Bull.[36] She took over the job from Eleanor Glyn-Jones, a neighbour in Wellington Square where the Bulls had rented a flat. Bull plunged into the job, 'crawling around Rhodes House checking references', carrying out 'Girl Friday' tasks and generally doing whatever was necessary to help Perham keep the Lugard project on the rails. Later, Perham would praise her research assistants for their interest in the project, their good humour, and 'their terrier-like pertinacity in hunting for elusive documents'.[37] Bull's relationship with Perham was warm and good, 'she was very motherly towards me', but Perham's hectic pace meant that she needed a lot of looking after too. Invariably, says Bull with a laugh, 'some institute in London would ring up to say that Margery had left her umbrella and would someone be coming round to collect it'. In working side-by-side with Perham – in the first instance until the autumn of 1955 – Bull was able to guage Perham's commitment to the project as well as her estimation of Lugard. It was clear, she recalls, that Perham had an enormous amount of admiration for him but that her own view of Africans was much more sympathetic and egalitarian than his had been. 'One worked for Africans', is how Bull describes Lugard's outlook, 'not with them', which is the way she encapsulates that of Perham.[38]

In 1956, *Lugard: The Years of Adventure 1858–1898* was published. The book was a major achievement, a massive compendium of 750 pages, narrating and analyzing the first forty years of Lugard's life. In part it read like *King Solomon's Mines*: 'As Lugard followed this route he was overwhelmed with the strangeness and beauty through which he passed. The Kwakwa river ran through high wooded banks, and he watched the trees as his native crew propelled the boat laboriously upstream.' Indeed, the first volume of the biography is mainly as the title of the book would have it, an adventure. In it, Perham's obvious literary abilities are given full rein, and because this half of Lugard's life was unknown except in bare outline to Perham she herself was engaged upon a kind of adventure in acquainting herself with all of its constituent parts and then weaving them together to try and tell the whole story of his early life.

As Bull notes, too, Perham's romantic sensibilities about Africa were reenlivened by her chronicling of Lugard's exploits and travels, so much so that at times in the book it becomes unclear whether or not it was Lugard's view that was being relayed, or that of Perham herself.[39] Regardless of some occasional criticisms, the book was well-received, and amongst its first readers no one was more pleased than the ninety-two year old Ned Lugard, who regarded it as 'a *wonderful* book – an amazing story'.[40] Its publication would prove to be a nice fillip to his life as he would die within a few months of its release. To today's reader the book's style is arch and moralistic, and its subject matter of the great white man on a mission in darkest Africa could not be less fashionable – notwithstanding the fact that today there remain many white men on missions in contemporary Africa; only the rationale for doing so has changed. Still, in its attempt to probe as fully as possible Lugard's actions in East, Central, and West Africa during that period of history when European rule was established throughout most of the continent, Perham constructed an impressive edifice of Imperial scholarship, well worth reading both then and now.

Almost concurrent with the writing of the second volume of the biography was the editing and publication of Lugard's diaries. Beginning in 1959 with three volumes (a fourth was added in 1963), the diaries comprised a million words of text, some of which came from the 'secret diary' that Lugard had instructed was to be embargoed and burnt and that, after much persuading by Perham, Ned had agreed to see in print. Finding a publisher for such a huge project proved to be difficult, however. Oxford University Press, for example, turned Perham down, 'even if a subsidy for their cost could be got'.[41] But Faber and Faber (and Northwestern University Press in Chicago for the fourth volume) brought them out to much acclaim.[42] In a glowing review in *The Observer* in October 1959 Elspeth Huxley called them 'the raw material of African history and, except for a good deal of repetition about shooting animals, more readable than most novels'.[43] A few years later, upon the publication of the fourth and final volume, Ronald Robinson, who would go on to hold a chair of history at Cambridge and then the Beit Chair in Commonwealth History at Oxford from 1980 until his retirement in 1987, just two years earlier had published *Africa and the Victorians*.[44] Written with Jack Gallagher and Alice Denny, it would prove to be one of the most important texts in the field of British Imperial history during the generation that followed. 'Margery Perham', he enthused in the *Sunday Telegraph* in February 1963, 'with her brilliant biography and scholarly edition of his copious African diaries, has raised a Taj Mahal to an empire builder'.[45]

Perham's assistant editor for the first three volumes of the Lugard diaries and co-editor of the last one was Mary Bull. Her work on the diaries intersected with that on the second volume of the biography, which came out in 1960 as *Lugard: The Years of Authority 1898–1945*.[46] Unlike the first volume, this one presented Perham with the problem of familiarity with both the man and the field. In that way the book became much more of a commentary on events that could be construed as almost 'current' and certainly, given the rapid move to independence by most of Britain's African colonies in the late 1950s and early 1960s (Nigeria, for example, declared its independence that year, 1960), Lugard's legacy was hardly something to be consigned to the annals of colourful late-Victorian history. Almost identical in length to the first volume (it was just two pages shorter), the second volume is given over almost wholly to Lugard's time in Nigeria and, as Bull notes, in it Perham expresses 'serious doubts of Lugard's achievements' – something virtually absent from *The Years of Adventure*.[47]

Bull is clearly right in saying that as Lugard's biographer 'her desire was to justify him'.[48] That said, however, Perham did not merely assert such justification but sought evidence for doing so. Volume two of the biography is a recounting of Lugard as an imperial administrator. And in researching it Perham found much to criticize in his thinking and conduct in this regard. In particular, Lugard's disregard of Africans as individuals and his inability to see them as worthy recipients of the eventual transfer of power were elements of his character that she found almost irredeemable. 'Still', Perham quotes him as saying about a couple of educated Africans that he met in Lagos in 1912, 'it is something to get a little in touch and hear their views'.[49]

Lugard's development of indirect rule is the point at which public criticism came most readily, both at the time of the biography's publication and since. Of the latter, one of the fiercest critics was I.F. Nicolson in *The Administration of Nigeria, 1900–1960: men, methods, and myths* (1969), who saw Lugard as nothing more than a shameless self-promoter.[50] John Flint, the biographer of Sir George Goldie, argues that indirect rule had a stultifying effect on Nigeria fixing it 'firmly in British policy as a conservative philosophy, hostile to the ambitions of educated Africans and those influenced by Christian missionaries, to urban growth, to the spread of the money economy, and to the vision that new African nations were in the making'.[51] Other, similar judgements continue to be made on indirect rule. Bob Shenton, a Marxist historian, for example, perhaps predictably describes it as a 'rigid, political structure' and a mere 'ceremony' whose imposition – on Southern Nigeria especially – was 'disastrous'.[52] Toyin Falola and A.D. Roberts deride it for being a 'policy of segregation, inasmuch as it was part of a broader strategy for restricting the influence of Africans who had been educated on Western lines'.[53] Perham, by way of contrast, was sure that indirect rule as designed and implemented by Lugard was 'the most comprehensive, coherent and renowned system of administration in our colonial history. This was his greatest and most famous work, the achievement of his prime'.[54]

The publication of the second and final volume of the biography in 1960 completed the task of preserving Lugard's record for posterity (save, as we saw, for volume four of his diaries, which came out three years later). Perham's main scholarly task of the preceding fifteen years – indeed of her whole life – was now finished. She had 'enhanced, but not irredeemably sanctified' Lugard's reputation, as the writer of his entry in the ODNB observes, which, it may be added, is usually the result of most good biographies. And with the closing out of her work on Lugard she was now approaching the end of her own career, at least in its official form. Perham turned sixty-five that year and as the Union Jack began to be hauled down around British Africa she was in the perfect position to offer the long view of its phenomenon, of which she had been a close observer now for some forty years. And in 1961, as we shall see, when Perham was named by the BBC to be its prestigious Reith Lecturer, she was given the opportunity to do exacty that.

8

BRITAIN'S 'CONSCIENCE ON AFRICA': PERHAM THE PUBLIC INTELLECTUAL

By the early 1960s Margery Perham was being hailed by some as 'Britain's African Queen'.[1] Hers was the best known and probably the most listened to voice on African affairs in the country, especially in the midst of the almost serial independence ceremonies taking place in Africa. Indeed, in 1960 alone seventeen European African colonies became independent – although only two of that number, Somaliland and Nigeria, were British. 'No woman (and few men)', remarked the same writer as above, 'know more about Africa; she has criss-crossed it on foot, camel, horse, jeep and plane, studied it, soaked it up, fallen in love with it'.[2] Slight journalistic hyperbole or no, Perham indeed had emerged as the most important commentator and public intellectual on African affairs in Britain because of half-a-lifetime of thinking and writing about the topic.

From the time of Perham's first contribution to *The Times* in April 1930 she never ceased to write for a wider audience than academics typically – and sometimes with good reason – usually address. The ways of the Academy are not the ways of the public at large, and to crossover from one to the other takes both intention and skill. Doing so can also cause resentment and depredation by colleagues, some of whom hold the view that engaging in debates about public policy can weaken and compromise the necessarily rarified works of scholarship that must remain at the heart of the academic enterprise. There is little doubt that Perham understood this distinction, but there is also clear evidence that she chose to disregard it in an attempt not only to contribute to the academic content of her chosen field, but to engage both the British public and government policymakers in debate. In making this choice Perham would be a constant voice on Africa, as well as on other questions of international import. But in so doing she would also be regarded by some of her colleagues, such as her successor as Reader in Colonial Administration at Oxford, Kenneth Robinson, as being less than a scholar because of it. To others, however, such as former Nuffield colleague, Frederick Madden, she simply 'combined the roles of publicist and scholar', and got on with it.[3]

The long forty-year arc of Perham's public engagement with Africa in the pages of British newspapers and magazines reveals an astonishing breadth of interest and knowledge. From her earliest days come writings on 'Tribal Rule in Africa' and 'The Future of East Africa', 'Nigeria Today', 'Obligations of British Policy in Ethiopia', 'Tanganyika Now', and 'Christian Missions in Africa'. These and some one hundred others formed the core of her understanding of the British Empire and native administration in the period before, during, and immediately after the Second World War. In the years that followed and until she wrote her last article for a newspaper – 'Dealings with African States' – which was published in *The Times* in 1973, Perham would produce about another hundred pieces in which she would make plain her views on Africa, and by so doing suggest a standard by which the continent should be understood by Britons at large. Occasionally, her writings would point out a particular event or injustice that yielded a marked public response. One of the most notable of these in the first half of her years of being a publicist on Africa was that concerning the Bechuanaland political dynasty, the Khamas, and the episode went some distance in reinforcing her stance as a critic of British colonial rule in Africa, perhaps even radically so.

As was seen in chapter four, Perham met and befriended Tshekedi Khama, Bechuanaland's regent, during her first visit to southern Africa in 1930. When, after the war, South Africa began to contemplate the annexation of the British mandated territory of Bechuanaland, Khama objected to it fiercely but was thwarted in his attempt to come to London in person in order to discuss the matter with the Labour government. Consequently, Perham took up his cause in the pages of *The Times* in August 1946. 'Nothing', she wrote, 'is more highly valued by colonial leaders than the opportunity, in matters of importance, to come to London and put the case before the highest authorities'. In this regard, she then went on to cite the case in 1895, when Tshekedi's grandfather, Khama III, had come to the Imperial capital in order to plead for his country against the attempt by Cecil Rhodes and the British South Africa Company to annex it. Joseph Chamberlain, Colonial Secretary at the time, indeed heard Khama's plea and ruled in his favour, an outcome vehemently opposed by Rhodes, who complained bitterly that 'it is humiliating to be utterly beaten by these niggers'.[4] In the event, half-a-century later Tshekedi did not come to London, but neither was South Africa's attempt at territorial aggrandizement successful. Yet only a few years later Perham would once again weigh into the Imperial fray over the Khamas, in a case of the intensely personal becoming the acutely political.

In 1947, while studying to become a barrister in London following a year spent in broader reading at Oxford, Seretse Khama, Tshekedi's nephew and heir to the Bechuanaland chieftainship, met a young Englishwoman named Ruth Williams. Since the death of his father, Sekgoma II, in 1925, when Khama was four years old, he had been *kgosi* (king) of the Bamangwato people and thereby effectively of Bechuanaland. In the meantime, his uncle Tshekedi, ruled as regent and chief and was his guardian until such time – thought to be after he had completed his studies in law – when he was ready to rule. A little over a year after Khama's meeting Williams, they married. The unconventional interracial union caused uproar, both among the tribal leadership in Bechuanaland and in neighbouring South Africa whose newly-elected National Party had introduced a system of apartheid under which interracial marriage was banned. Having the future king of Bechuanaland so obviously defy what was legally normative just across the border, caused the South African government of D.F. Malan (having recently succeeded the aging Jan Christian Smuts) to protest loudly. In a similarly vociferous protestation, Tshekedi Khama demanded that the marriage be annulled and that Seretse return to Bechuanaland to face a series of *kgotlas* (public meetings) to determine whether or not the Bamangwato elders still considered him fit to be king. In due course the young man did so, bringing his English wife with him, and after a raucous series of meetings, the elders reaffirmed Khama's right to rule. Their decision was objected to by Tshekedi, but admitting (local) defeat he went into exile and Seretse returned to London and his law studies in 1949.[5]

The issue continued to simmer, however, with South Africa making threats of various sorts, including the restriction or repricing of gold and uranium exports to Britain, still in recovery from the deleterious financial impact of the Second World War. The Attlee government was also fearful that perhaps South Africa might launch economic sanctions against the Bechuanaland Protectorate or even resort to a military invasion. As a result, a parliamentary enquiry was called to investigate the fitness of Seretse's future chieftainship of Bechuanaland. On 8 March 1950, with the parliamentary report embargoed, the government chose to suspend his chieftainship and ban him from his homeland for five years. Ten days later, a letter from an outraged Perham appeared in *The Times*.

In a passionately argued thousand-word epistle Perham was sure that in
defence of Seretse 'Britain must shake herself clear of all the muddle and
misunderstanding which seem to have dimmed her reputation for good
faith and humane administration'. She reached this conclusion by pointing
out that there were both political and administrative problems connected
with the case – not to mention the clear issue of social justice – making
the none too comfortable point for her that the old tribal hierarchies left in
place by indirect rule were proving to be the 'most difficult to democratize'.
But beyond the Bamangwato elders, whose opposition to the marriage was
traditionally cultural, lay the British government's decision to revoke and
banish Seretse and here there simply must be a 'reversal of policy' to set it
right, she maintained. If nothing else, a demonstration of such would be a
reaffirmation of 'British Fairplay'.[6]

Alas, the British government did not reverse its course but with Perham's
help the opposition of Tshekedi himself to his nephew's status was dropped.
This outcome was achieved through personal diplomacy. Tshekedi visited
Britain beginning in April of 1950 and during part of his stay was Perham's
guest at her Bardwell Road home in Oxford. From the moment of his arrival
in England and their meeting at Paddington Station Perham worked both
to convince the British government to change its policy and to effect reconciliation between regent and king. To this initial end she was in touch with
Arthur Creech Jones. Though just out of office as Colonial Secretary (and
out of Parliament too) after the general election of February 1950, Perham
valued his counsel highly and she consulted him about Tshekedi and then,
later, had the two men meet in person: 'I am so glad you saw Tshekedi.
Your advice will be more valuable than anybody's. I am so afraid of him
getting into the wrong hands, and having premature publicity and offend-
ing Gordon-Walker [the Secretary of State for Commonwealth Relations]
before this may be necessary!'[7]

Even more closely did she work with a trio of African sympathizers,
whose later work as colonial liberationists would make them well-known
figures in the 1960s and 70s, to bring about a partial reconciliation between
Tshekedi and Seretse. The Reverend Michael Scott, an Anglican priest
from Johannesburg, Mary Benson, who would become Tshekedi's assistant
and biographer, and David Astor, editor of the *Observer*, joined her for a
face to face meeting between the estranged uncle and nephew in May at
Astor's house outside the historic village of Sutton Courtney, just south of
Abingdon near Oxford.[8] The meeting was able to restore a degree of amity
between the two men. But such was not the case, ultimately, with the British
government, which, in August of 1950, had chosen also to ban Tshekedi

from Bechuanaland for, in Perham's view 'no defensible reason', and then in May 1951 decided to renew the banishment. Perham's views were clear: 'Here is a man innocent of any offence ... who has proved himself in his twenty years of regency to be probably the most intelligent, enlightened and determined chief in Africa'.[9]

An obvious structural problem with the case also was of concern to Perham. She regarded the Commonwealth Relations Office, of which Patrick Gordon-Walker was head, as unsuited to deal with the Bechuanaland question. In existence only since 1947 when it was established to succeed the Dominions Office, its essentially diplomatic function meant that in her view it lacked the knowledge and wisdom to deal with 'this one, small, but difficult task of African administration'. As a protectorate Bechuanaland did not lie under Colonial Office control and therefore could not now be the beneficiary of its 'wide experience' in matters such as these, she contended in protest.[10] Perham joined others, therefore, in demanding a Parliamentary inquiry, which was refused. Not long afterwards, however, in August 1952, the banishment order against Tshekedi was lifted by the Churchill Conservatives, in office from the previous October, and he returned to the Bamangwato Reserve where he would live until dying prematurely from kidney disease in 1959. Meanwhile, Seretse and his wife were allowed to return home in 1956 as private citizens only and it would take ten years of skillful political work and, ultimately, independence, for Seretse to achieve the political leadership of both the Bamangwato and of Bechuanaland – known as Botswana beginning in 1966.

Perham's intervention in the Tshekedi Khama case was a clear example of how she managed the line between (radical) publicist and academic. For Mary Benson, it was indicative too of 'her deep Christian conviction', which, from time to time, overcame her academic detachment allowing her to take 'a notable part in fighting for justice in certain African causes'.[11] The Khama episode occurred just as another colonial crisis had begun to flare, only this one was violent, widespread, and in a colony about which Perham knew much and to which she felt a strong connection. Mau Mau had erupted in Kenya in 1952, drawing in both the white settlers and their particular nemesis, the highly politicized Kikuyu. Perham's earlier critical view of the settlers' position in Kenya, first articulated in the early 1930s, had not changed over the succeeding twenty years. Indeed, it had congealed and hardened during a lively wartime correspondence with one of the great champions of the settler cause, Elspeth Huxley.

In later life Huxley became well-known for her writings on colonial Kenya, especially her memoir of growing up there in the earliest days of white settlement, *The Flame Trees of Thika: Memories of an African Childhood* (1959). But in the 1940s when Perham first knew her she had already carved out something of a reputation as an author. Born in 1907, Huxley moved from England to British East Africa with her parents in 1912. They were determined – as was Karen Blixen at almost exactly the same time – to find success as coffee farmers, which, for a time, they did. After a childhood and youth of living amongst both the settlers and the Kikuyu Huxley returned to England in 1925 to read for a degree in agriculture at Reading University. Afterwards she took a job as a press officer at the Empire Marketing Board, got married to fellow employee Gervase Huxley, a grandson of Thomas Huxley – famous in the nineteenth century as 'Darwin's Bulldog' – and with him embarked on a life of intermittent travel before returning to England in 1944 to settle more or less permanently.[12] By that time Huxley had published a number of books, including her first, *White Man's Country: Lord Delamere and the Making of Kenya* (1935) and had crossed paths with Margery Perham, whose views on the subject of the white settlers in Kenya diverged sharply from her own.

Perham and Huxley met at Oxford in the summer of 1941 and came away from their first meeting contemplating the possibility of a full discussion of 'the tangled problem of Kenya and its future', as the latter put it in a letter in March of 1942. Perham responded with enthusiasm: 'there is no one with whom I would more gladly discuss the Kenya situation', and a close correspondence ensued, one that would last until August of 1943.[13] The letters between the two women, which totalled fifty-five over this period, are detailed, impassioned, and polemical. They are also unfailingly polite and of a high literary quality. Nonetheless, and unsurprisingly, the two women reached a deadlock in their views in January 1943, at which time Huxley chose to break off their correspondence: 'The affairs of Kenya, after all, will work themselves out according to the trends of history and the pull of human effort without the intervention of you or me'.[14] But less than three weeks later Huxley reconsidered and was back at it, writing to Perham 'and wondering whether we couldn't, after all, find some points of agreement on this Kenya question?' Perham was 'delighted' to restart their letter-writing and it went on for another eight months until ceasing almost for good seven months later.[15] Having then 'emptied our quivers' in Perham's phrase, they agreed to stand down from their debate, both of them considerably more enlightened than heretofore, but neither one willing to concede much to the other.[16] The interminably knotty question of race relations remained impervious to appeals from both sides, it seemed, and in this part especially of their wide-ranging debate Perham and Huxley most clearly anticipated the crisis that would erupt in Kenya in 1952.

Partway through this mostly enjoyable correspondence, however, they conceived of the idea of publishing their letters. Indeed, on the day after Huxley had written initially to close off their protracted exchange of views in January of 1943, Perham wrote to the aging Lugard to see whether he might be willing to compose an introduction to their proposed book along the lines 'that, having looked at our letters, you advised us to publish them'.[17] Huxley's letter, which arrived a few days later, must have deflated Perham, but once the correspondence resumed she was again in touch with Lugard who agreed to write the requested introduction. Given his close friendship with Perham, however, he was concerned about impartiality and also about the fact that his reading of the letters did not pre-date the idea that they were 'important' and therefore ought to be published![18] In any event, once the two authors had decided upon the book's title, *Race and Politics in Kenya*: 'Best congratulations on thinking of it', Huxley wrote to Perham, the manuscript was finished and printed and on bookstore shelves in May of 1944.[19] Readily and roundly reviewed it received an especially astringent assessment by Leonard Woolf in *The New Statesmen*. His sympathies lay clearly with Perham whom he praised for putting 'all her cards upon the table' whereas 'Mrs. Huxley always goes off at a tangent when Miss Perham attempts to make her say exactly what she means'. Woolf, who had spent eight unhappy years as a member of the Ceylon Civil Service before the First World War, spoke with considerable though contested authority on Imperial questions but nevertheless was sure that Kenya was 'the test case of British colonial policy toward backward peoples'.[20] He seems to have written with some measure of foresight because by the time Perham and Huxley's book was reissued in 1956 – with the two authors each providing a 'reassessment' – Kenya had come through the worst of the Mau Mau crisis, which, at base, was a violent distillation of half-a-century of 'race and politics in Kenya'.

Mau Mau has been written of thoroughly and, recently, highly controversially, and requires no full reprise here.[21] In 1952, attacks upon White Highlands farmers by members of Mau Mau, an essentially Kikuyu-based rebel movement, began. At the same time more frequent attacks upon Christian and otherwise 'loyalist' Kikuyu also began, sending the country into a State of Emergency and launching a counter-insurgency that would last for most of the rest of the decade, although its severest period was over by 1955. Naturally, Perham was keenly interested in it and in her 1956 'reassessment' referred to above she spent considerable time trying to understand Mau Mau's impact and its ramifications on the totality of Kenyan society. In the first instance, it was to Perham like so many others in Britain and around the world a 'horrible movement'.[22] Replete with stories of blood oaths and animal sacrifice, Mau Mau seemed to make real the sorts of fantastical interpretations put on Africa in the Victorian era and earlier. Perham was keenly aware that what she might have to say on the subject was being written while 'sitting comfortably in an Oxford study'.[23] But perhaps that is all the more reason for her bald statement that 'in a historical perspective we, as a nation and through our local representatives, are very much responsible for what the Kikuyu are today'.[24] Elsewhere, she called the atmosphere that had grown up between the white settler farmers and their descendants and the Kikuyu 'pathological', and the violence and fear that gripped Kenya, especially up-country from Nairobi after 1952, provided ample evidence of that.[25] But writing from the perspective of 1955 it was clear that the violence, if nothing else in Perham's view, had clarified the racial issue: 'the truth stands clearly that a minority of one race cannot *at this date* prosper in the middle of another and much more numerous race which has come to hate them'.[26] Reform of government was the only way, the right way, forward implored Perham. And a few years later in 1963, when Kenyan independence took place, she wrote the foreword to a book by a former Mau Mau prisoner, Josiah Mwangi Kariuki. The book was the first of its type to emerge from the Mau Mau period, and was harsh in its condemnation of British tactics, especially during the period of the Emergency. Still, Perham did not shy away from writing the foreword even though the book's content was 'deeply disturbing' for her to read. *'Mau Mau' Detainee*, in her estimation, was an 'African *De Profundis*' and therefore needed to be read by anyone with a genuine interest in Kenya and in African colonial politics more generally.[27]

For some years already Perham had been thinking hard about the prospect of colonial independence in Africa. But the gradualist move out from under British control which she favoured was simply not going to be the way that empire ended in Africa, if Mau Mau was any indication. The Second World War and American opposition to British Imperialism, in a sense, had seen to that. But it was the internal logic and irresistible dynamic of African nationalism itself that was propelling the move to independence at a rapidly increasing rate. In 1951, in the Gold Coast, for example, Africans were successful in winning control of a British colonial legislative council for the first time, sending, as Perham put it in a long article in *Foreign Affairs*, 'a shock right through Africa'.[28] The newly-formed Convention People's Party under the charismatic leadership of Kwame Nkrumah had won the election, even while he suffered through imprisonment at the hands of the colonial state. Subsequently released, in 1952 Nkrumah became Prime Minister and together with his CPP colleagues fought two more elections before demanding and receiving independence for the new state of Ghana in 1957, the first British African colony to throw off the yolk of imperial control.[29] After that, it seems that the floodgates opened and African independence became unstoppable, even if the will to do so had been there, which, for the British at least, it was not.

The mid-late 1950s, therefore, opened up an enormously exciting time for Perham, as for all those interested in the fate of a decolonizing Africa. Once Ghana had gained independence it seemed only a matter of time before her peer colonies would do the same. As Perham worked away on the second volume of the Lugard biography, all around her intimations of the end of empire could be felt and seen. As she wrote in December 1954, 'Africa will take from the West all she needs to replace her own crumbling tribal past'.[30] The salient issue for Perham was what, in fact, were those things that were being taken? As for Britain's intention, that, in her mind, was clear. 'There can be no dispute', she stated categorically, 'about the general nature of Britain's colonial purpose: to develop self-government in the colonies, and to do it in such a way that their peoples remain voluntarily within the Commonwealth'.[31] Now that the final transaction was at hand – the transfer of power itself – what would be the shape and outcome of this process, she wondered? For Perham, nothing could be worse than what was just then beginning to happen in Algeria where the Imperial French had allowed themselves to be pulled into a war with colonial nationalists. This 'savage war of peace', as Alistair Horne later called it, would drag on for the next eight years, cost the lives of some one-million Algerians – ten percent of the population – and poison relations between France and its former colony for years to come.[32]

Much of Perham's popular writing during these years was done to prepare her fellow Britons for the fact that, as Dean Acheson, US Secretary of State under President Harry Truman, would put it so bluntly in 1962: 'Great Britain has lost an empire and has not yet not yet found a role'. She may not have been necessarily intentional about performing this interpretive function, but a scan through her writings between 1955 and 1960 show this to have been the end result all the same. 'Nigeria Prepares for Independence'; 'Economics versus Race'; 'Sudan after the Southern Rebellion'; 'The Future of the Somalis'; 'Britain's Pledges in Central Africa'; 'The Psychology of African Nationalism'; 'Staffing the Transfer of Power'; these titles represent only a handful of those written, but they are clearly suggestive of what

Perham was sending into the public domain in the last critical years before the decade of African independence that was the 1960s began.

The first British colony to gain its independence in this decade was Somaliland, which, of course, represented Perham's initial exposure to Africa and in that way remained close in heart and mind to what she had first felt when she had disembarked at Berbera back in 1921. Its independence on 26 June 1960 came just in advance of the expiration of Italy's trusteeship over Somalia and together on 1 July the two erstwhile colonial territories became the Somalia Democratic Republic. Perham, who was in Mogadishu on that day as a guest of the new government of the former Somali Youth League nationalist leader, President Aden Abdullah Osman Daar, was pessimistic about its future, however, something that she had written about as early as 1957, calling the various territorial and ethnic claims in Somalia 'the ingredients for an international witches' cauldron'.[33] Subsequent events all the way down to today would bear out her description. But as much as she feared for Somalia's future and could become nostalgic about its past, the imminent independence of Nigeria is what lay ahead as the major event in British Africa for Perham in 1960.

Of all the British African colonies Nigeria always occupied a place near top of mind for Perham. The country's tangled history; Lugard's impact on it; her own intimate experience of it on foot and by road and rail; Nigeria, along with Kenya, preoccupied her like none of the other colonial territories in Africa, save, perhaps, for the Sudan. Like in Somalia a few months earlier, she attended the Nigerian independence celebrations in Lagos in late-September and early-October as a guest of the new government of Prime Minister Sir Abubakar Tafawa Balewa. She spent ten days there, flying in on 24 September and driving with great anticipation through the familiar 'oil palms, kola nut trees and the heavy green bush' on the way into Lagos from the airport. British royal representation – a key feature of almost all African independence ceremonies – came in the form of Princess Alexandra, the Queen's cousin, who struck Perham 'as being very simple and friendly' and with whom she had 'a long talk, as she asked me a lot of questions about Nigeria'.[34] A few days later the princess would open the new Nigerian Federal Parliament. Perham's visit climaxed with the moment of independence, which was celebrated at Lagos Racecourse on 1 October in what she described as 'the great national pageant of Nigeria'. She wrote about the experience shortly thereafter in an article published in *The Listener*. As part of the climatic warmth of the night was the warmth of the tributes paid to Britain by Nigerians for the part it had played in the 'making of their country'. Unity was the key to the future, and the forty-six years of it provided by the British dating back to Lugard's amalgamation of Northern and Southern Nigeria in 1914 was a foundation that boded well for the new country's success, she believed. To that end 'the future lies in the gradual dissolution of the tribal and regional solids into a true fluid Nigerian electorate'. But she was not unduly optimistic about this process. What England and the old democratic countries in Europe and elsewhere had taken hundreds of years to do, Nigerians and other Africans were trying to do in just sixty years. 'But in Nigeria the democratic colours are on the mast …,' she enthused nonetheless, 'they [Nigerians] enter the African stage like some chief actor for whom the world audience has been impatiently waiting while the minor characters played their parts'.[35]

In 1961, Sierra Leone and Tanganyika (modern Tanzania) would achieve their independence followed by nine more British African colonies from 1962–68. The rush to independence was on. The wind of change that Prime Minister Harold Macmillan had said was blowing through Africa in a speech given first in Accra and then famously so in Cape Town in 1960, was doing exactly that as the decade unfolded. For Perham, these events provided much scope for prediction, as well as for summation, and in that year, she was given the opportunity especially for the latter when she was invited to give the prestigious Reith Lectures for 1961.

Inaugurated by the BBC in 1948 to honour its first Director-General, Sir John (later Lord) Reith, the lecture series broadcast on radio had quickly become one of the most important and certainly one of the most listened to public lectures in Britain, which it continues to be to this day. The first Reith Lecturer was Bertrand Russell, then seventy-six years of age but still two years away from being awarded the Nobel Prize in Literature. In the years that followed other notable intellectuals had given the lectures including Arnold Toynbee and Robert Oppenheimer. Now, at the height of her public profile and in the midst of Africa dominating the news, Perham sounded forth on her subject, 'The End of Britain's African Empire', which, when published the following year, came out under the rather forbidding title of, 'The Colonial Reckoning'.

By this point in her life Perham was a veteran of radio broadcasting. Indeed, by 1961 she had been presenting for almost thirty years and in so doing had become very good at it. Indeed, her election that year as a fellow of the British Academy was based in part on her accomplishments that cut across scholarly boundaries. Initially, the demands that the media always make for wide accessibility made her wonder that 'it will be very difficult to be 'popular' and yet correct enough'.[36] But she worked steadily on that element of radio performance and altogether, she would, over her entire career, give some one hundred and ten separate broadcasts. The Reith Lectures were, arguably, the best of them all. They certainly demanded the most meticulous preparation. They also were facilitated by the presence at the BBC of talks producer Prudence Smith, who both suggested to her superiors that Perham be invited to give the lectures, and then helped her to plan their form and content.[37]

The lectures, six of them in total, were given in October and November of 1961. In the lectures, delivered in Perham's deep, sometimes sonorous, and always clipped voice, she ranged across the history of the British Empire concentrating, inevitably, on twentieth-century Africa. The lectures do not exactly comprise an *apologia pro vita sua*, in the style of the one-time Anglican turned Roman Catholic, John Henry Newman, but clearly she attempted to bring to the subject a broad and largely sympathetic understanding of the European, and more pointedly, the British Imperial presence in Africa and in so doing make plain her own lifelong investment in it. This task was not easy, and it would become even less easy as the decade wore on. After all, 'few Africans', she observed, 'are ready to rationalize about our record or their own, still less to appreciate the services of colonialism'.[38] To post-colonial ears used to a constant, often reflexive, denunciation of empire in all its forms, Perham's choice of words – 'the services of colonialism' – might seem intentionally provocative, the sort of language that would suit a 1990s neo-conservative, perhaps. The reality, however, was much different. In measured form in these six lectures, as in so much of the rest of her writing, Perham pulls and pushes, probes and understands in ways that belie the simple consignment of the colonial record to the trash heap of history. Perham's phraseology here is the kind that causes post-colonial scholars to cringe, if not do worse, when it is read. But her desire to really understand Africa, and her obvious bona fides of having studied it and traveled it for, ultimately, half-a-century, mitigates the rush to judgement of those who populated the field of African history then or do so today.[39]

The lectures carried the headings: 'Colonialism and Anti-Colonialism'; 'African Nationalism'; 'The Politics of Emancipation'; 'The Problems of White Settlement'; 'The Colonial Account'; and 'The Prospect.' When published in 1962 they comprised a mere one hundred and sixty pages, but brevity of her presentation belies the capaciousness of the argument. In the same way that the tip of the iceberg obscures the behemoth floating beneath the waterline, so too is Perham's vast learning and first-hand experience somewhat obscured by the brief way – demanded by the lecture format of course – that she elucidates her subject. The most important of the lectures – because it is the most revealing of her summative view of the record of the British in Africa – is the fifth of them, 'The Colonial Account'. In it, she recognizes the enormity, even the impossibility, of the task she has given herself. As she puts it: 'To attempt to judge an empire would be rather like approaching an elephant with a tape measure'.[40] But measure it she does anyhow, attempting initially to build slowly a well-rounded means of interpreting the reasons why the British constructed an empire in the first place. Sir John Seeley's famous 1883 aphorism that Britain did so 'in a fit of absence of mind' simply does not square with the intentionality of what Perham says are the reasons that lay behind the empire's foundation and growth. She lists these reasons as trade, security, emigration, power and prestige, and philanthropy. They were neither consecutive nor did they all occur at the same time, but throughout the long course of British expansion abroad, from the days of the East India Company at Surat in the seventeenth century to the lowering of the Union Jack in a host of African colonial capitals some 350 years later, these forces under-girded British imperialism.[41]

Once having established her terms of reference Perham proceeds to flesh out her argument arriving, ultimately, at the unsurprising conclusion that in Africa 'Britain's record is mixed'. But this summation is hardly that of an apologist for empire, but rather it is one of a historical realist who, in recognizing that once modernity had come to Africa, there was no turning back the clock. Here she quotes Albert Schweitzer: 'The independence of the primitive is lost at the moment when the first white man's boat arrives with powder or rum, salt or fabrics'.[42] In this sense, the story of the British in Africa is an age-old one and therefore similar to that of the Spanish in the Caribbean in the closing years of the fifteenth century or the Chinese in Tibet – or the Sudan – today. Indeed, she argues that if the British had had more time in Africa – if they had not been taken over by the irresistible forces of colonial nationalism – they might have helped prepare their colonies to be that much better equipped for independence in the contemporary world.[43] As patronizing as this argument may sound to some, it was one that was common at the time and remains so today in quarters ranging from the Marxist to the neo-Conservative.[44]

The view that the end of empire for Africans had come too quickly that 'we had not given them enough time', as she said on numerous occasions in later life, is one that came to govern Perham's personal roll-call of British Imperialism in Africa.[45] Her experience with writing and then presenting *The Colonial Reckoning*, had helped to telescope the idea, and regardless of her regret in this regard the Reith Lectures were a personally gratifying and publicly timely event. As she wrote to Prudence Smith, not long after their broadcast, 'I enjoyed enormously giving those. They came just at the right moment when I was ready to think over all I had been working upon, and generalize about it at what was, probably, the right historical moment'.[46]

The historical moment indeed was ideal and as target dates for independence became firm in London and in various African colonial capitals, Perham invariably found herself on the list of invited guests to witness the transfer of power. Since 15 August 1947 and India's 'tryst with destiny', as Jawaharlal Nehru had put it so eloquently, independence ceremonies had become a standard set-piece in international affairs. To her, attendance at those marking the inauguration of the new states of Somalia and Nigeria were added others, particularly that of Kenya on 12 December 1963. Nine years earlier she had written perspicaciously that 'Independence cannot be given but must be taken. It has to be demanded ...' .[47] All over Africa the collapse of British and European rule now bore witness to this piece of prophecy. For Perham, however, owing to her extensive knowledge of Africa, and because since the Second World War especially she had begun to move beyond the occupants of Government House and the members of the Colonial Service into friendships with Africans themselves, she had gained real insight into the dynamic of what 'demanding' independence had come to mean. In the Kenyan context, in addition to her close following of Mau Mau, can be found her friendship with one of the young men of Kenyan nationalism, Tom Mboya, who would go on to become a Cabinet minister in the government of Kenya's first prime minister and later president, Jomo Kenyatta, before being assassinated in a still-unsolved case dating from 1969.

Years earlier, in 1955, as a young, bright and politicized Luo tribesman, Mboya had taken up a scholarship awarded to him by Britain's Trades Union Congress to attend Ruskin College, Oxford to study industrial management. Mboya's year at the University was a formative one for the twenty-five year old, not least because he was befriended by Margery Perham. He arrived in Oxford an already seasoned trade unionist but eager to add some formal post-secondary education to his resume. Perham had been informed by the Colonial Office that Mboya was coming and upon meeting him she was immediately impressed by both his intelligence and his persistence, in the same way that Tshekedi Khama had done upon their first meeting back in 1930.

Mboya's year at Oxford brought him into the University's circle of Imperial historians and he used it also to widen his contacts with British trade unionists, which, owing to his position as General Secretary of the Kenya Federation of Labour, was an easy thing to do. During his time in Oxford Mboya also wrote a pamphlet that attempted to explain the situation in Kenya – just then past the hottest phase of Mau Mau – and for which Perham wrote the foreword. Her motive in doing so was 'the desire that the views of Africa's potential leaders should be widely read and, if possible, sympathetically understood'.[48] The pamphlet was probing and mature but over it Mboya and Perham would disagree on one important point: the speed at which Kenya and all other of Britain's African colonies were travelling toward independence made it imperative for there to be 'a period of graduation' in the lead up to it. In this given period she recommended that Britain should act as a kind of arbiter in the transition from Kenyan colonial government to Kenyan national government. However, both events and Mboya's own position would cause him to reject this advice.[49]

After Mboya left Oxford – where to this day his presence is still remembered by some as 'striking' – to return to Kenya in 1956 Perham kept in touch with him.[50] She was keen to have a direct connection with a prominent African nationalist, one who would, in 1957, be among the first Africans elected to Kenya's legislative council. She also made it clear to the Governor of Kenya, Sir Evelyn Baring, that in Mboya the colonial government would find exactly the right kind of nationalist with whom it could deal profitably after the extreme strain of Mau Mau.[51]

In March of that year Perham and Mboya embarked on a close correspondence. 'This may be the wrong time to ask this question when you are in the full flush of your election', she wrote to Mboya, 'but I will risk it. Would you like to collaborate with me in writing letters to each other which we would publish in book form?' A short time later he replied, expressing 'deep interest' in Perham's suggestion, and promising 'to do my best to keep up with the correspondence.' Thus ensued their conversation through the mails that would last until the autumn of 1958, and sporadically thereafter. Alison Smith has shown well how the letters that passed 'between the middle-aged establishment figure in an Oxford college and the hard-headed young Luo populist in a Nairobi location' enlightened the understanding of both participants as to the salient questions of eventual Kenyan independence.[52] For Perham, the correspondence with Mboya was faintly disappointing, however, partly because she realized that effecting real amity of purpose between the colonizers and the colonized was very difficult, regardless of good intentions, and partly because, as she noted in a letter to the Colonial Secretary, Alan Lennox-Boyd, 'I don't flatter myself that I have much influence with him'.[53] In the main, however, for Perham this latest attempt at understanding Kenya more fully through an intimate exchange of views was useful and enjoyable, not least because unlike her experience with Elspeth Huxley, she and Mboya were in essential agreement with one another over Kenya's future.

That future came to pass five years later when Kenya achieved self-government in April of 1963 followed by independence in December. Again, Perham would attend a ceremony marking the lowering of the Union Jack in Africa and the handing over of power to nationalist leaders. 'We must hope and pray', she said in anticipation of Kenya's independence, 'that they will rise to the test, and that old tribalism will be swallowed up by the new nationalism'.[54]

The year 1963 also presented a watershed in Perham's personal life as it marked her retirement from teaching and the many administrative respon-sibilities that had come over the course of what had been a forty-six year academic career. As she approached her sixty-eighth birthday in December she was in robust health and even though she would be leaving Oxford University and her Official Nuffield Fellowship, she was by no means leav-ing her African vocation. She was made an Honourary Fellow and given a splendid retirement dinner by Nuffield in July, presided over by its warden, Sir Norman Chester, who praised Perham highly: 'In Britain, no voice car-ries greater weight than hers when speaking on African issues'.[55] And a very appreciative University awarded her the prized honourary degree of D.Litt. She also moved out of her suite of rooms at the college, as she and Ethel took up residence at 5 Rawlinson Road, a rambling North Oxford house not far from her previous one on the Bardwell Road.

Now to some degree at liberty Perham accepted election to the presidency of the newly-founded African Studies Association of the United Kingdom. The first formal meeting of the membership would follow in September 1964 at the University of Birmingham over which she presided and at which attended some one hundred Africanists, many of whom were either in the midst of influential academic careers or on the cusp of them.[56] Perham's presidential address was a superb distillation of a lifetime's work in the field and, perhaps astounded herself by the length and breadth of it all, she con-cluded by remarking that 'it seems a long trek from the days of Africa's attraction to my teenage romanticism all the way to this platform'.[57]

Earlier in November of 1962, she had also accepted the request of the Universities Mission to Central Africa to be its president for the year 1963–64. Saying yes to the UMCA, however, was not done as readily as that of the African Studies Association. Having just passed its hundredth anniversary, the UMCA was in the midst of reconstituting itself by amalgamating with its much older sister missionary organization, the Society for the Propagation of the Gospel. As was seen in chapter six, Perham's Christian faith had been renewed in 1942 and while she was honoured to have been asked to helm the mission for a year, she was not sure about taking on such a task, especially during a time of institutional reconstruction. Moreover, when first approached back in 1960 to join the UMCA board as vice-president she had contemplated saying no owing to the 'intense pressure of work' she felt at the time. She had immediately reconsidered, however, pushed aside her scruples about probably not being able to take an active part in its running, and replied: 'I think I might swallow my principles on this occasion'.[58]

The vice-presidency led to the request to be president, one which 'overwhelmed' her.[59] But after much discussion with the mission's persuasive General Secretary, the Rev'd J.S. Kingsnorth, she agreed to take it on for a year during which she duly and smoothly presided over the proposed amalgamation as the UMCA's first woman president and travelled again to East Africa, this time on the mission's behalf.

At roughly the same time as she was engaged in these activities, Perham was helping a former student bring out a book. The publication of *The Colonial Reckoning* in 1962 anticipated the release of a book the following year by a young American academic named Robert Heussler that would chronicle the history of Perham's lifetime subject, the Colonial Service. Heussler had come to Oxford in 1959 as a Fulbright Scholar to earn a D. Phil. under her supervision. After a period of exhaustive research, which included the extensive interviewing of Sir Ralph Furse, now quietly retired in Devon and, like Perham, feeling the slings and arrows of the growing disaffection and even denunciation of the so-called British Imperial project, the thesis was finished just two years later. In November of 1961, in the midst of giving the Reith Lectures, Perham had read it in its final form: 'Recruitment and Training of the British Colonial Administrative Service, 1920–1945'. 'I think it is an amazing piece of work ...', she enthused immediately to Heussler. 'I can write and say whole-heartedly that I think it should be published'. She expressed some concern for the way it might be received by Furse, however. Nevertheless, 'these things', she stated simply, 'have to be. In my later dealings with my beloved Lugard I was bound often to hurt him'. In any event, Perham remarked lightly to Heussler that 'your book convincingly proves that we should all retire at sixty, if not before'.[60] Shortly thereafter, in a more serious tone in a letter to Furse that accompanied the thesis, she wrote: 'This is an extraordinary book ... . Looking back upon my own small part in all these affairs I do feel that many of us were blind to the change that was happening in the colonies, and for which in the end we were far too little prepared'.[61] A week later Furse responded from the refined precincts of the Savile Club in London. Given that Heussler's work was a

systematic critique of what Furse had given his life to building, his words to
Perham are astonishingly even-tempered in content, and barely defensive in
tone. Describing it as 'a remarkable tour de force' he proceeds to comment
on the 'strange experience' of watching myself being 'turned into a myth!'
Furse's tone then deepens as he opines to Perham, 'of course we made mis-
takes: who wouldn't? And did not see through the mists in time – but they
were pretty thick!'[62] If nothing else the experience shows both Perham and
Furse to be remarkably elephant-skinned in the face of (balanced) criticism
of the historical record of the Colonial Service.

Heussler's thesis – with an introduction by Perham – was published two
years later as *Yesterday's Rulers: The Making of the British Colonial Service*.[63]
The book became the standard text on the subject – which it remains – and
was a worthy companion volume to Philip Mason's outstanding study of the
Indian Civil Service, *The Men who Ruled India*, which had been published
about ten years earlier in the aftermath of Indian independence.[64]

As Perham's first year of official retirement drew to a close, paradoxically
she seemed as busy and productive as ever. The year 1963 saw her turn
her attention also to the establishment of the Oxford University Colonial
Records Project, over which she would preside as Director until 1972. One
of her pressing concerns, seen first in her discussions with Lugard about
the proper disposition of his papers after his death, was the possibility of
documentary evidence from the colonial period being lost, mishandled or
even destroyed in what her successor as Director, John Tawney, called 'the
prevalent anti-colonial atmosphere' of the 1960s and the rapid dismantling
of the Colonial Service.[65] To this end, and with the particular assistance of
the then Director of the Institute of Commonwealth Studies at Oxford,
Frederick Madden, she set about ensuring that Rhodes House Library
would become the depository for as much colonial-era material held in
private possession as could be gathered. The Project was a great success, far
outlasting her directorship and even her lifetime, and only recently did it
finally complete its work.

As Perham reached the mid-1960s she would encounter the full brunt of
the anti-colonial onslaught that was, as she saw it, 'an essential springboard
for young nationalism'.[66] Symbolic of the radically different political landscape she now inhabited was the closing down of the Colonial Office, just
two years after one of its finest chief occupants, in her view, Arthur Creech
Jones, had died. Known to Perham and his other friends as 'Jon,' she gave
the eulogy at his funeral in October of 1964 in which she praised him as
supremely adept at adjusting 'a historic office for its changing functions'.
Near the end of her remarks she felt compelled to turn to the essentials of

her own faith in coming to terms with Creech Jones's passing. 'I believe that the souls of the righteous', she concluded powerfully, 'are in the hands of God. I know that this was a righteous man. I am very sure that this is not the end'.[67]

For Perham, she now seemed indeed to have entered the valedictory phase of her life. Her influence on government policy was over, as was her active academic career. But she continued to write on Africa for public consumption, as well as the occasional foreword or introduction for scholarly books in her subject area such as the new (5th) edition of Lugard's *Dual Mandate* (1965) and Tony Kirk-Greene's edited volume, *Principles of Native Administration in Nigeria* (1965).[68] And the series of honours – 'gongs' – that had begun to come her way in recent years continued. In 1961, the Royal Scottish Geographical Society had awarded her its Mungo Park Medal for studies in Africa. The next year it was St. Hugh's College bestowing upon their former history don an Honourary Fellowship – something that really pleased her. A few years after that it was Cambridge University awarding her the D. Litt., and though conscious of the anti-colonialism of the day choosing to cite her rather grandly as someone who may have learned 'her craft from Julius Caesar himself. At one time she kept his *Commentaries* at her bedside … .' Then it was the Royal African Society's turn, which, in 1967, awarded her its Wellcome Medal for 'distinguished service to Africa'. By then too, she had become Dame Margery Perham, owing to her appointment in 1965 as dame commander in the Most Distinguished Order of St Michael and St George, a singular honour bestowed by the Queen and putting her at the same level as many of those in her longtime gubernatorial circle.[69]

Events in the former British Empire turned Commonwealth continued to attract a great deal of public attention as the decade wore on. Independence ceremonies in the remaining British African colonies occurred regularly with the new states of Malawi (Nyasaland), Zambia (Northern Rhodesia), and Botswana (Bechuanaland) attracting Perham's especial notice in the years 1964–66. The future of Southern Rhodesia, with its own version of Kenya's white settler problem, was an issue that had begun to burn hotly too, most clearly after the decision in November 1965 by its white-dominated Rhodesian Front Party government of Ian Smith to declare a Unilateral Declaration of Independence in the face of ferocious denunciation by the British government and the international community alike. Harold Wilson's Labour government had refused to grant independence to Southern Rhodesia without a move to majority rule first. The result was a protracted crisis that would not be resolved ultimately until 1980 when the old Southern Rhodesia became the new state of Zimbabwe. From the beginning Perham was firmly in the liberationist camp. White minority rule had no future, nor should it, she wrote to *The Times* just before Christmas 1965. 'The white Rhodesians, like other minorities, through little or no fault of their own, have been cut off by the tide of history'.[70] Tragically, and unlike in most other British African territories on the eve of independence, it would take a war to prove history right.

At the same time that the UDI crisis in Southern Rhodesia came to the fore, a crisis of equal proportions, though of a different quality, had emerged in Nigeria, now five years independent and for whom Perham had carried such cautious hopes as she looked out over the celebrations at Lagos Racecourse marking that independence back in October of 1960. Since that time the old fissures that had cleaved Nigeria since the days of Lugard had worsened leaving the infant state in a precarious position in its ongoing attempt to weave together a workable modern federation. Prime Minister Balewa's coalition government based on an alliance between his Northern People's Congress party and the Eastern Region's National Council for Nigeria and the Cameroons had had some early success, but the ascendancy of these two parties at the time of independence and beyond meant that the third major region, the Western, represented by the Action Group party, was marginalized politically and ethnically, even though much of Nigeria's new wealth emanated from its oil rich delta. When, in 1962, the Action Group's leader, Chief Obefemi Awolowo of the Yoruba, was arrested for treason and imprisoned, it set off large-scale protests in the Western Region of Nigeria, which weakened further the authority of the federal government in its attempts to hold the centre together.

Over the next couple of years the political situation deteriorated in lock-step with the social and economic. Inflation was rampant, and in December 1964 the federal elections in which the NCNC was excluded from power were openly corrupt. So too were the elections that took place in the Western Region in October of the next year. In this tension-wracked atmosphere country-wide protests and strikes became endemic, and on the pretext of an impending complete breakdown in law and order the Eastern-based and Ibo-led military moved to take control of the country by staging a coup in January of 1966. The coup was bloody, with the assassination of Balewa on 15 January – his body not found until six days later strewn on a Lagos roadside – as well as that of the Finance Minister, Festus Okotie-Eboh. Dying too at the hands of the military was Sir Ahmadu Bello, Premier of the Northern Region and the Sardauna of Sokoto and, like Balewa, a Muslim.

At home in Oxford Perham reacted with 'deep shock' over what had transpired in Nigeria. In a piece published on 23 January in *The Listener*, the day of Balewa's funeral, she decried the events of the previous week and in so doing attempted to rouse outrage in her potentially complacent readers by pointing out that 'it would be an insult to Africans to make a calm acceptance of murder as their natural way of changing governments'. She then proceeded to pick her way through the last hundred years of Nigerian history in order to put into perspective the violent events that now threatened the future of Africa's most populous country. She masterfully distilled this history, especially its ethnic and regional basis, before asking the cardinal (rhetorical) question: 'was Britain right to bring these contrasting people and regions into one state?' She answers yes, of course, but not, it would seem, because of a sole desire to vindicate Lugard and indirect rule and the whole panoply of British colonial rule in Nigeria, but rather because such is what the modern world, what modern Africa itself, requires. She pours scorn on the notion that the coup means that 'Africans are incapable of democracy' – a conclusion that she draws rightly was on the lips at the time of many white South Africans and Rhodesians. Britain's similar political maturation, she argues stingingly, may be a few hundred years in the past, but there was a time when it, too, killed its leaders, such as Charles I. Typically, Perham ends the piece on a note of optimism, charging the British people, especially the 'generous young', not to 'lose faith in independent Africa or Britain's work in creating that independence'.[71]

Unfortunately, over the next couple of years the violent and unstable situation in Nigeria would leave both Perham and many others in Britain and elsewhere with plenty of reasons to 'lose faith' in Nigerian independence. As is often the case when the military attempts to enforce order, disorder is the result. At the head of the new Ibo-led Federal Military Government and Supreme Commander of the Armed Forces was Major-General Johnson Aguiyi-Ironsi. A career soldier who had headed the Nigerian contingent under United Nations command in the Congo in the early 1960s, for six months until July of 1966 he led Nigeria only to die at the hands of a group of fellow military officers under the direction of Theophilus Danjuma. They feared that their chief – who seemed to reinforce his dictatorial tendencies by never going anywhere without a swagger stick that displayed a stuffed crocodile mascot – was arrogating all power personally after his move in May to recreate Nigeria as a unitary rather than a federal state. On 29 July, after just one hundred and ninety-four days in office, Aguiyi-Ironsi and the Military Governor of the Western region, Adekunle Fajuyi, were assassinated, sparking the renewal of the political crisis.[72]

The July counter-coup had been a move by Northerners to reassert their position in the face of what they understood to be Ibo-ascendancy, and in the aftermath of the discovery of Aguiyi-Ironsi's bullet-riddled body, his former Army Chief of Staff, General Yakubu Gowon, was chosen by his fellow officers to head the new government. This he would do for the next nine years, the first few of which would bring him into close contact with Margery Perham.

Gowon was young, just thirty-one years of age when he became Nigeria's third head of state in six years. He was a Northerner, but ethnically an Ngas and religiously a Christian and therefore deemed to be a safe choice to lead the new government. His parents were Church of England missionaries in Zaria, where he was raised and educated and where he had excelled as a football player and boxer. In 1954, aged twenty-one, he joined the Nigerian army, and commenced a rapid ascent that included a stint spent at the Royal Military Academy Sandhurst in the years before Nigerian independence. Like his erstwhile chief Aguiyi-Ironsi, Gowon served in the Congo under United Nations command in the early 1960s. By 1966 he had made Lieutenant-Colonel and was a battalion commander. He was a career soldier, emphatically so. But the first coup changed that and Gowon was drawn into politics, a course solidified by the second coup that would see him win the confidence of its plotters.[73]

Gowon, though close to the scene of the murderous action in July 1966 and its aftermath, was not part of the coup and came into office as a reasonably irenic figure. Upon taking office, he immediately reversed his predecessor's decision to abrogate the federal principle in Nigeria. Though his installation as head of state on 1 August 1966 brought with it a measure of calm and stability, Gowon could do little to stem the tide of anti-Ibo violence that swept the North in September and October as a result of the coup. Thousands of Ibo were killed and as many as a million fled to their ancestral homelands in the Eastern Region of the country. The military governor there, Lieutenant-Colonel Chukwuemeka Ojukwu – an Oxford-educated Ibo who had been appointed to the post earlier that year by Aguiyi-Ironsi – stood firmly against such reprisals to his people locally. He then began to argue that if the Nigerian state did not have the will or the capacity to protect the Ibo throughout the country – especially in the Eastern Region – then they had the right to establish their own state and secede from the federation. In May of 1967 the Ibo consultative assembly duly gave Ojukwu the authority to declare the secession of the Eastern Region and its reconstitution as the Republic of Biafra.

Named for the Bight of Biafra off its southeast coast, the new state was enormously provocative from its inception. International recognition and support were offered quickly by Britain's old colonial rivals, Portugal and France. Within Africa – and in attempt to help exacerbate the split in the continent's largest nation – South Africa and Rhodesia recognized it too. But so also did Gabon, the Ivory Coast, Tanzania, and Zambia, politics, as always, making for strange bedfellows. Critically, Britain did not recognize its legitimacy although there was plenty of debate and outrage at what was rapidly perceived as a David and Goliath situation in which the valiant 'Biafrans' were being destroyed by a violently intolerant and undemocratic federal Nigerian government.

Initially, Perham's sympathies lay with the federal government. Her centrist and unifying instincts were sure in this regard. But as the Biafrans moved from their declaration of secession and independence in May of 1967 to the outbreak of fighting in July her sympathies began to turn towards them. In August, she wrote two letters published in *The Times*, first to plead for a ceasefire, and the second time to demand that the British government outlaw all shipments of arms to the Nigerian state.[74] Throughout that year and into 1968 her views were made public, particularly her sadness and outrage at the death and displacement of so many Ibo.[75]

What happened next was to act as a kind of capstone in the life of Perham as the greatest British publicist on African affairs of her generation. On 23 August 1968 the Commissioner for Information at the Nigerian High Commission in London, Chief Anthony Enahoro, wrote to her. He opened his letter by saying that she was held in 'much esteem and respect in Nigeria' despite views that 'have not been complimentary to the Federal Government'. He then went on to blame her views on the 'inadequacy of facts at your disposal' and suggested that to remedy this problem the Nigerian government would like her to come out to the country as its guest in order to see for herself exactly what was happening. Complete freedom to travel and to observe was offered, as was a guarantee of her personal safety.[76]

Perham veritably leapt at the opportunity to return to Nigeria for the first time since 1960. And at seventy-two years of age it would very likely be her last trip to Nigeria and probably to Africa altogether. An itinerary was put together quickly and she flew off to Lagos within a week, arriving on 30 August and staying in Nigeria until 9 September. She checked into the Federal Palace Hotel in the capital and immediately wrote to Ethel back home on Rawlinson Road: 'Here I am in an enormous & luxurious suite, with private bathroom looking over the harbour, the view I so often saw from Gov't House'. Both excited by the prospect of commencing her visit and jet-lagged by the ten-hour flight, she reported that 'I had an absolutely sleepless night, never even dozed for one moment'.[77] The next morning she attended Holy Communion at St. Saviour's, the oldest Anglican church in Lagos dating from 1909, and then plunged into 'an amazing city. Nothing like it in my experience', she reported to Ethel – and a round of touring the war zones – not without danger – and attendance at multifarious meetings and interviews, the most important of which was the three hours she spent with General Gowon at his barracks headquarters in Lagos.

Shortly after that meeting, on 7 September, and at the invitation of Gowon, she made a radio address broadcast throughout Nigeria but targeted at Biafra. 'I am speaking to you, Emeka Ojukwu', she began, 'and to the Ibo people with you'. The address was short – barely four hundred words – but she had laboured over it through two drafts and one sleepless night. Conscious of presenting herself as independent, fair-minded, and speaking 'upon my own judgement and initiative, and as a Christian', she enjoined Ojukwu to surrender, otherwise 'many thousands of lives which Nigeria cannot spare will be lost'. The address was simple, heartfelt and characteristically direct. 'You must know', she pleaded with Ojukwu, 'even if your people do not, that an immense effort is now being made to prepare the way back for your people into life in Nigeria. I therefore beg you not take upon yourself the terrible responsibility of refusing to surrender and of fighting to the end'.[78]

Two days later, and after seeing her historic visit and broadcast recorded prominently in the local newspapers, especially the *Lagos Daily Times*, Perham flew home to England, there to write a testimonial article for *The Times* – 'Nigeria needs the Ibos; even more the Ibos need Nigeria' – on her remarkable experiences over the preceding two weeks and to reverse her previous public stand in favour of the breakaway Biafran state.[79] On the same day, 12 September, she wrote to General Gowon thanking him for the visit and for their own detailed conversation (of which, unfortunately, no written record was kept), and for his promise made 'to deal justly and humanely with the Ibo should they surrender'.[80] She would continue to weigh in on what was now being called the Nigerian Civil War, and was deeply relieved when it finally came to an end in January 1970 upon the Biafrans' surrender. The human cost of the war had been extremely high: about 100,000 military casualties and perhaps as many as two-million civilian casualties from a combination of fighting, starvation and disease. After the surrender Gowon lived up to his word and did endeavour rather successfully to heal the wounds inflicted by the war and make good on the personal promise he had made to Perham in his reply to her September letter when he had stated that 'I will use all the forces at my command to fight anti-Ibo discrimination in all forms'.[81]

In the spring of 1969, in an even more personal follow-up to her Nigerian visit, Perham was invited to attend the bachelor Gowon's April wedding in Lagos. She declined, but encouraged him in his 'great problem', as she called the war, which by then was in sight of a conclusion, and reminded him once again 'to show mercy and moderation in victory'.[82] And with this fillip Perham's lifetime direct involvement with Nigeria – an intense one to the end – came to a close. In her understanding of the issues at stake, in her correspondence with leading figures in the conflict as well as with ordinary Nigerians – especially a number of Ibo students in Britain who wrote to her – and in sustaining criticism by some, notably the great Nigerian and Ibo novelist Chinua Achebe, who unjustly accused her of having no more interest in Biafra than a 'vast pile of documentation' in her study – Perham had proved herself once again to be a remarkable figure in the history of the British Empire in Africa.[83] As her last significant moment as an Africanist, Perham's public engagement over Biafra may well have been her finest hour.

9

LAST THINGS

On 6 September 1970 Margery Perham turned seventy-five years old. She was in good health, her body still strong and her mind acute. She and Ethel continued to live together on Rawlinson Road, which, for students of Africa and for occasional visitors from the same, had become something of a place of pilgrimage. In addition, the two sisters would often stay at their cottage, driving the short distance to Farnborough near Wantage on the Berkshire Downs, especially at the weekend. They were devoted to one another, the divorcee who never remarried and the lifelong spinster unlucky in love. Perham experienced a happy 'sense of duty' about their terminal living arrangement, driven at least in part by the fact that over the years all domestic chores had fallen to Ethel, which had freed Perham almost completely to pursue her own work. Her voluminous papers, collected over a lifetime of research and writing, were stuffed into drawers and piled high along shelves in their main floor five-room Rawlinson flat – the upper two floors were let – although slowly the papers were being transferred to Rhodes House, an enormous task that would not be completed until after her death.[1] Likewise, she kept burgeoning newspaper clippings files, the filling of which remained a feature of the job of her part-time assistant, the last of whom, Madge Switzer, was employed for two to three days per week until 1979. Perham's bicycle, long her preferred method to travel about Oxford, had been put away, but she remained physically active in a manner that accorded with her earlier, athletic self.[2] As she aged the genteel game of croquet became a favourite relaxation, although, characteristically, she played it with a competitive edge. 'You know', Ethel commented once to Perham's former assistant, Isabel Roberts, 'my sister has to win'.[3]

If her 1968 journey to Nigeria had marked her true retirement Perham nonetheless continued to write and be consulted on African affairs. The BBC, especially, remained interested in her views – and in her memories.

In January 1970, Radio 4 broadcast 'The Time of My Life', a wonderfully evocative recounting by Perham of her passion for Africa all begun by that initial visit to British Somaliland in 1921. She ended her remarks with something close to an elegy: 'Nothing can change my purely personal and perhaps egotistical attitude to Somaliland as the place where I fulfilled so ecstatically my childhood's dream and also found a guiding purpose for my life and work'.[4] That broadcast was followed in the summer of 1971 with a four-part series – again on Radio 4 – called 'Travelling on Trust', which chronicled her round-the-world journey of 1929–30. In addition, Faber and Faber, the publisher with whom she had become most identified over the years, was keen to keep her in print and in 1974 brought out the diaries from her Rhodes Trust-sponsored original journey through Southern Africa as the aptly-titled *African Apprenticeship*.[5] In an article in the *Oxford Mail* that ran shortly after the book's publication, Perham was presented admiringly as an almost exotic specimen from the high noon of the British Empire, an interpretation that she herself did nothing to dispel. Her early exposure to Africa was thoroughly enjoyable, she explained, 'I delighted even in the costume needed then for the part I was playing – the high leather boots, the breeches, the short circular khaki shirt, the becoming double terai hat – long since discarded as an unnecessary protection; above all the rifle over the shoulder and the pistol under the pillow'.[6] Two years later Fabers published *East African Journey*, doing for that part of her first major trip through Africa what *African Apprenticeship* had done for the earlier period.[7]

Despite her name appearing from time to time in the media in this way, Perham's star naturally had waned. As far back as 1961 in a profile of her published in the *Observer* this declension in influence on affairs was noted, only to have it confounded at nearly the same time by her deeply learned and manifestly current Reith Lectures.[8] But as the 1970s wore on, and as increasing age became more problematic, there was no denying that the slippery term 'influence' was no match for the inexorable passage of time. As such, these years were mainly ones of domestic consolidation and private correspondence. Friends stayed in touch, some from Africa, others from her long academic career, especially former students. To her students and colleagues especially, Perham had often been a formidable presence upon first meeting her. 'Dead scared', is how David Fieldhouse – not a man easily cowed – describes his feelings upon an early encounter with Perham.[9] An essential business-like quality to her manner of interaction could sometimes become brusque to the point of rudeness. Helen Kirk-Greene, Tony's wife, upon being introduced to her in the mid-1960s, was asked whether she had ever been to Africa or knew much about it. When the honest answer 'no' was given, Perham simply turned away and sought out fresh, and presumably, more 'African' company.[10] Perhaps this forthright manner came from a lifetime of having lived and worked mostly around men. Patricia Pugh surmises that her formative years spent in the midst of a passel of brothers allowed her to 'handle' men.[11] Wm. Roger Louis, today's pre-eminent historian of the British Empire and a student of Perham's in the early 1960s, has observed bluntly though affectionately that 'she preferred male company'.[12] Whatever the congeries of reasons that made her widely viewed as formidable, she was always uncommonly clear and precise in expressing her beliefs, positions, likes, and dislikes. This extended to her understanding of how to operate in what, for her, especially, was a man's world and to this end she believed that for a woman there were only two, mutually exclusive, choices: career or marriage.[13] In her time, which came in advance of when women began to be awarded professorial appointments, she was likewise passed over. There's little doubt that she would have made a superb chairholder at Oxford, but such was not to be; indeed, it would only be in 1988, a quarter-century after Perham's retirement and six years after her death, that the first female appointee to the Beit Chair in Commonwealth History, Judith Brown, was made. From time to time during her career Perham had been seen as eminently suitable to head a (women's) college – such as when Newnham College, Cambridge, shortlisted her for Principal in 1941.[14] But ultimately, heavily administrative positions did not fire her aspirations in the same way as her academic work and her wider sustained commentary on African affairs, and she declined all such offers.

It is true too that Perham had little time and even less sympathy for modern feminism, and certainly the so-called second wave feminism of the 1960s with its focus on self-proclaimed sexual liberation and on the profound questioning of authority was completely uncongenial to her, notwithstanding the fact that the life-long independence and dogged pursuit of professional goals that marked her character were otherwise traits which contemporary feminists extolled. Earlier, in her writings, she had spent some time considering the social and political position of African women – notably with reference to the issue of genital mutilation in Kenya in the 1930s – that she encountered on her various journeys, but even here her interest is muted and she sees them, naturally perhaps given her own intellectual formation, mainly through the Victorian and Edwardian lens of conventional womanhood.[15]

As for her romantic attachments to men, as we have seen earlier they were sometimes intense, never ultimately fulfilling, often impossible to pursue, and almost certainly unconsummated. Mary Bull, in her charmingly honest manner, remarks that one of the favourite topics of discussion amongst Perham's succession of research assistants was whether or not she was a virgin. The consensus view was that yes, she had remained so throughout her life.[16] In the Perham Papers there is a handwritten poetic ditty, without either date or attribution, which suggests something essential about Perham's persona and sexuality:

> Men said of a lady called Perham
> That she made it her business to entrap them;
> But she hunted the Snark, like her hero Bismarck,
> When she joined the Bras d'Or Sultan's Society of Celibates.[17]

Clearly, her Christian faith and the conventional morality under which she had been raised militated against sex outside marriage, much less anything that a subsequent generation would call 'casual sex'. Accordingly, the probability that she always remained sexually inexperienced is comprehensible when understood in these terms. In this way too her presumed virginity was maintained in much the same way as that seen in the life of Gertrude Bell.[18]

Just as former students continued to stay in touch – such as Perham's last graduate student, Christopher Clapham, whose doctoral thesis on Ethiopia was published in 1969 and for which she wrote the foreword, so too did many of her friends and acquaintances from Africa.[19] Whether it was Mekki Abbas, the ex-Sudanese government minister who found himself in desperate straits in the late-1960s, that she helped land in Oxford in 1970 where he became a visiting fellow at the Institute of Commonwealth Studies at Queen Elizabeth House, or Florence Lubega, her former student from the late-1940s and a sometime member of Uganda's colonial legislative council, whose exile from her home country under the criminal regime of Idi Amin would turn her into an asylum-seeking refugee in Britain. Later, in 1977, Perham vouched for Lubega and she was able to remain in the country.[20] Meanwhile, General Gowon, who had been ousted from power in Nigeria in a bloodless coup in 1975, had come to Britain to undertake a PhD in politics at the University of Warwick. Perham wished him well: 'I deeply admire the restraint and courage you have shown over your exile, and I only hope that the work you are doing as an academic is satisfying'.[21] Closest to home, Tony Kirk-Greene, whose acquaintance Perham had first made in 1955, had returned from Nigeria and half-a-career as a District Officer turned university lecturer and, in part with her help, moved into an Oxford lectureship in the Government and Politics of New States (Africa) and a fellowship at St. Antony's College from which a long and highly productive second career would emanate. 'I know Kirk-Greene very well', she had written to Oxford University Press in relation to what would become his first major edited book, *Native Administration in Nigeria* (1965), 'and he is of course soaked in Northern Nigerian affairs ... . I would certainly support the proposal and wish I had thought of it myself'.[22]

Despite her sometimes gruff manner there was an essential kindliness about Perham that shone through, as evidenced above and in her later years especially where it concerned animal welfare. She was a frequent dog-owner, with perhaps Guerda, the Alsatian that she kept while living at Nuffield, being the most obvious evidence of her love of animals. She took a keen interest in societies that protected animals and in the 1970s became – in advance of her time – intensely exercised by the plight of battery hens and the crowded conditions under which they were housed and the means by which they were slaughtered, as well as with the ill-treatment of horses and ponies. As usual, she went public with her concerns, writing in the *Guardian* and the *Observer* among other newspapers.[23] She saw this concern as being in accord with her Christian principles of caring for the earth and for God's creatures, and in her weekly attendance at the Church of St. Philip and St. James in North Oxford – 'Phil and Jim' as it was called by parishioners and locals alike – and by her adoption in later years of near-vegetarianism, she bore witness to her version of the faith.

Earlier, her Christianity had demonstrated itself in a different way when it had spurred her to take a leading role in ensuring that Nuffield College contained a chapel, in the face of stiff opposition from some of the other fellows, such as the socialist G.D.H. Cole, who hoped that the new foundation would be resolutely secular.[24] Her interest in the chapel was thorough, extending to its design and furbishment, and in this regard she hoped to commission the brilliant Italian sculptor Giovanni Novaresio to do a crucifixion scene set in bronze with Ste. Mary and St. John. She had seen an example of his work in the university college at Mogadishu, Somalia, and thought it perfect for Nuffield.[25] In the end, and in part owing to cost considerations, the well-known English painter and printmaker – and sometime fellow of the college – John Piper, designed the chapel and made the windows, including within it also the work of John Hoskin. Regardless, the dedication of the chapel by the bishop of Oxford in December 1961 – a small, but beautifully appointed liturgical space – was a singular triumph for Perham.[26]

Occasionally, however, her dedication to Christian principles and its accompanying sense of moral rectitude could become almost comic, and one perhaps can see the smile curving her lips as she wrote the following few exculpatory words for publication in the *Oxford Times* in December 1972: 'Dame Margery Perham wishes to apologize to the man whom she supplanted in the Summertown Shoppers Car Park on Tuesday, Dec. 5'.[27]

Perham's inveterate travelling fell off in these retirement years too. Her last trip to Africa came in the spring of 1969 when she visited Kenya and came home to report on how the country was faring in the early years of its independence. In August, she gave a talk on BBC Radio 3 for its 'Third Programme' in which she described the progress made in Kenya since that glorious night back in December of 1963 when from the reviewing stand in Nairobi's Uhuru Stadium she had witnessed 'the new flag of independent Kenya run up amid wild rejoicing'. She referred to that 'hero, President Kenyatta', and his presiding over the Kenyan Parliament, 'perhaps the nearest thing to a real parliament in any new African state'. Perham's talk is full of knowledge and insight and optimism, her words becoming dark only when she turns to the tragic slaying of Tom Mboya, which had occurred only the month before. Perham had visited Mboya while in Kenya and his death 'is a terrible loss,' because 'he was not only a great Kenyan but a great African, a man both of his own world and of the international world, calm, resolute, rational, restrained, with a magnificent brain ... . The Afrikaners and Rhodesians should study such a man and realize what potential ability they are suffocating with their blind, destructive repression'.[28]

By the mid-1970s almost all of Perham's public engagements had come to an end. In June of 1972 and again in March of 1973 she was invited to dine at 10 Downing Street in honour of, respectively, Leopold Senghor, President of Senegal, and President Kenyatta of Kenya.[29] These dinners were like old times for Perham. But such events ceased, as did her media appearances, the final one being an interview on Radio Oxford in June of 1976 to mark the recent publication of *East African Journey*. Travelling now was restricted to local holidays, which together with Ethel, often meant going to the seaside, as they did for the last time in the summer of 1977, to the Isle of Wight.[30] Perham's health remained good, and she was vigilant about it, having long kept a detailed medical file amongst the plethora of others at Rawlinson Road and by making regular trips to the doctor.[31] The same could not be said, however, for her aging sister. Ethel had begun to slide into the ravaging grip of Alzheimer's disease and as she did so Perham's closest friend and domestic helpmeet for half of her life became incapacitated. In the autumn of 1977 this meant that Ethel was moved into a rest home by her daughter Margery Mumford. The home, called The Close, was located not far from Oxford near Abingdon in the village of Burcot, and there she died two years later in 1979.

By this time too, all participation on committees had long since been relinquished and like many elderly people, the parameters of life had narrowed for Perham. In the summer of 1979, Sir Michael Brock, appointed the Warden of Nuffield the year before, held a dinner in Perham's honour to mark the fortieth anniversary of her becoming a fellow of the college. The event was her last significant public social occasion. The next year, in April, she was taken by her niece, Margery, for a final nostalgic trip to Harrogate. There she visited her childhood home on the Kent Road, still looking much as it had eighty years earlier when she had grown up in it, as well as to her old parish church, St. Wilfrid's, which her long-dead father had helped build.[32] These years were marked by a slow diminishment in Perham's mental functioning. Sadly, in the same way that Ethel had developed Alzheimer's, so too did she, the effects of which became clear in 1981 when the Rawlinson Road house was sold. Perham then moved into The Close, where Ethel had spent her last years. Perham's memory had now failed to the point where even the photo of Lugard that he had given her and which she had always kept in a prominent place could not be recognized.[33] In September of that year she turned eighty-six years old. Victimized by Alzheimers, an especially cruel disease for someone whose mind had been as lively and capacious as Perham's, she lived on for another five months before dying at Burcot on 19 February 1982.

Margery Perham's death brought with it an end to a particular kind of arc in British Imperial history. Her life had spanned the Empire's climax and denoument, which her work on Africa had done so much to illumine. In the days that followed her passing Perham's body was cremated with the ashes being scattered over her beloved Berkshire Downs. On 5 March in the chapel at Nuffield, whose existence she had worked so hard to ensure, a memorial service was held. The intimate room was full for the occasion and her former colleague, Frederick Madden, delivered a moving address in which he captured her spirit well. 'She saw life', he said, 'clearly and sternly as a pilgrimage, beset by challenges, which would of course be overcome. Her approach was disciplined and stern but nevertheless rewardingly warm and humble'. The service ended with the singing of a John Bunyan hymn – her favourite – 'Mr Valiant-for-Truth'.[34]

Later, on 1 May in the University Church of St. Mary the Virgin, Oxford honoured Perham with a Memorial Service during which two addresses were given, including that by Roland Oliver, Professor of the History of Africa at the University of London. As a longtime friend and colleague, Perham had welcomed Oliver's appointment in 1964 to 'the first chair of African history in this country... . This is not only a new chair but its post-holder is a new kind of academic... . Professor Oliver and his colleagues represent a wholly new and more valid and scholarly approach – one which puts the colonial period in its proper place'.[35] Now, almost twenty years later and at a somber occasion unlike his own installation, Oliver returned the compliment. In a wide-ranging, and at times humourous address, he encapsulated her life story with its profound 'services to Africa' ending with his own understanding of her as 'a simple and a singularly *cheerful* Christian'.[36]

Her faith is one of the things that became inescapable about the post-1942 Perham and it accounts in large measure for her moral approach to African affairs. In his address at her Memorial Service Sir Norman Chester, Nuffield's warden for a good part of Perham's fellowship there, closed by calling her 'one of the last of the Eminent Victorians'.[37] Notwithstanding Lytton Strachey's withering satire of the same name, the idea of progress, so central to the Victorian mind, was one that Perham had imbibed fully in her childhood and youth and subsequently had attempted to live out in Africa and Oxford. Indisputably, she was a moralist in her approach to African affairs, believing deeply that any analysis of the history of European Imperialism in Africa must be viewed through such a lens. However, in so doing she was no simple apologist for the European – especially the British – record in Africa. Whether in writings as polished and summative as those contained in *The Colonial Reckoning*, or when addressing a group of young students at Putney High School, as she did in the early 1960s – 'Africa: a whole continent in three-quarters of an hour!' – Perham stressed the whelming complexity of analyzing imperialism in Africa, 'a controversial subject, hot with emotions'.[38] Throughout it all she kept returning to her main point, however; that being, the ultimate purpose of British colonial rule in Africa was to enable Africans themselves to establish a form of self-government which would allow them to function successfully in the modern world. As she remarked to a meeting of members of the Universities Mission to Central Africa in 1963, genuine 'sincerity' in this aspiration was the key to African independence and therefore to the proper process of British decolonization.[39]

Thirty years after Perham's death it is this moral insistence, communicated over her long career to governors, Colonial Service officers, soldiers, settlers, students, Africans, missionaries, and the British public that comes through in a defining way as comprising the essence of her life and legacy. Andrew Porter writes well of the moral dimension of Perham's understanding of British colonialism in Africa and of her reevaluation of the importance of the work of missionaries, for example, both there and elsewhere, including her view that the early ones worked, as she put it bluntly, 'on wrong or mistaken lines' because they were wholly insensitive to, or even disparaging of, the pre-colonial culture and morality of Africans.[40] In more general terms Roland Oliver rightly positions her historical significance in the same way, and D.A. Low reinforces the point when he observes that Perham was 'Britain's conscience on Africa … what remains so striking is the massive consistency of her approach … . She was a consistent, and untiring, opponent of every move to transfer any control over the destiny of Africans to settler hands'.[41]

Margery Perham's 'Time of my Life', those indelible months spent in British Somaliland in 1921, marked the beginning of a tireless devotion to Africa that culminated in her becoming the chief British public voice on the continent's affairs in the era of its independence from European rule. In the same way that Mary Kingsley could never again live happily in England after going to West Africa in the 1890s, and Gertrude Bell found her passion for the Middle East sated in the sands of Arabia and Iraq a generation later, Perham too had achieved that moment when aspiration and circumstance ally while galloping her horse along a blinding-white beach in Berbera. And it sustained her passion for Africa over the next sixty years.

CHRONOLOGY

1895   Born 6 September at Bury, Lancashire

1908   Sent to school at Windsor and then to Staffordshire

1914   Went up to St. Hugh's College, Oxford

1917   Graduated from Oxford with First Class Honours in Modern History

1917   Appointed Assistant Lecturer in History at Sheffield University

1921   On leave in British Somaliland

1924   Appointed Fellow and Tutor in Modern History at St. Hugh's College, Oxford

1925   Published *Major Dane's Garden*

1929   Awarded a Rhodes Trust Travelling Fellowship

1935   Appointed Research Lecturer in Colonial Administration, Oxford

1939   Elected first Fellow of Nuffield College, Oxford

1945   Appointed first Director of the Institute of Colonial Studies, Oxford

1948   Made a Companion of the British Empire (CBE)

1956   Published *Lugard: The Years of Adventure, 1858–1898*

1960   Published *Lugard: The Years of Authority, 1899–1945*

1961   Gave the BBC Reith Lectures

1963   Retired from teaching at Oxford University

   Elected first President of the African Studies Association of the UK

   Appointed President of the Universities Mission to Central Africa

1965 Created Dame Commander of the Order of St. Michael and St. George

1968 Public Involvement in the Nigerian Civil War

1982 Died at Burcot, Oxfordshire, 19 February

NOTES

Chapter One

1 Perham Papers, Box 1/File1/Folio 1.
2 PP, 1/2/1–2.
3 PP, 5/2/2.
4 PP, 5/2/4.
5 PP, 5/2/1.
6 PP, 1/2/5–8.
7 PP, 4/4/1–5.
8 PP, 3/4/50.
9 Georgina Howell (2006). *Daughter of the Desert: The Remarkable Life of Gertrude Bell* (London, Macmillan), 40.
10 PP, 1/2/11–12.

Chapter Two

1 Perham Papers, Box 5/File 2/Folio 2.
2 See M.G. Brock and M.C. Curthoys, eds. (2000). *The History of the University of Oxford, Vol. VII: The Nineteenth Century, Part 2*, ch. 10, "'In Oxford but … not of Oxford': The Women's Colleges" (Oxford, Oxford University Press).
3 Margery Perham, BBC Radio 4 Talk, 11 January 1970, 'The Time of My Life'.
4 Ibid.
5 PP, 33/2/13.
6 PP, 2/2/5.
7 PP, 1/2/45.
8 PP, 33/2/8.

9 PP, 278/4/15.
10 PP, 33/2/9.
11 'The Time of My Life'.
12 PP, 4/9/28–32.
13 PP, 1/2/23–26.
14 See, for example, Peter Hart (2006). *The Somme* (London, Cassell).
15 PP, 1/3/15; 1/2/47–48.
16 Ibid.
17 Ibid.
18 PP 1/3/10; Paul Fussell (1977). *The Great War and Modern Memory* (London, Oxford University Press), 36.
19 PP, 1/2/83.
20 PP, 1/2/95, 96, 102.
21 PP, 1/2/108.
22 See Bill Nasson (2007). *Springboks on the Somme* (London, Penguin).
23 PP, 1/2/115–116.
24 Ibid.
25 PP, 2/3/1.
26 *Oxford University Calendar 1919*, 239.
27 'The Time of My Life'.
28 Ibid.

Chapter Three

1 Margery Perham, BBC Radio 4, 11 January 1970, 'The Time of My Life'.
2 Perham Papers, Box 1/File 5/Folios 4–5.
3 'The Time of My Life'.
4 PP, 1/5/4–5.
5 'The Time of My Life'.
6 PP, 1/5/1–3.
7 'The Time of My Life'.
8 PP, 1/5/4.
9 PP, 5/2/7.
10 PP, 1/5/1–3.
11 PP, 1/5/3.
12 PP, 5/4/4.
13 PP, 5/4/4.
14 PP, 5/4/1.
15 PP, 1/5/3.

16 Ibid.
17 PP, 6/1/15–16.
18 PP, 1/4/2.
19 'The Time of My Life'.
20 See Ioan Lewis (2008). *Understanding Somalia and Somaliland* (London, Hurst & Company).
21 'The Time of My Life'.
22 Karen Blixen did much same thing, marrying Bror Blixen a few years later in January 1914.
23 The best account of Hassan and the British is that by Douglas Jardine (1969; first published in 1923). *The Mad Mullah of Somaliland* (New York, Negro Universities Press). See, also, Ralph E. Drake-Brockman (2007; first published in 1912). *British Somaliland* (Mansfield Centre, CT, Martino Publishing).
24 Burton's account of the journey is found in *First Footsteps in East Africa* (1856); Speke's is in *What Led to the Discovery of the Source of the Nile* (1864).
25 H. Rayne (1921). *Sun, Sand and Somals: Leaves from the Note-book of a District Commissioner in British Somaliland* (London, H.F & G. Witherby), 213.
26 Ibid., 223.
27 PP, 34/1/1–72 (Hereafter, 'Somaliland Diary').
28 Ibid.
29 Ibid.
30 Ibid.
31 See Roxani Eleni Margariti (2007). *Aden and the Indian Ocean Trade: 150 Years in the Life of a Medieval Arabian Port* (Chapel Hill, University of North Carolina).
32 'Somaliland Diary'
33 See, for example, Wm. Roger Louis (2006), *Ends of British Imperialism* (London, I.B.Tauris), 529.
34 'Somaliland Diary'.
35 See Edward Rice (1991). *Captain Sir Richard Francis Burton* (New York, HarperPerennial), 341.
36 'Somaliland Diary'.
37 Ibid.
38 See A.H.M. Kirk-Greene (1980). *A Biographical Dictionary of the British Colonial Governor* (Stanford, CA, Hoover Institution Press, Stanford University).
39 'Somaliland Diary'.

40 See Martin Gilbert (1991). *Churchill: A Life* (London, Heinemann), 431–38.
41 'Somaliland Diary'.
42 Ibid.
43 Ibid., PP, 6/1/1.
44 See, for example, Georgina Howell (2006). *Daughter of the Desert: The Remarkable Life of Gertrude Bell* (London, Macmillan), 256–94.
45 'Somaliland Diary'.
45 Ibid.
46 Ibid.
47 'The Time of My Life'.
48 PP, 14/1/5–8.
49 See Isak Dinesen (1981). *Letters from Africa, 1914–1931.* Frans Lasson, ed. Trans. by Anne Born. (Chicago, University of Chicago Press), 1–28.
50 'The Time of My Life'.
51 'Somaliland Diary'.
52 Ibid.
53 'The Time of My Life'.
54 Ibid.
55 Ibid.
56 PP, 226/1/1.
57 See, for example, a recent short study by A.H.M. Kirk-Greene, 'Entente Cordiale ou Enquete Colonial? Margery Perham Hands Down Her Suspended Judgement.' *The Journal of Imperial and Commonwealth History*, vol. 37, no. 1, March 2009, 119–126.
58 PP, 227/2/1–16.
59 PP, 281/2/9–27.
60 PP, 9/6/6.
61 PP, 14/4/1–8.
62 PP, 8/1/6.
63 'The Time of My Life'.
64 Ibid.

Chapter Four

1 Quoted in Brian Harrison, ed. (1994). *The History of the University of Oxford, Vol. VIII, The Twentieth Century* (Oxford, Clarendon Press), 81.
2 Quoted in Penny Griffin, ed. (1986). *St. Hugh's: One Hundred Years of Women's Education in Oxford* (Basingstoke, Macmillan), 59.
3 Perham Papers, Box 6/File 3/Folios 1–38.

4 Quoted in Harrison, ed., *The History of the University of Oxford*, 355.

5 PP, 227/3/19.

6 See, for example, Margaret MacMillan (2003). *Paris 1919: Six Months that Changed the World* (New York, Random House), 98–106.

7 PP, 17/1/1.

8 PP, 283/2/4–7.

9 'The Time of My Life'.

10 PP, 283/4/11.

11 PP, 1/5/8.

12 Quoted in Margery Perham (1970). *Major Dane's Garden* (New York, Africana Publishing Corporation).

13 PP, 283/6/6.

14 W. David McIntyre (2009). *The Britannic Vision: Historians and the Making of the British Commonwealth of Nations, 1907–48* (Basingstoke, Palgrave Macmillan).

15 Margery Perham (1983). *West African Passage: A Journey through Nigeria, Chad, and the Cameroons, 1931–1932*. A.H.M. Kirk-Greene, ed. (London and Boston, Peter Owen), 53.

16 Richard Symonds (1986). *Oxford and Empire: The Last Lost Cause?* (London, Macmillan), 28.

17 See, for example, Philip Ziegler (2008). *Legacy: Cecil Rhodes, the Rhodes Trust and Rhodes Scholarships* (New Haven, CT, Yale University Press). See, also, Colin Newbury, "Cecil Rhodes and the South African Connection: 'A Great Imperial University?'", in Frederick Madden and D.K. Fieldhouse, eds. (1982). *Oxford and the Idea of Commonwealth* (London, Croom Helm), 75–96.

18 Symonds, *Oxford and Empire*, 51.

19 Frederick Madden, 'The Commonwealth, Commonwealth History, and Oxford, 1905–1971', in Madden and Fieldhouse, eds. *Oxford and the Idea of Commonwealth*, 7–29.

20 Margery Perham (1988). *Pacific Prelude: A Journey to Samoa and Australasia, 1929*. A.H.M. Kirk-Greene, ed. (London, Peter Owen), 14–20.

21 Ibid., 15–18.

22 Ibid., 35.

23 Ibid.

24 Ibid.

25 Ibid.

26 Ibid., 36–37.

27 Ibid., 43.

28 Ibid., 61.

29 Ibid., 40.

30 Ibid., 42–43.

31 Ibid., 43.

32 Ibid., 47.

33 Eugene D. Genovese (1976). *Roll, Jordan, Roll: The World the Slaves Made* (New York, Vintage), 413–431.

34 Perham, *Pacific Prelude*, 58.

35 Ibid., 69.

36 Ibid., 71, 83.

37 Ibid., 73.

38 Ibid., 235.

39 Ibid., 226.

40 See James Wightman Davidson (1967). *Samoa ma Samoa: The Emergence of the Independent State of Western Samoa* (Melbourne, Oxford University Press).

41 Perham, *Pacific Prelude*, 179, 203.

42 Ibid., 209.

43 Margery Perham (1974). *African Apprenticeship: An Autobiographical Journey in Southern Africa 1929* (London, Faber and Faber), 30–31.

44 See Leonard Thompson (1985). *The Political Mythology of Apartheid* (New Haven, CT and London, Yale University Press), 37–38.

45 Perham, *African Apprenticeship*, 37.

46 Ibid., 38.

47 Ibid., 45.

48 Ibid., 50–51.

49 Ibid., 65.

50 See T.R.H. Davenport (1987). *South Africa: A Modern History* 3rd ed. (Toronto, University of Toronto Press), 138–41.

51 Perham, *African Apprenticeship*, 77.

52 Ibid., 87.

53 Ibid., 89.

54 A.H.M. Kirk-Greene, ed. (1980). *A Biographical Dictionary of the British Colonial Governor, Volume I: Africa* (Stanford, CA, Hoover Institution Press), 271.

55 Perham, *African Apprenticeship*, 88.

56 Ibid., 106–07; PP, 7/1–2.

57 Ibid., 120.

58 PP, 7/2/8. Perham, *African Apprenticeship*, 130.

59 See Margaret Ballinger (1969). *From Union to Apartheid: A Trek to Isolation* (Cape Town, Juta).

60 Perham, *African Apprenticeship*, 138.
61 Ibid., 141.
62 Ibid., 157.
63 See Doreen E. Greig (1970). *Herbert Baker in South Africa* (Cape Town, Purnell).
64 Perham, *African Apprenticeship*, 159.
65 Ibid., 171.
66 PP, 9/2/2–11; Perham *African Apprenticeship*, 189.
67 Perham, *African Apprenticeship*, 192–200.
68 See Susan A. Williams (2006). *Colour Bar: The Triumph of Seretse Khama and his Nation* (London, Allen Lane).
69 Perham, *African Apprenticeship*, 202–06.
70 Ibid., 206.
71 Ibid., 213.
72 Ibid., 235–38.
73 Ibid., 240.
74 Ibid., 241.
75 Ibid., 263.
76 PP, 9/1/1, 17.
77 Margery Perham (1976). *East African Journey: Kenya and Tanganyika, 1929–30* (London, Faber and Faber), 24.
78 Ibid.
79 Ernest Hemingway (September 1936). *Cosmopolitan* magazine.
80 Ulf Aschan (1987). *The Man whom Women Loved: the Life of Bror Blixen* (New York, St. Martin's Press).
81 Perham, *East African Journey*, 157. Some years ago I wrote a story for a Toronto newspaper on Karen Blixen's brother, Thomas Dinesen, who had won the Victoria Cross while fighting for the Canadian Army during the First World War. Over lunch at the Dinesen family home, Folehave, near Rungsted, Denmark Thomas's then 99-year-old wife, Jonna, and their daughter, Ingeborg, talked to me at length about Thomas, Tanne (as they called Karen), and Bror. More than half-a-century after his death Bror still had the power to charm. 'What a rogue,' they laughed. 'Definitely not the man for Tanne!'
82 See Frances Osborne (2008). *The Bolter* (London, Virago), and James Fox (1982). *White Mischief* (London, Jonathan Cape). Perham, *East African Journey*, 107.
83 Perham, ibid., 109–12.
84 Ibid., 209.
85 PP, 9/6/10 and 9/5/4; Ibid., 29.

86 Perham, *East African Journey*, 44.
87 Ibid., 138–40. She would see Blixen once more, in Kenya in 1936. By that time he had, in her somewhat disappointed estimation, 'gone respectable with adversity'. PP, 49/1/75.
88 Perham, *East African Journey*, 32–4; see, also, David Anderson (2005). *Histories of the Hanged: Britain's Dirty War in Kenya and the End of Empire* (London, Weidenfeld & Nicolson), 18–20.
89 PP, 9/6/ 3; Perham, *East African Journey*, 53.

Chapter Five

1 Perham Papers, Box 9/File 1/Folios 12–13.
2 PP, 2/4/1–3.
3 *St. Hugh's College Chronicle* 1929–30, No. 2.
4 PP, 105/1–166.
5 PP, 9/1/20–1.
6 PP, 9/1/13.
7 Margery Perham (1983). *West African Passage: A Journey through Nigeria, Chad and the Cameroons*. A.H.M. Kirk-Greene, ed. (London and Boston, Peter Owen Publishers), 217.
8 Ibid., 218–19.
9 PP, 9/6/1.
10 Perham, *West African Passage*, 24.
11 Ibid., 25.
12 See John E. Flint (1960). *Sir George Goldie and the Making of Nigeria* (London, Oxford University Press).
13 See A.H.M. Kirk-Greene (1984). 'Canada in Africa: Sir Percy Girouard, Neglected Colonial Governor'. *African Affairs*, v. 83, no. 331, pp. 207–39.
14 Lugard, Lord Frederick D. (1965). *The Dual Mandate in British Tropical Africa*. 5ᵗʰ ed. (London, Frank Cass).
15 Perham, *West African Passage*, 53.
16 Ibid., 25.
17 Ibid., 32.
18 Ibid., 35.
19 Ibid., 36.
20 David Fieldhouse, a colleague of Perham's at Oxford and formerly Vere Harmsworth Professor of Imperial and Naval History at Cambridge University, remarked that she 'was a strong, physical person who loved horses' and would still, near the end of her life, say occasionally that she

'wanted to go leg-over a horse'. Interview with the author, 2 July 2009, Jesus College, Cambridge.

21 Ife, with evidence of human habitation going as far back as 350 BCE, in Yoruba mythology is the home of the founding deities Oduduwa and Obatala who jointly began the creation of the world. The Yoruba claim descent from them. Anthropological discoveries at Ife – as noted by Perham in 1931– have since become a highly important and valuable part of the way in which Nigerian art and religion have been presented to the world.

22 See Henry Barth (1857–58). *Travels and Discoveries in North and Central Africa: Being a Journal of an Expedition Undertaken under the Auspices of H.B.M.'s Government, in the Years 1849–55*. 5 vols. (London, Longmans, Green). See, also, A.H.M. Kirk-Greene, ed. (1962). *Barth's Travels in Nigeria* (London, Oxford University Press).

23 Perham, *West African Passage*, 51.

24 Ibid., 55.

25 Ibid., 56.

26 PP, 9/6/1–35.

27 Perham, *West African Passage*, 56–58.

28 Ibid., 61.

29 See Paul Lovejoy (1983). *Transformations in Slavery: A History of Slavery in Africa* (Cambridge, Cambridge University Press).

30 Perham, *West African Passage*, 66.

31 Ibid., 70–80.

32 Ibid., 86–7, 91.

33 Ibid., 104–6.

34 Ibid., 116.

35 PP, 9/6/1–35; Ibid., 122–27.

36 See Margaret MacMillan (2003). *Paris 1919: Six Months that Changed the World* (New York, Random House), 98–105.

37 Perham, *West African Passage*, 129–35.

38 As Isabel Roberts (nee Ferguson), Perham's research assistant and secretary from 1955–59, recalled: 'Margery and her sister Mrs. Rayne had a romantic Victorian/Edwardian view of personal beauty and regarded it almost a calamity in life, for both sexes, not to be good looking.' From 'Working for Margery Perham,' an unpublished paper presented at the Margery Perham Seminar, Rhodes House, Oxford, 3–4 July 1989.

39 For a more detailed examination of Perham's views of French colonial practice see A.H.M. Kirk-Greene, 'Entente Cordiale ou Enquete Coloniale? Margery Perham Hands Down Her Suspended Judgement'.

The Journal of Imperial and Commonwealth History, vol. 37, no. 1, March 2009, 119–26.

40 Perham, *West African Passage*, 141.

41 Ibid., 163.

42 Ibid., 185.

43 Ibid., 190.

44 Ibid., 212.

45 PP, 8/2/1.

46 PP, 9/6/1–35.

47 Deborah Lavin, 'Margery Perham's Initiation into African Affairs'. *The Journal of Imperial and Commonwealth History*, vol. 19, no. 3, October 1991, 45.

48 As I write, Geldof and Bono, lead singer of the rock band U2, have just finished 'guest editing' *The Globe and Mail*, Canada's newspaper of record published in Toronto. The focus of their efforts? A full edition (10 May 2010) of the newspaper, with follow up reports, given over to the 'African Century'.

49 PP, 9/1/16.

50 PP, 22/1/33.

51 PP, 9/6/1–35.

52 Margery Perham and Lionel Curtis (1935). *The Protectorates of South Africa* (London, Oxford University Press).

53 Lavin, 'Margery's Perham's Initiation into African Affairs', 57.

54 Philip Ziegler (2008). *Legacy: Cecil Rhodes, The Rhodes Trust and Rhodes Scholarships* (New Haven and London, Yale University Press), 113–14.

Chapter Six

1 Perham Papers, Box 8/File 3/Folio 1.

2 PP, 9/6/1–35.

3 *Oxford Magazine*, 16 February 1933, 426–27.

4 Margery Perham, ed. (1936). *Ten Africans* (London, Faber and Faber).

5 *African Affairs*, vol. 35, (1936), 461.

6 PP, 286/1/1. Margery Perham (1937). *Native Administration in Nigeria* (London, Oxford University Press).

7 PP, 287/3/1.

8 PP, 287/4/31–32.

9 Margery Perham (1962). *Native Administration in Nigeria*. Reprint. (London, Oxford University Press), 363.

10 Anthony Kirk-Greene, 'Forging a Relationship with the Colonial Administrative Service, 1921–1939'. *The Journal of Imperial and Commonwealth History*, vol. 19, no. 3 (October 1991), 74.

11 Ibid., 63.

12 See Richard Symonds (1986). *Oxford and Empire: The Last Lost Cause?* (London, Macmillan, 1986).

13 Margery Perham, 'War and the Colonies', *The Spectator*, 6 October 1939.

14 *The History of the University of Oxford, Volume VIII: The Twentieth Century* (1994). Brian Harrison, ed. (Oxford, Clarendon Press), 647–48.

15 PP, 8/3/22–26.

16 PP, 8/3/28.

17 David Fieldhouse, interview with the author, Jesus College, Cambridge, 2 July 2009.

18 PP, 8/6/1.

19 Margery Perham (1941). *Africans and British Rule* (London, Oxford University Press).

20 PP, 288/3/1–19.

21 Roland Oliver, 'Prologue: the Two Miss Perhams', *The Journal of Imperial and Commonwealth History*, vol. 19, no. 3 (October 1991), 21–26.

22 Michael Twaddle, 'Margery Perham and *Africans and British Rule*: a Wartime Publication', vol. 19, no. 3 (October 1991), 100–11.

23 Margery Perham and J. Simmons, eds. (1942). *African Discovery: an Anthology of Exploration* (London, Faber and Faber).

24 PP, 1/6/1, 4. Patricia Pugh, interview with the author, Abingdon, 8 September 2009.

25 PP, 1/12, 21–38. Ibid.

26 PP, 33/4/1–127.

27 PP, 34/6/14; 14/1/4.

28 One such friend was Mary Bull, sometime research assistant and co-editor of *The Lugard Diaries*. Interview with the author, Oxford, 28 April 2010.

29 See Peter Thompson (2005). *The Battle for Singapore* (London, Portrait).

30 Roland Oliver, 'Prologue: the Two Miss Perhams', 23.

31 Margery Perham, 'The Colonial Empire: the need for Stocktaking and Review', *The Times*, 13 March 1942. The second article was called 'Capital, Labour and the Colour Bar'.

32 Ibid.

33 See Robert Heussler (1963). *Yesterday's Rulers: The Making of the British Colonial Service* (Syracuse, Syracuse University Press).

34 Ibid., 136.

35 Anthony Kirk-Greene (1999). *On Crown Service: A History of HM Colonial and Overseas Civil Services, 1837–1997* (London, I.B.Tauris), 46.

36 PP, 49/7/27.

37 See C. Brad Faught (2008). *Gordon: Victorian Hero* (Washington, DC, Potomac).

38 PP, 50/3/55–59.

39 See A.H.M. Kirk-Greene (1982). 'The Sudan Political Service: A Preliminary Profile', (Oxford, Parchment).

40 Ibid., 23.

41 'N.A.' is a reference to Native Affairs. PP, 536/6/1–15.

42 As told to Mary Bull, interview with the author, Oxford, 28 April 2010.

43 Patricia Pugh, interview with the author, Abingdon, 8 September 2009.

44 K.D.D. Anderson (1953). *The Making of the Modern Sudan: The Life and Letters of Sir Douglas Newbold* (London, Faber and Faber), xv.

45 Mary Bull, interview with the author, Oxford, 9 September 2009.

46 Isabel Roberts (nee Ferguson), 'Working for Margery Perham', an unpublished paper presented at the Margery Perham Seminar, Rhodes House, Oxford, 3–4 July 1989.

47 Fieldhouse, interview with the author, 2 July 2009.

48 Isabel Roberts, 'Working for Margery Perham.'

49 Margery Perham (1948). *The Government of Ethiopia* (London, Faber and Faber).

50 See Wm. Roger Louis, 'The Dissolution of the British Empire', *The Oxford History of the British Empire, vol. IV, The Twentieth Century* (1999). Judith M. Brown and Wm. Roger Louis, eds. (Oxford and New York, Oxford University Press), 329–56. See, also, *The Transfer of Power in Africa* (1982). Prosser Gifford and Wm. Roger Louis, eds. (New Haven and London, Yale University Press).

51 Louis, 'The Dissolution of the British Empire', 329.

52 Ibid., 330. Patricia Pugh, interview with the author, Abingdon, 8 September 2009.

53 See Henry Franklin (1963). *Unholy Wedlock: The Failure of the Central African Federation* (London, G. Allen & Unwin). See, also, Robert Blake (1977). *A History of Rhodesia* (London, Methuen).

54 See Sir Andrew Cohen (1959). *British Policy in Changing Africa* (London, Routledge & Kegan Paul).

55 *The Times*, 26 February 1953; For this recounting of Perham's involvement in the lead-up to Sudanese independence I have relied heavily on Wm. Roger Louis's, 'The Coming of Independence in the Sudan,' *Ends of British Imperialism: The Scramble for Empire, Suez and Decolonization: Collected Essays* (2006). (London, I.B. Tauris), 529–51.

56 Kirk-Greene, 'The Sudan Political Service', 36.

57 Quoted in Louis, 'The Coming of Independence in the Sudan', 536.

58 *The Times*, 10 December 1946.

59 Quoted in Louis, 'The Coming of Independence in the Sudan', 543.

60 See Glen Balfour-Paul (1991). *The End of Empire in the Middle East: Britain's Relinquishment of Power in Her Last Three Arab Dependencies* (Cambridge, Cambridge University Press), 16–48.

61 Quoted in Louis, 'The Coming of Independence in the Sudan', 546, 549–50.

62 *Manchester Guardian*, 22 December 1955.

63 Quoted in Louis, 'The Coming of Independence in the Sudan', 551.

64 Kenneth Robinson, 'Margery Perham and the Colonial Office', *The Journal of Imperial and Commonwealth History*, vol. 19, no. 3 (October 1991), 194. See, also, Philip Murphy (1999). *Alan Lennox-Boyd: A Biography* (London, I.B. Tauris).

Chapter Seven

1 James Morris, *Farewell the Trumpets: An Imperial Retreat* (London: Penguin, 1979), 386–7.

2 David Fieldhouse, interview with the author, Jesus College, Cambridge, 2 July 2009.

3 Margery Perham (1956). *Lugard: The Years of Adventure 1858–1898* (London, Collins), 23.

4 Ibid, 31.

5 Ibid, 34.

6 Ibid, 48.

7 Ibid, 62.

8 Ibid, 59.

9 A.A. Thomson and Dorothy Middleton (1959). *Lugard in Africa* (London, Robert Hale), 29, 43.

10 See C. Brad Faught, 'The Uganda Business': Gladstone and Africa Revisited,' Peter Francis, ed. (2001). *The Gladstone Umbrella* (Hawarden, Monad Press/ St. Deiniol's Library), 156–74.

11 Frederick D. Lugard (1893). *The Rise of our East African Empire: early efforts in Nyasaland and Uganda* (London, W. Blackwood and Sons).

12 Perham, *Lugard: The Years of Adventure 1858–1898*, 477. See, also, John E. Flint (1960). *Sir George Goldie and the making of Nigeria* (Oxford, Oxford University Press).

13 Thomson and Middleton, *Lugard in Africa* , 139.

14 Ibid., 144.

15 Perham, *Lugard: The Years of Adventure*, 25.

16 Lugard, Lord Frederick (1965). *The Dual Mandate in British Tropical Africa* 5th ed. (London, Frank Cass), 194.

17 Today known as Dorlin and Little Parkhurst, the property dates back to around 1760 and offers a stunning combination of rural privacy and ready access to Guildford, Dorking, and London. The house sits in the middle of almost four acres of woodland and is spread over about 8,500 square feet of living space. Recently renovated within, it retains the same exterior style as in Lugard's day and at the time of writing was on the market for sale at £3,750,000.

18 Perham Papers, Box 9/File 6/Folio 6.

19 Perham, *Lugard: The Years of Adventure*, v.

20 PP, 22/1/14.

21 PP, 22/1/4.

22 PP, 22/1/27.

23 PP, 22/1/40.

24 Mary Bull, 'Writing the Biography of Lord Lugard" *The Journal of Imperial and Commonwealth History*, vol. 19, no. 3 (October 1991), 118.

25 Coupland, Sir Reginald (1928). *Kirk on the Zambesi: a chapter of African history* (Oxford, Clarendon Press).

26 Bull, 'Writing the Biography of Lord Lugard', 118–19.

27 PP, 22/2/75.

28 PP, 22/5/28, 68.

29 PP, 22/4/11, 33.

30 PP, 22/4/2.

31 PP, 22/5/94.

32 Patricia Pugh, interview with the author, Abingdon, 8 September 2009.

33 Bull, 'Writing the biography of Lord Lugard', 120.

34 Ibid, 118.

35 Ibid, 123.

36 Australian National University, memoir of Hedley Bull. Mary Bull, 'Chapter 1. Early Years: Sydney and Oxford', 3.

37 Perham, *Lugard: The Years of Adventure*, viii.

38 Mary Bull, interview with the author, Oxford, 9 September 2009.

39 Bull, 'Writing the Biography of Lord Lugard,' 126.

40 Ibid, 122.

41 PP, 318/7/80.

42 Margery Perham, ed. (1959). *The Diaries of Lord Lugard*, vols 1–3. Mary Bull, asst. ed. (London, Faber and Faber); Perham (1963). *The Diaries of Lord Lugard*, vol. 4. Mary Bull, co-ed. (Evanston, Northwestern University Press).

43 PP, 318/8/4.

44 Ronald Robinson and John Gallagher with Alice Denny (1961). *Africa and the Victorians: The Official Mind of Imperialism* (London, Macmillan).

45 PP, 318/9/7.

46 Margery Perham (1960). *Lugard: The Years of Authority 1898–1945* (London, Collins).

47 Bull, 'Writing the Biography of Lord Lugard', 128.

48 Ibid, 131.

49 Perham, *Lugard: The Years of Authority*, 390.

50 I.F. Nicoloson (1969). *The Administration of Nigeria 1900–1960: men ,methods and myths* (Oxford, Clarendon Press).

51 Bull, 'Writing the Biography of Lord Lugard', 133.

52 Robert Shenton (1986). *The Development of Capitalism in Northern Nigeria* (Toronto, University of Toronto Press), 108, 122, 70.

53 Toyin Falola and A.D. Roberts, 'West Africa', in Judith M. Brown and Wm. Roger Louis, eds. (1999). *The Oxford History of the British Empire: The Twentieth Century* (Oxford and New York, Oxford University Press), 519.

54 Perham, *Lugard: The Years of Authority*, 138.

Chapter Eight

1 Perham Papers, Box 8/File 3/Folio 19. 'Newscheck on South Africa and Africa,' 12 October 1962.

2 Ibid.

3 Frederick Madden, 'Commonwealth Government at Oxford: Some Reflections', *The Journal of Commonwealth and Comparative Politics*, vol. XXXI, no. 1 (March 1993), 38.

4 Margery Perham, letter to *The Times*, 10 August 1946.

5 This brief recounting of the case is drawn from Susan Williams (2006). *Colour Bar: The triumph of Seretse Khama and his nation* (London, Allen

Lane), and Eric Robins (1967). *White Queen in Africa* (London, Robert Hale).

6 Perham, letter to *The Times*, 18 March 1950.

7 PP, 23/1/126.

8 See Anne Yates and Lewis Chester (2006). *The Troublemaker: Michael Scott and his lonely struggle against injustice* (London, Aurum Press), and Mary Benson (1960). *Tshekedi Khama* (London, Faber and Faber). Benson died in London in 2000. One of her last visitors was Nelson Mandela.

9 Perham, letter to *The Times*, 29 May 1951.

10 Ibid.

11 Benson, *Tshekedi Khama*, 215.

12 See C.S. Nicholls (2002). *Elspeth Huxley: A Biography* (London, HarperCollins).

13 Elspeth Huxley and Margery Perham (1944). *Race and Politics in Kenya* (London, Faber and Faber), 22, 24.

14 Ibid., 125.

15 Ibid., 126–27.

16 Ibid., 235.

17 PP, 290/1/1.

18 PP, 290/1/4.

19 PP, 290/1/77.

20 Leonard Woolf, *The New Statesman*, 3 June 1944.

21 See David Anderson (2005). *Histories of the Hanged: Britain's Dirty War in Kenya and the End of Empire* (London, Weidenfeld & Nicolson). See, also, Caroline Elkins (2005). *Imperial Reckoning: The Untold Story of Britain's Gulag in Kenya* (New York, Henry Holt).

22 Huxley and Perham (1956). *Race and Politics in Kenya*, rev. ed., 271.

23 Ibid.

24 Ibid., 272.

25 Anderson, *Histories of the Hanged*, 328.

26 Huxley and Perham, *Race and Politics in Kenya*, 274.

27 Josiah Mwangi Kariuki (1963). *'Mau Mau' Detainee: The Account by a Kenya African of his Experiences in Detention Camps 1953–1960* (London, Oxford University Press), xi, xxi.

28 Margery Perham, 'The British Problem in Africa', *Foreign Affairs* (July 1951).

29 See Dennis Austin (1970). *Politics in Ghana: 1946–1960* (London, Oxford University Press).

30 Margery Perham, 'Britain's Response to the End of Colonialism,' *The Listener*, 10 December 1954.

31 Ibid.
32 Alistair Horne (1977). *A Savage War of Peace: Algeria, 1954–1962* (London, Macmillan).
33 Perham, letter to *The Times*, 16 December 1957.
34 PP, 58/4/2, 8–9.
35 Margery Perham, 'A Prospect of Nigeria', *The Listener*, 20 October 1960.
36 Prudence Smith, 'Margery Perham and Broadcasting: a personal reminiscence', *The Journal of Imperial and Commonwealth History*, vol. 19, no. 3 (October 1991), 198.
37 Ibid., 197, 199.
38 Margery Perham (1962). *The Colonial Reckoning* (London, Collins), 160.
39 One such person, an Africanist at a leading British university, recently referred to Perham as 'that old biddy' [!] when I mentioned I was writing her biography.
40 Perham, *The Colonial Reckoning*, 102.
41 Ibid., 103.
42 Ibid., 134.
43 Ibid., 135.
44 See, for example, Bill Freund (1984). *The Making of Contemporary Africa: The Development of African Society since 1800* (Bloomington, Indiana University Press), and Niall Ferguson (2002). *Empire: The Rise and Demise of the British World Order and the Lessons for Global Power* (New York, Basic Books).
45 Patricia Pugh, interview with the author, Abingdon, 8 September 2009.
46 Smith, 'Margery Perham and Broadcasting', 199.
47 Margery Perham, 'Britain's Response to the End of Colonialism', *The Listener*, 10 December 1954.
48 Margery Perham, Foreword, *The Kenya Question: an African answer* by Tom Mboya (Fabian Society, 1956).
49 Ibid.
50 In a recent issue of the *Times Literary Supplement* the writer of a letter to the editor on a new biography of Barack Obama points out Mboya's selection of Obama's Kenyan eponymous father to be awarded a scholarship to study in the United States in the 1960s. Fifty-four years after Mboya's fleeting presence in Oxford, and in a time when there very few Africans at the University, the writer recalls that 'his presence in central Oxford and in Old Headington was striking'. *TLS*, no. 5591 (28 May 2010).

51 PP, 457/1/2.

52 PP, 343/2/2, 199. Alison Smith, 'Dear Mr Mboya: correspondence with a Kenya nationalist', *The Journal of Imperial and Commonwealth History*, vol. 19, no. 3 (October 1991), 159–184.

53 PP, 457/1/13.

54 Margery Perham, 'Kenya in Travail', *The Listener*, 21 March 1963.

55 PP, 11/3/1.

56 'African Studies Association of the UK: The 1964 Conference', *African Studies Bulletin*, vol. 7, no. 3 (Oct., 1964), 13–15. Among many others in attendance at this meeting were Professors Roland Oliver, J.D. Fage, David Anthony Low, and K.E. Robinson. The meeting also marked the opening of the Centre of West African Studies at Birmingham University. Later, in 1969, she would supplicate there for the Hon. D.Litt.

57 Ibid.

58 PP, 15/1/2.

59 PP, 15/1/4.

60 PP, 320/1/1.

61 PP, 320/1/3.

62 PP, 320/1/4.

63 Robert Heussler (1963). *Yesterday's Rulers: The Making of the British Colonial Service* (Syracuse, Syracuse University Press).

64 Philip Mason (1953–54). *The Men who Ruled India* 2 vols. (London, Jonathan Cape).

65 John J. Tawney, 'Personal Thoughts on a Rescue Operation,' *African Affairs*, vol. 67 (1968), 345.

66 Perham, letter to *The Times*, 4 August 1966.

67 PP, 23/3/3.

68 A.H.M. Kirk-Greene, ed. (1965). *The Principles of Native Administration in Nigeria: Selected Documents, 1900–1947* (London, Oxford University Press).

69 PP, 8/6/1, 2, 6.

70 Perham, letter to *The Times*, 20 December 1965.

71 Perham, 'The Nigerian Crisis and After', *The Listener*, 23 January 1966.

72 See Robert J.M. Collis (1970). *Nigeria in Conflict* (London, Secker & Warburg). See, also, Chimamanda Ngozi Adichie (2006). *Half of a Yellow Sun* (London, Fourth Estate/HarperCollins).

73 See John D. Clarke (1987). *Yakubu Gowon: Faith in a United Nigeria* (London, Frank Cass).

74 Perham, letters to *The Times*, 4 and 19 August 1967.

75 See Martin Dent, 'The Nigerian Civil War', *The Journal of Imperial and Commonwealth History*, vol. 19, no. 3 (October 1991), 201–11.
76 PP, 415/1/2.
77 PP, 415/2/1.
78 PP, 415/5/5–9.
79 PP, 415/7/n.f. Perham, 'The Nigerian War', *The Times*, 12 September 1968.
80 PP, 416/1/2.
81 PP, 416/1/4.
82 PP, 416/3/2.
83 Dent, 'The Nigerian Civil War'. Chinua Achebe, letter to *The Times*, 19 September 1968.

Chapter Nine

1 Patricia Pugh, 'Margery Perham and her Archive', *The Journal of Imperial and Commonwealth History*, vol. 19, no. 3 (October 1991), 212–28.
2 Deryck Schreuder, a South African Rhodes Scholar in the 1960s, who went on to have a long and distinguished career as an historian and administrator at various Australian universities, remembers well Perham beckoning him and other students to cycle along with her to the weekly Commonwealth history seminar. In conversation with the author, Chester, 6 July 2009.
3 Isabel Roberts, 'Working for Margery Perham', an unpublished paper from the Margery Perham Seminar, Rhodes House, Oxford, 3–4 July 1989.
4 Margery Perham, 'The Time of My Life', BBC Radio 4, 11 January 1970.
5 Margery Perham (1974). *African Apprenticeship: an autobiographical journey in South Africa 1929* (London, Faber and Faber).
6 Anthony Wood, 'How a don served her African apprenticeship', *Oxford Mail*, 16 September 1974.
7 Margery Perham (1976). *East African Journey: Kenya and Tanganyika 1929–30* (London, Faber and Faber). Later, and posthumously, Tony Kirk-Greene would edit and see to it that two of her other travel diaries were also published: Margery Perham (1983). *West African Passage: a journey through Nigeria, Chad, and the Cameroons, 1931–1932*. A.H.M. Kirk-Greene, ed. (London, Peter Owen), and Perham (1988). *Pacific Prelude: travels in Samoa and Australasia, 1929* (London, Peter Owen).

8   'Profile: Margery Perham', *Observer*, 26 November 1961.

9   David Fieldhouse, interview with the author, Jesus College, Cambridge, 2 July 2009.

10 Helen Kirk Greene, in conversation with the author, Oxford, 10 September 2009.

11 Patricia Pugh, interview with the author, Abingdon, 8 September 2009.

12 Wm. Roger Louis, 'Historians I Have Known', American Historical Association *Perspectives* (May 2001).

13 Mary Bull, interview with the author, Oxford, 28 April 2010.

14 Perham Papers, Box 8/File 7/Folio 1.

15 Ashley Leech goes some distance in probing this question in 'Writing Gender: Representations of Women in Margery Perham's Personal Papers.' Unpublished M.Sc. thesis, University of Oxford, 2008.

16 Bull, ibid.

17 PP, 14/1/9.

18 See Georgina Howell (2006). *Daughter of the Desert: The Remarkable Life of Gertrude Bell* (London, Macmillan), 146.

19 Christopher Clapham (1969). *Haile-Selassie's Government* (London, Longmans, Green). Over forty years later, and as of writing, Clapham remains a member of the Centre of African Studies at Cambridge University where he edits the *Journal of Modern African Studies*.

20 PP, 8/4/5; 8/1/108.

21 PP, 416/1/4.

22 PP, 264/2/11.

23 Margery Perham, 'Chicken Imports,' *Observer*, 21 July 1965; 'Life or death – in a battery,' *Observer*, 7 November 1968; 'Death of ponies in road accidents in Gower,' *South Wales Evening Post*, 27 June 1971.

24 Fieldhouse, ibid.

25 PP, 11/1/1.

26 Derick Grigs, 'Chapel an Unexpected Contrast at Nuffield,' *Oxford Mail*, 5 January 1962. A plaque in Perham's honour now adorns one of the chapel walls, describing her accurately, if unfashionably, as a 'pioneer' in the study of Africa.

27 PP, 8/12/81.

28 Margery Perham, 'Kenya Revisited', BBC Third Programme, 14 August 1969.

29 PP, 8/1/70, 75.

30 PP, 31/4/2.

31 PP, 31/2/1.

32 PP, 14/9/2.

33 Bull, ibid.
34 St. Hugh's College *Chronicle*, no. 55 (1982–83).
35 PP, 240/19/1.
36 St. Hugh's College *Chronicle*, ibid.
37 Ibid.
38 PP, 241/17/1; 241/16/3.
39 PP, 240/12/1.
40 Andrew Porter, 'Margery Perham, Indirect Rule and Christian Missions', *The Journal of Imperial and Commonwealth History*, vol. 19, no. 3 (October 1991), 94. Of these, she included her own uncle, John Perham, who had been a missionary for the Society for the Propagation of the Gospel in Foreign Parts in Borneo in the late nineteenth century.
41 Roland Oliver, 'The Historical Significance of Margery Perham', an unpublished paper from the Margery Perham Seminar, Rhodes House, Oxford, 3–4 July 1989, and D.A. Low, 'Britain's Conscience on Africa', *African Affairs* (1971) 70: 172–75.

BIBLIOGRAPHY OF BOOKS BY MARGERY PERHAM

Major Dane's Garden (1925). London, Hutchinson & Co.

Josie Vine (1927). London, Hutchinson & Co.

The Protectorates of South Africa (1935). Co-authored with Lionel Curtis. London, Oxford University Press.

Ten Africans (1936). Ed. London, Faber and Faber.

Native Administration in Nigeria (1937). London, Oxford University Press.

Africans and British Rule (1941). London, Oxford University Press.

African Discovery: An Anthology of Exploration (1942). Co-edited with Jack Simmons. London, Faber and Faber.

Race and Politics in Kenya (1944). Co-authored with Elspeth Huxley. London, Faber and Faber.

The Government of Ethiopia (1948). London, Faber and Faber.

Lugard: The Years of Adventure, 1858–1898 (1956). London, Collins.

The Diaries of Lord Lugard, vols. 1–3, East Africa (1959). Asst. ed., Mary Bull. London, Faber and Faber.

Lugard: The Years of Authority, 1898–1945 (1960). London, Collins.

The Colonial Reckoning (1962). London, Collins.

The Diaries of Lord Lugard, vol. 4, West Africa (1963). Co-edited with Mary Bull. London, Faber and Faber.

African Outline (1966). London, Oxford University Press.

Colonial Sequence, 1930–1949 (1967). London, Methuen.

Colonial Sequence, 1949–1969 (1970). London, Methuen.

African Apprenticeship: An Autobiographical Journey in South Africa, 1929 (1974). London, Faber and Faber.

East African Journey, 1929–30 (1976). London, Faber and Faber.

West African Passage: A Journey through Nigeria, Chad and the Cameroons, 1931–32 (1983). Ed. by A.H.M. Kirk-Greene. London, Peter Owen.

Pacific Prelude: Travels in Samoa and Australasia, 1929 (1988). Ed. by A.H.M. Kirk-Greene. London, Peter Owen.

INDEX

A casual Perham family pose taken about 1902 when Margery was seven: Edwardian respectability exemplified. Courtesy of the Bodleian Library, Oxford.

Perham on camelback at the pyramids at Giza, Egypt with unidentified group, 1930.
As Napoleon had said to his troops in 1798: 'From the heights of these pyramids,
forty centuries look down upon you'. Courtesy of the Bodleian Library, Oxford.

Perham on horseback in Darfur, Sudan, 1937: then and now, the country's most desolate
province. Courtesy of the Bodleian Library, Oxford.

Perham *c.* 1900. Even as a child of five she was
highly self-assured.
Courtesy of the Bodleian Library, Oxford.

Harry Rayne as a lieutenant in the King's
African Rifles, Nairobi, 1915. Handsome
and adventurous, it's easy to see why he
had such great appeal to the opposite sex.
Courtesy of the Bodleian Library, Oxford.

Lord Lugard, the great man of African empire, as Perham knew him in 1935. Courtesy of the Bodleian Library, Oxford.

Perham on horseback at Hargeisa, British Somaliland in 1921. She was an accomplished horsewoman all her life. Courtesy of the Bodleian Library, Oxford.

Perham with Bror Blixen (far right) and two unidentified hunters, in Tanganyika, 1930. Blixen was 'The Man Whom Women Loved', according to his biographer, but not Perham. Courtesy of the Bodleian Library, Oxford.

Perham with General Yakubu Gowon, Head of State of Nigeria, in Lagos, 1968. Her visit to Nigeria during its civil war was Perham's last significant intervention in African affairs. Courtesy of the Bodleian Library, Oxford.

A characteristically animated Perham talking with native women in Darfur, Sudan, 1937. Courtesy of the Bodleian Library, Oxford.

Edgar Perham c. 1915 in the uniform of the West Yorkshire Regiment. The beloved brother who was lost at the Somme. Courtesy of the Bodleian Library, Oxford.

Perham on camelback in Hargeisa, British Somaliland, 1921. In those days a gun was usually near to hand. Courtesy of the Bodleian Library, Oxford.

Hugh Cholmondeley, 3rd Baron Delamere, by Bassano, 1930. 'They call me D, if I'm lucky'. Perham respected Delamere, but could not accept his view of Kenya's future. Courtesy of the National Portrait Gallery, London.

Ever the sportswoman, Perham (middle row, second from right) with the other members of the St. Hugh's College, Oxford, Women's Hockey 1st XI, 1916.
Courtesy of St. Hugh's College, Oxford.

Perham (top row, second from left), as a new history don, recently returned from Sheffield, St. Hugh's College, Oxford, 1925. Courtesy of St. Hugh's College, Oxford.